CLASSICAL ARMENIAN CULTURE

University of Pennsylvania
Armenian Texts and Studies

Supported by the Sarkes Tarzian Fund

SERIES EDITOR
Michael E. Stone

Number 4

CLASSICAL ARMENIAN CULTURE
Influences and Creativity

Proceedings of the First Dr. H. Markarian
Conference on Armenian Culture

CLASSICAL ARMENIAN CULTURE
Influences and Creativity

edited by
Thomas J. Samuelian

SCHOLARS PRESS

Published by
Scholars Press

CLASSICAL ARMENIAN CULTURE
Influences and Creativity
Proceedings of the First Dr. H. Markarian Conference on Armenian Culture

Edited by
Thomas J. Samuelian

© 1982
University of Pennsylvania
Armenian Texts and Studies

Library of Congress Cataloging in Publication Data

Dr. H. Markarian Conference on Armenian Culture
  (1st : 1979 : University of Pennsylvania)
  Classical Armenian culture.

  (University of Pennsylvania Armenian texts and studies ;
no. 4)
  "Proceedings of the First Dr. H. Markarian Conference
on Armenian Culture"—T.p. verso.
    1. Armenia—Civilization—Congresses.
I. Samuelian, Thomas J. II. Title. III. Series.
DS171.D7   1979   306'.09566'2   82-776
ISBN 0-89130-565-3   AACR2
ISBN 0-89130-566-1 (pbk.)

Printed in the United States of America

CONTENTS

ACKNOWLEDGEMENTS

Robert W. Thomson, trans. & comment. Agathangelos' History of the Armenians. p. 137, para. 124. Copyright © 1976 by Robert W. Thomson. Reprinted by permission of State University of New York Press.

Editor's Preface

The First Dr. H. Markarian Conference on Armenian Culture was held November 4 - 6, 1979 at the University of Pennsylvania under the auspices of the Tarzian Chair in Armenian History and Culture. At the conclusion of the conference, when these papers were first read, it was decided that they deserved wider and more permanent distribution. Thereafter, they were transformed by authors and editors into the present collection. To make the book easier to read and use, notes and names have been standardized as far as possible, and an index of proper names, including place names and titles of classical and Biblical books, has been provided.

Since a comprehensive bibliography was not economical for a book of such diverse contents, the names of authors cited--whether mentioned explicitly in the text or only in the notes--have been listed in the index along with all other proper names. If an author's name has been cited in more than one form, the name is given as it appeared in the work cited and any other spelling is given in parentheses. Throughout the book, Armenian forms of proper and place names have been preferred and have been transliterated according to the practice of the Revue des Études Arméniennes, with the exceptions of ը, which for typographic reasons had to be transliterated ĕ instead of ə, and օ, which has been transliterated ō. A transliteration chart has been provided below for the reader's convenience. Persian names have been standardized according to the Encyclopaedia Britannica (1974), and Greek has been transliterated according to one of the two systems set forth in the same edition.

Many thanks are due Lou Ann Matossian, who as preliminary editor gave the collection the first semblance of a coherent volume; Michael Stone, who gave much invaluable advice on the preparation of the text, standardization of notes and names, and production of the book itself; and Vartan Gregorian, who saw to making the book possible.

TJS

Convenors' Preface

The papers collected in this volume have three things in common: they were all presented at the First Dr. H. Markarian Conference on Armenian Culture held at the University of Pennsylvania in November 1979; they all deal with Armenian culture through the seventh century; and they all address the same theme—influences and creativity. Sensitive to their surroundings yet steadfast in their individuality, the Armenian people in each period of their history have created a colorful, coherent, supple yet enduring culture all their own. In specialized studies in their respective disciplines, the participants in the conference focused on the independence and interdependence of Armenian culture—art, architecture, literature, language and religion—among the cultures of the Mediterranean and the Middle East.

No single conference, nor any single volume could be expected to exhaust a subject of such breadth and complexity. The aim of this collective probing of Classical Armenian culture was more to cite and illustrate than to survey or define. As a ground-breaking effort, this conference has given the convenors a deep appreciation of the unity and variety of international scholarship, and we are indeed indebted to all the contributors for shedding new light on many facets of Classical Armenian culture.

Vartan Gregorian   Michael Stone
                    Convenors

LIST OF ILLUSTRATIONS

Armenian Transliteration Key

Ս	Բ	Գ	Դ	Ե	Զ	Է	Ը	Թ	Ժ
ա	բ	գ	դ	ե	զ	է	ը	թ	ժ
a	b	g	d	e	z	ē	ĕ	t'	ž

Ի	Լ	Խ	Ծ	Կ	Հ	Ձ	Ղ	Ճ	Մ
ի	լ	խ	ծ	կ	հ	ձ	ղ	ճ	մ
i	l	x	c	k	h	j	ł	č	m

Յ	Ն	Շ	Ո	Չ	Պ	Ջ	Ռ	Ս	Վ
յ	ն	շ	ո	չ	պ	ջ	ռ	ս	վ
y	n	š	o	č'	p	ǰ	ř	s	v

Տ	Ր	Ց	Ւ	Փ	Ք	Օ	Ֆ	Ու
տ	ր	ց	ւ	փ	ք	o	ֆ	ու
t	r	c'	w	p'	k'	ō	f	u

Classical Armenian Culture:
Influences and Creativity

ZOROASTRIAN PROBLEMS IN ARMENIA: MIHR AND VAHAGN

James R. Russell

Columbia University (USA)

Artaxerxes II (404-359 B. C.) was the first Achaemenian king to invoke the triad of Ahuramazdā, Anāhitā and Mithra, rather than Ahuramazdā alone, as his predecessors had done. Of all the Zoroastrian yazatas, it is Mithra who has received the greatest scholarly attention, largely because of the development of Mithraism in the Roman Empire. Within Iran itself, Mithra is a divinity of unquestioned importance. As one of the three ahuras, Ahura Mazdā and *Vouruna-Apąm Napāt being the other two,[1] he stands at the head of the Zoroastrian pantheon.[2] As a judge of souls,[3] a guardian of covenants[4] and a fighter against evil,[5] he epitomizes the Zoroastrian ethic and world-view. Zoroastrian temples are called 'gates of Mithra' (New Persian dar-i Mihr).[6] Mihragān was a festival second in importance in Sasanian Iran only to Nō Rōz, which was consecrated to Ohrmazd,[7] and Zoroastrian tradition holds that by presiding over the second half of the month through the sixteenth day which bears his name, Mithra is subordinate only to Ohrmazd,[8] the Creator, of whose creations he is the Protector. In the Parthian period, Mithra, whose earlier identification had been with fire and the various luminaries of Heaven, came pre-eminently to represent the Sun, and thrice daily Zoroastrians invoke Mihr and Xwaršēd (the Sun) together.[9]

In Armenia, Mithra appears to have enjoyed similar prominence in the Zoroastrian cult of the Orontid, Artaxiad and Arsacid kings. The common Armenian word for a non-Christian temple, mehean, has been derived from Old Iranian *māithryāna—'Place of Mithra.'[10] In his famous visit to the Emperor Nero, the Armenian Arsacid king Trdat I invoked Mithra as witness to his covenant with Rome, and in his inscription in Greek at Garni he calls himself Hēlios 'the Sun,' i.e., Mithra.[11] Armenian proper names containing the element mihr- are numerous: Mher, a hero of the Armenian national epic, probably represents the yazata himself; and Mithraustēs, an Armenian hero, fought the armies of Alexander,[12] according to Arrian. The Armenians

1

celebrated Mihragān; the name of their seventh month, Mehekan, resembles that of the Zoroastrian month.[13]   To this day, the Zoroastrians of Iran celebrate the ancient feast of fire, *Āthrakāna, now called the jašn-i Şade 'feast of a hundred days,' by kindling an immense bonfire in the courtyard of the dar-i Mihr, while the Armenians, who call the festival Teaṙn ĕnd aṙaj, 'The Presentation of Our Lord to the Temple,' perform the same ritual in the courtyards of their churches on February 13th (corresponding to the Armenian month of Ahekan, derived from Iranian *Āthrakāna).[14]

Although one would expect, therefore, to find prominent mention of Mihr amongst the other yazatas described by the Classical Armenian historians, he is conspicuously absent. In a ceremonial invocation, witnessed by no less a personage than St. Gregory the Illuminator, King Trdat III, in the late third century, asks the blessings of Aramazd (Old Persian Ahuramazdā; Avestan Ahura Mazdā; Zoroastrian Pahlavi Ohrmazd), Anahit (Old Persian Anāhitā) and Vahagn.[15] The latter is the Zoroastrian yazata Verethraghna; the Armenian form is a loan-word from Parthian.[16] It was on the ruins of Vahagn's temple, at Aštišat, that St. Gregory chose to establish the See of the Armenian Church whence he journeyed to Bagawan (where the royal temple of Aramazd had stood) to celebrate Nawasard with the king[17] and thereby to affirm the balance of ecclesiastical and temporal power in the newly Christian kingdom. Mihr's mehean at Bagayaṙič, an out-of-the-way village, does not seem to rate such an honor. We find also that the Mithraustēs of Arrian is called by Armenian historians Vahē, a name apparently derived from Vahagn.[18] Mihr is not identified as the Sun in Armenian texts, but as Hephaestus, the Greek god of fire.[19] Vahagn is called the Sun, however, and one mediaeval Armenian text relates that omank' zaregakn paštec'in ew Vahagn koč'ec'in 'some worshipped the Sun and called it Vahagn.'[20] The pre-Christian Armenian hymn on the birth of Vahagn transcribed by Movsēs Xorenac'i[21] would seem to depict a sun god.

The eclipse of Mihr in Armenian Zoroastrianism in the first century of the Sasanian period poses a problem. Verethraghna, whose name contains the Avestan word vərəθra--'resistance' and gan--'to strike,' is the Zoroastrian yazata of victory. He is considered a protector of travellers, the sick and the demon-afflicted; his warlike stature makes him the "standard-bearer" of the other divinities in the fight against evil.[22] In the Avestan Hymn to Mithra, he appears as a powerful, raging boar (Avestan varāza-, Armenian varaz) who destroys any man false to the covenant sanctified by Mithra. In

Armenia, Vahagn was called višapak'ał 'dragon-reaper.'[23] Anania Širakac'i explained the expression višap hanel as used in legends to mean a storm.[24] In modern Armenian folklore, Gabriel and the other angels drag up to Heaven those višaps who have grown large enough to threaten the existence of the world. The thrashing about of the monsters causes turbulence in the seas they inhabit, and the angels battle them with swords of lightning before casting them into the Sun, which burns them to cinders. Only the ones that are "ripe" are "reaped" thus (hence the -k'ał of Vahagn's epithet). They are so heavy that Gabriel needs other angels to help him drag them across the sky.[25]

Second to Ḩaldi in the Urartian pantheon was Teišeba, the Hurrian Tešub, a weather god who gave his name to Tušpa, the capital of Bianili (cf. Armenian Tosp, Van), Assyrian Urartu. In a chariot drawn by an ox, Tešub vanquishes the monster Ullikummi, who is depicted on a golden bowl found at Hasanlu in Iranian Azerbaidzhan as a half-human creature with three canine-headed snakes sprouting from the lower half of his body, the whole immersed in water. Tešub and his bull are approaching in the sky above, and water pours from the bull's mouth: the weather is stormy.[26]

In Armenia, the great stones called višaps have wavy lines carved into them to represent water; some of them also bear carvings of the hide of an ox.[27] It would seem from the protest of Eznik Kołbac'i that 'if such a višap be lifted up, it is not by any so-called oxen (ezambk') but by some hidden power [of God],'[28] that the reaper of višaps had the help of oxen. It appears that Vahagn assumed the ancient prestige of Tešub. It has been suggested that the name of the latter's consort, Hepit, survives in Armenian htptank';[29] Vahagn's consort is Astłik, whose name, 'Little Star,' is probably a translation of Syriac kaukabta with the affectionate honorofic suffix -ik.[30] The yazata Vahagn was certainly Zoroastrian, but with a strongly local color to his personality. Armenian writers use the Middle Persian form vṙamakan[31] in referring to fires of Verethraghna established by the iconoclastic Sasanian church, as though emphasizing the distinction between the ancestral faith they had shared with the Parthians and the aggressive, proselytizing instrument the Persians made of it. Similarly, Armenian writers distinguish "Armenian" Aramazd from Middle Persian Ormizd.[32]

The name of Mithra is found in a version of the legend of the contest between Tešub and Ullikummi related by Pseudo-Plutarchus in his description of the Armenian river Arax: Mithra, he says, impregnated a rock on the banks of the Arax, and the rock later gave birth to a monster, Diorphos by name, who challenged Arēs to a contest of valor, and was slain. According to Hittite legend, Kummarbi, the parent of Tešub, wishing to regain the kingship he had lost to his son, impregnated a rock which gave birth to Ullikummi, whom Tešub destroyed.[33]

It is possible that Pseudo-Plutarchus's tale was a propaganda piece fashioned by the Vah(n)unis, the hereditary k'rmapetut'iwn 'high priesthood' of Aštišat, to secure the primacy of their cult against the popular Mihr. Political considerations, such as the constant wariness of the Armenian naxarars against encroachments on their sovereignty, their sense of regional pride, and even a certain hostility toward the Parthian Arsacids may have played a part. For the cult of Mihr in Armenia was strong indeed, and it has been proposed that the Roman legion XV Apollinaris, stationed in the country, was profoundly impressed by it and carried it west, where, with suitable adaptations, it became a major religious force, Mithraism.[34]

The accession to power of the Sasanians changed everything. Ardašīr's family were priests in the temple of Anāhīd at Staxr; Movsēs Xorenac'i places in his mouth an invocation to Mihr mec astuac 'Mihr, the great god.'[35] The Armenian Anahit was very prominent; the cult of the oskemayr 'golden mother' at Erēz probably drew upon autochthonous traditions of a fertility goddess. Aramazd, whose cult center moved with the kings of Armenia from Ani to Bagawan, was of course held in great reverence. An effective way of expressing opposition to the encroachments of Kartīr and his brand of Sasanian catholicism was to promote the cult of Vahagn, a yazata similar in many respects to Mihr and of like militant and triumphant aspect, yet also quite Armenian in character.

There is one place in Armenia, however, where the cult of Mihr has survived down to our own day. On Ascension Day and on the feast of the Transfiguration of Jesus Christ (Armenian Vardavaṙ), the Gate of Mihr (Armenian Mheri duṙn) is said to open on Agṙawuc' k'ar, the Ravens' Rock, at Van. The origin of the New Persian term dar-i Mihr is unknown, so the Armenian term Mheri duṙn is striking and suggestive, In side a cave sits Mihr, or Mher, astride his horse, waiting for the end of the world and its evil.[36] The raven which figures in this tradition, related in the Epic of Sasun, has been compared to the Avestan karšiptar 'black-winged,' who expounds Avestic lore in the var of Yima beneath the earth.[37] Mher's vigil recalls the role of Mithra as judge after death and at Frašegird, the

Zoroastrian final day of judgement, when the world is to be restored to purity.

None of what we know of Mihr in Armenia either contradicts his Zoroastrian essence or contributes to an understanding of the origin of those aspects of western Mithraism which are inconsistent with the teachings of the "Good Religion"; explanation of such phenomena must be sought in the local European cults Mithraism absorbed, rather than in Armenia or Iran.[38] Vahagn's Armenian character may be compared to the regional characteristics assigned to prominent saints of the Roman Catholic Church by Christians in various countries; Armenian Zoroastrianism permitted the use of images in temples, and this feature must have strengthened further the preservation of local traditions. If our hypotheses as to the reasons for the eclipse of Mithra in Armenia are true, they are testimony to the vitality of naxarar sovereignty even in matters of religion, and to Zoroastrian opposition to the Sasanians.   One thing, however, may be stated with certainty: Mithra's importance in Armenia waned in proportion to the popularity of Verethraghna.

NOTES

[1]M. Boyce, A History of Zoroastrianism (Leiden, 1975), 1, 40-52.

[2]Ibid., 49, 52.

[3]M. Boyce, "On Mithra's Part in Zoroastrianism," BSOAS 32 (1969), 1.23.

[4]Boyce, History, 26-7.

[5]Ibid., 86 and "On Mithra's Part in Zoroastrianism," 17 n. 35, 26 n. 82.

[6]M. Boyce, Zoroastrians: Their Religious Beliefs and Practices (London, 1979), 180, 187.   This term is attested only after the Islamic conquest.

[7]Boyce, "On Mithra's Part in Zoroastrianism," 25.

[8]Ibid., 24.

[9]Ibid., 25.

[10]A. Meillet, "Sur les termes religieux iraniens en arménien," REArm 1 (1920), 233-6.

[11]Cassius Dio 63.5; Pliny 1.6; F. Cumont, "L'iniziazione di Nerone da parte di Tiridate d'Armenia," Rivista di Filologia 61 (1933). On the inscription, see M.-L. Chaumont, Recherches sur l'histoire d'Arménie (Paris, 1969), 179; B. Aŕak'elyan, "Excavations at Gaŕni, 1949-50, 1951-55," Contributions to the Archaeology of Armenia (Cambridge, Mass., 1968), 3, 3.13-199; K. V. Trever, Nadpis' o postroenii armjanskoj kreposti Garni (Leningrad, 1949); A. G. Abrahamyan, Hay gri ev grč'ut'yan patmut'yun (Erevan, 1959), 30.

[12]H. Hübschmann, Armenische Grammatik (Leipzig, 1897), 53-4; T'. Avdalbegyan, "Mihrĕ Hayoc' meĵ," Hayagitakan hetazotut'yunner (Erevan, 1969), 14-16; on Mithraustes, see L. P'. Šahinyan, "Movsēs Xorenac'u Patmut'yan meĵ hišatakvoł Vahei masin," Patmabanasirakan Handes (1973), 4.173.

[13]S. H. Taqizadeh, "The Iranian Festivals adopted by the Christians and condemned by the Jews," BSOAS 10 (1940-42), 642.

[14]Hübschmann, Armenische Grammatik, 95; A. G. Abrahamyan, (ed.), Hovhannes Imastaseri matenagrut'yunĕ (Erevan, 1956), 81, 163; M. Y. Ananikian, "Teaŕnĕndaraĵ ew erknayin hurĕ," K'nnakan usumnasirut'iwnner (New York, 1932); L. H. Gray, "On Certain Persian and Armenian Month-Names as Influenced by the Avesta Calendar," JAOS 28 (1907), 339.

[15]Agat'angełos, 127.

[16]E. Benveniste, L. Rénou, Vr̥tra et Vr̥thragna (Paris, 1934), 70, 82; Thieme in JAOS 80 (1960), 312, cited by V. N. Toporov, "Ob otraženii odnogo indoevropejskogo mifa v drevnearmjanskoj tradicii," Patmabanasirakan Handes (1977), 3.98 n. 61.

[17]Agat'angełos, 809-36.

[18]See n. 12 above.

[19]Movsēs Xorenac'i 3.17 describes the temple at Bagayaŕič as dedicated to Hep'estos, whom T'ovma Arcruni 1.3 identifies with the Sun, however.

[20]Nor Baŕgirk' Haykazean Lezui, s. v. Vahagn; on Vahagn's identifica-

tion with the Sun, see also Movsēs Xorenac'i 2.14 and Manuk Abełyan, Erker (Erevan, 1966), 1.75.

[21]Movsēs Xorenac'i 1.31.

[22]Boyce, History, 266; A Persian Stronghold of Zoroastrianism (Oxford, 1977), 71.

[23]Agat'angełos, 809; Movsēs Xorenac'i, 2.12.

[24]L. Ališan, Hin hawatk' kam het'anosakan kronk' Hayoc' (Venice, 1910), 73 n. 1.

[25]Abełyan, Erker, 1.88.

[26]E. Porada, Ancient Iran: The Art of Pre-Islamic Times (London: 1965), 96-101, Figs. 63-4, Pl. 24.

[27]N. Marr, Ya. Smirnov, Les Vichaps (Leningrad, 1931).

[28]A. G. Abrahamyan (trans.), Eznik Kołbac'i: Ełc Ałandoc' (Erevan, 1970), 81.

[29]G. Kapancjan (Łap'anc'yan), Istoriko-lingvističeskie raboty (Erevan, 1956), 1.276. Kapancjan's suggestion is not important to our argument, and it must be noted that his methods were often unreliable.

[30]Agat'angełos, 809.

[31]Ališan, Hin hawatk', 51.

[32]Anania Širakac'i, Mnac'ordk' banic' (St. Petersburg, 1877), 31.

[33]Psuedo-Plutarchus, De fluviis 23.4, discussed by Schwartz, Mithraic Studies 2.416.

[34]C. M. Daniels, "The Role of the Roman Army in the Spread and Practice of Mithraism," Mithraic Studies 2.251.

[35]Movsēs Xorenac'i 3.17.

[36]Abełyan, Erker (Erevan, 1975), 7.54; H. Orbeli, Haykakan herosakan eposě (Erevan, 1956), 52-3; Avdalbegyan, "Mihrě Hayoc' meǰ," 63.

[37]I. Gershevitch, "Die Sonne das Beste," Mithraic Studies 1.88.

[38]Boyce, "On Mithra's Part in Zoroastrianism," 16, suggests that the darker aspects of Western Mithraism cannot have any Zoroastrian source.

CHANGE AND CONTINUITY IN THE RELIGION OF ANCIENT ARMENIA WITH PARTICULAR REFERENCE TO THE VISION OF ST. GREGORY (AGATHANGELOS §731-755)

Anders Hultgård

Uppsala University (Sweden)

When a new religion becomes established in a given region, a change, of course, takes place which may be more or less profound. There is a clear tendency on the part of the new religion to reduce the importance of the previous religion and to make the "conversion" appear as a total and sudden rupture with the ancient faith. In reality, however, the establishment of a new religion would more accurately be described as a process of transformation which requires a rather long time. It is the task of the historian to elucidate this process as far as it is still possible to do so.

The conversion of Armenia to Christianity, as described in Agat'-angełos,[1] clearly shows the tendency indicated above. The work of converting the Armenians is ascribed to one Gregory, called the Illuminator, who, on the order of King Trdat II after refusing to worship the goddess Anahit, is thrown into a deep pit. Gregory's miraculous survival in this prison for nearly 15 years plays a decisive role in convincing the king and the nobles of the superiority of Christianity. The time of the conversion is compressed to the period of Gregory's missionary activity and the idea of a total conversion is conveyed by stressing the unanimity with which the nation acts and is acted upon. Thus, we often read phrases like "the king, the nobles and the common people," or "all the people and the king,"[2] where there is no question of exceptions or opposing groups. Such an effect is achieved by the story of the punishment of all non-believers. The king is transformed into a beast and beset by evil spirits, and all other non-believers, princes and commoners, possessed by demons. This episode also serves to sharpen the contrast between the earlier period of "paganism" and the later period of Christianity, when the Armenians, having been cured by Gregory, accepted

8

the new doctrine.   The contrast is reinforced in the description of the country as a whole.   The punishment of the king and the people was said to have been accompanied by "a terrible desolation upon the country" (§213), but after the conversion to Christianity, it is said:

> At that time this land of Armenia was blessed,
> desirable and immensely admired (§854).

Similarly, the ancient faith is described in terms of the useless worship of idols made of stone and wood, a false lawless cult instituted by Satan and the demons.[3]   These are conventional arguments taken from the polemics directed by Jews and Christians against the polytheistic religions.   Although the heathen Armenians are ignorant and barbarous,[4] they undergo a great transformation once they are converted, becoming spiritual, sober, and instructed.[5]   To sum up, Agat'angełos' leading principle in presenting the history of Armenia's conversion is to show that there was a total and sudden change in religion and civilization.   The allegorical vision of Gregory expresses this idea with the image of herds of black goats who pass through waters and thereby turn into white, shining sheep (§740).

The conversion of Armenia was, in reality, more complicated.   On the one hand, there were Christians in Armenia long before the missionary work of Gregory at the beginning of the fourth century.[6]   On the other hand, some early Armenian writers preserve accounts which point to a strong influence of the pre-Christian religion long after the official conversion of the country. In the biography of Mesrob, for example, Koriwn reports that in his time (the early fifth century) there were many "pagans" in the province of Gołt'n, in the eastern part of Armenia, who were converted by Mesrob.   Again, the picture of the majority of the Armenians given by P'awstos Buzand in one passage of his historical work clearly reveals the persistence of the ancient religion among people.   Long after the conversion, he maintains, the Armenians still devoted themselves to the mythology and the cult of the pre-Christian period.[7]   The civilizing power of Christianity, as described by Agat'angełos, had evidently not been able to transform the people in the way expected by the Christian church.   Other evidence shows the conversion to have been a gradual process of cultural transformation during which much pre-Christian material was preserved and assimilated into the new Christian culture of Armenia.[8]   Here we are concerned with a particular text which reveals a continuity in one aspect hitherto unrecognized.

The conversion of Armenia and the founding of the first Christian monuments are prefigured in a vision that appears to St. Gregory. By virtue of its content, this famous text holds an important position in the work of Agat'angełos.   In an arrangement which corresponds to the traditional presentation of apocalyptic visions in early Jewish and Christian literatures, the vision of Gregory is divided into two parts: that which is seen by the visionary (§733-740) and its subsequent explanation by an interpreting angel (§741-755).

In the vision, the importance given to light and fire images is striking. The firmament of heaven opens and a man in the form of light descends (§733: ew iǰeal ayr mi i kerparans lusoy). Gregory sees a stream of light flowing out from heaven, accompanied by numberless shining figures with wings like fire. The place where they arrive becomes radiant with light.[9] In the middle of the city of Vałaršapat,[10] the visionary sees a tall column of light or fire (§736: siwn mi hrełēn, §737: lusełēn seann) with a capital of cloud, surmounted by a cross of light. Three columns of cloud, with fiery capitals and crosses of light above, surround the column of light, which shines out among the other, lower columns. Above the four columns, which form something like a building with wondrous vaults, there appears a throne of fire with the Lord's Cross above, which spreads light all around. A multitude of fiery altars, each with a column and a cross, become visible, shining out like stars (§736-738).

This prominence of light and fire symbols distinguishes the vision in Agat'angełos from similar Biblical traditions taken over by the Christians of Armenia.   Some of the terms used by Agat'angełos may allude to the tradition of the column of cloud and the column of fire in which the God of Israel appeared to his people, during the wanderings in the desert.   In Exod 13: 21-22 and Neh 9: 19, to mention the principal passages, it is said that in the night, God guided the Israelites by the column of fire, illuminating their way.   While the terminology is similar, though not identical,[11] the differences in meaning and content clearly assure the independence of Agat'angełos from the Exodus tradition.   The idea of the "glory" (Hebrew: kābōd) of YHWH, which spreads light around it (Ezek 1: 27, 10: 4, and 43: 2) presents a certain similarity to the description in Gregory's vision of the throne of fire, above the columns, extending light in every direction (§738). With its evocation of the flaming throne of God in Dan 7: 9, the imagery of this particular passage in the vision of Gregory may be influenced by the Biblical concept of the shining kābōd of God or that of his fiery throne.[12]

It seems difficult, at any rate, to explain the stress laid on the imagery of light in Agat'angełos solely by reference to Jewish and Christian sources. More important in differentiating the vision of Gregory are the two precise functions ascribed to the light and fire phenomena in general.

Firstly, they transmit in a quite material way a divine messenger and other celestial beings from heaven down to the earth. Secondly, the light which flows down and which also appears in the form of a column marks a particular place in the middle of the city, above a circular base of gold, which is to be a place of worship.   This is explicitly stated later in Agat'angełos (§769-770):   Gregory, together with the king and the people, goes to the place where the column of light or fire appears and they enclose the spot where the "house of the Lord" is to be built later. The importance and the characteristic use in Agat'angełos of the light and fire imagery express, I think, a continuity in the religious symbolism of ancient Armenia.

We know little about the pre-Christian faith of the Armenians. The scanty evidence which has come down to us, however, shows a thorough influence of Iranian religion.[13] One of its characteristic features appears to be a complex of light and fire symbolism is intimately bound up with the birth or appearance of a divine figure or messenger. In some variants, this complex contains the idea of the fire or light descending from heaven to indicate a place of worship. The light and fire symbolism may be associated with different figures, such as the god Mithra, the prophet Zoroaster, the coming saviour (particularly the Saoshyant), or the Iranian king. A brief survey of the principal texts where this symbolism is to be found will give an idea of its various expressions.

Dio Chrysostomus of Asia Minor, the Greek rhetor and philosopher of the late first century A. D., has preserved an account of an Iranian cult-myth transmitted to him by the western Magi.[14] Fire from heaven, we are told, descends and lights a hill which burns perpetually. The king, with the Persian nobles, approaches the flaming hill in order to pray to the divinity. A man, in this case Zoroaster, comes out of the fire and exhorts the king and his men to be confident and to perform sacrifices "as if one had come to the place of the god."

The birth of Zoroaster, as described in the Pahlavi texts, is accompanied by several light phenomena.   According to the Dēnkart,[15] during the three nights preceding the birth of the prophet, the village of his father Purusasp, is completely illuminated.   The inhabitants run away, thinking the village has caught fire, but when returning, they find that "a man radiant of light"[16] has been born there. The Selections of Zātspram likewise report that the xvarnah of Zoroaster comes down to the earth in the manner of fire "from the endless light."[17] The fiery xvarnah enters Zoroaster's mother, who becomes radiant, and the place where he is born emits a great light which shines out even to distant places.[18] The passages in Dēnkart and in the Selections of Zātspram which are concerned with this theme refer to earlier authoritative traditions written in the Avestan language.[19]

The royal legend connected with Mithridates Eupator of Pontus (121-63 B. C.) shows the importance given to the light symbolism. During the year he was born and the year he was enthroned, a great, shining star appeared, which was so large that it occupied a fourth of the heavens. The light of the star was so intense that the entire firmament seemed to catch fire.[20]

Finally, there is the tradition of the Magi and the Star. Although this tradition has been preserved only in Christian writings,[21] it is nevertheless obvious that we are dealing with an authentically Iranian tradition.[22] According to the chief texts, the Opus imperfectum in Matthaeum[23] and the Chronicle of Zuqnin,[24] the Magi, during a certain feast, gather on a hill called the mountain of victory (mons victorialis; in the Syriac text twr nšhn'), where there is a cave with a fountain and wonderful trees. Having purified themselves in the fountain, they pray in silence and wait for the appearance of a great light announcing the coming of a divine figure. Then a star above a column of light appears, the light descends and fills the cave, and the entire mountain becomes luminous. The heavens are opened, like a large gate, and radiant beings in human form descend, carrying the light of the star in their hands.[25] A little man (Syriac: 'nš' z'wr')[26] descends through the column of light and comes forth in the cave with the flaming light.

The texts do not tell us who this divine being, manifesting himself through the light, might be, because at this point the Iranian tradition has been superseded by the Christian legend of the birth of Jesus in Bethlehem. Most probably, the radiant figure appearing through the column of light is none other than the god Mithra or his incarnation in a savior king. In the Mysteries of Mithra the birth of the god is often depicted showing a little man coming out of the rock, holding a burning torch in his hand.[27] Sometimes flames appearing out of the the rock underline the fiery character of the god being born,[28] who is also called genitor luminis.[29]   In late Achaemenian and Parthian times, the connection of Mithra with light and the sun is common in Iran even outside the Mysteries.   It is also during this period that the Iranian king becomes associated particularly with Mithra. The king is styled "the great light of Mithra"[30] or "he who is enthroned with Mithra and rising together with the sun."[31]

In the tradition of the Magi and the star, the mountain with its cave where the light descends is clearly considered as a place of worship.   This is evident in the praying and the ritual washing of the Magi.   Further evidence of the cultic setting is found in the account of Porphyry referring to Eubolus who says that Zoroaster consecrated a cave and a fountain in the hills of Persis for the worship of Mithra.[32]

We are thus presented with a clear pre-Christian background which explains the emphasis placed on the light and fire phenomena as well as their central functions in the vision of Gregory.   Some of the characteristic details, such as the appearance of the column of light or fire,[33] and the descent of a divine messenger and radiant beings with the light, have their closest equivalents in Iranian traditions.   It may furthermore be significant that in Agat'angełos the golden base on which the column of light appears is compared to a large hill.[34]

Our conclusion is that in the vision of Gregory Agat'angełos draws on pre-Christian symbolism which has been adapted to a new context   and interpreted more explicitly along Christian lines in the second part of the vision.   The most plausible explanation of this influence is that the light and fire symbolism, as evidenced in the Iranian traditions, was part of the Armenian pre-Christian religion too.

A fragment of the mythical complex concerning the appearance of a divine figure through light and fire has in fact been preserved by the Armenian tradition.   This is the famous passage in Movsēs Xorenac'i describing the birth of Vahagn, the hero-god whose name is derived from the old Iranian Verethraghna.   In the few lines quoted by Xorenac'i from an ancient poem (erg), it is said that Vahagn manifests himself as a young child (or little man?), a patanekik in Armenian, rushing out (vazēr) from the reeds in flames and fire.[35]   There is much evidence in favor of the supposition that the epiphany of Mithra, described along the lines of the Iranian light and fire symbolism, was known and used also in ancient Armenia.[36]

During the Hellenistic and Roman periods, Mithra (Armenian: Mihr)

seems to have been, together with the goddess Anahit, the principal divinity
of Armenia. Although the materials concerning Mihr and his cult that have
come down to us are sparse, we get a hint of his importance to the
Armenians. We know of two temples dedicated to the cult of Mihr: one in
Bagayaric in western Armenia, probably going back to Achaemenian times,[37]
the other in Garni in the northeastern part of the country, dating from the
first century A. D.[38]   One of the general terms for "temple" in old
Armenian, mehean, derives from the name of Mihr (Middle Iranian:
mihriyan),[39] thus attesting the importance of this god among the Armenians.[40]   A month, mehekan, is named after the god Mihr.[41] The Armenian
king Trdat who, accompanied by Magi, came to Rome to visit Nero, is said
to have adored Mithra.[42] A Greek geographical writing connects Mithra with
the river Arax in the heart of Armenia.[43]   Last but not least, the popular
epic cycle, known as David of Sasun, seems to have preserved important
traditions about the god Mihr-Mithra, pertaining to his eschatological role as
well as to his cult in western Mithraism.[44]   In one of these traditions,
centered around the figure of Mher (= Mihr), we are told that once a year,
at midnight on Ascension Day,

> heaven and earth come together,
> they embrace one another in the light[45]

whereupon the rock in which Mher dwells, miraculously opens and Mher
comes out with his horse. This recalls the first line of the poem on the birth
of Vahagn "heaven and earth were in travail" and the myth of Mithra being
born in light out of the rock, celebrated in an annual feast by the Magi.

In central and eastern Asia Minor, the cult of Mithra seems to have
been already well established in the second century B. C. The royal dynasty
of Pontus, the Mithridates, stands under the protection of the god from whom
they derive their name.[46] In Commagene the god Mithra plays a prominent
role on the monuments of the royal dynasty. Mithra is the god who institutes
the king in his dignity as shown by the scenes of their dexiosis. In the royal
decrees, Mithra, identified with Apollo-Helios, is second to Zeus-Oro-
mazdes.[47] An inscription in Ariamneia from the first century B. C. mentions
a person who was a Magus of Mithra.[48] Other inscriptions dating from the
first centuries of our era demonstrate the continuity of the cult of Mithra
in Asia Minor.[49]

To sum up the result of our investigation so far, we may say that
there is a continuity of religious symbolism in the use that Agat'angełos

makes of the light and fire imagery.   There is more to say about the continuity of symbolism in the vision of Gregory.   The fiery altars mentioned in §739 probably allude to the Iranian pyreia of which it is said in the angel's interpretation that they will be truly the altars of God (§752).[50]   The description of the fiery columns in Agat'angełos has in fact been associated with the particular form of the Mazdean fire-altars in the Sasanian period.[51] The tall and fearful man who comes swiftly down from heaven like an eagle and strikes the ground of the earth with his golden hammer, as seen by Gregory in §735, has certainly pre-Christian models.[52]   One may point to Vahagn who as "dragon-handler" (višapak'ał)[53] must have had a weapon like the club of the Iranian Verethraghna or the hammer of the ancient Scandinavian god Thórr.   Resemblances to more ancient native deities, such as the one whose image has been found in Karmir Blur, holding in his right hand an object which looks like a hammer and in his left hand an axe, cannot be ignored.   This image may depict Teišeba, the god of war and thunder who gave his name to the ancient fortress of Karmir Blur, Teišebani;[54] or perhaps it represents another god connected with forging and warfare.

A continuity in religious matters manifests itself also in the persistence of sacred times and places of worship.   Agat'angełos offers a good example of the impact of the ancient religious feasts on the Christian calendar.   After the baptism of the royal house and a multitude of people in the Euphrates, it is said that Gregory instituted a commemoration of the martyrs and that he fixed the date for celebrating this festival at the same time as the worship of the former gods Amanor and Vanatur (§836).   This passage illustrates also the continuity of the cult in one and the same place although there has been a change of religion.   The text states that the Christian feast should be celebrated in the same place where they previously used to worship the pagan gods.

Such a cultic continuity seems to have occurred in more than one place.   A Christian church was, according to Agat'angełos, erected on the foundations of the temple of Vahagn in Aštišat.[55]   When mentioning this church P'awstos Buzand makes the statement that the Armenians generally transformed pagan cult-centers into Christian places of worship.   Archaeological excavations have also revealed the existence of pre-Christian remnants below the churches of St. Hṙip'simē and the basilica of Kassakh.[56]

In the Iranian religion, as we have seen, the myth of a descending light or fire also has the function of marking a sacred place where a cult will be performed. Now, the use made by Agat'angełos of this myth in its cultic setting strongly suggests that the place in the middle of Vałaršapat where the light-stream descended and the column of light appeared, was a center of worship before a Christian church was built on the same spot.

What does the archaeological evidence tell us?[57] The excavations made under the present cathedral of Ējmiacin in the late fifties have shown that the actual plan of the church goes back to a building from the fifth century, in all probability the church erected by Vahan Mamikonian a short time after 480. Below this fifth-century church there were found remnants of an earlier construction, showing four somewhat irregular bases for pillars and an apse, to mention the most important remnants. In the eastern apse, within the oldest part and below the altar-stone from the fifth century, a fire-altar was found. Furthermore, in front of the bema of the same apse an Urartian stele with a cross carved on the upper part was discovered.

How to interpret these findings? The earliest remnants found below the present cathedral are generally interpreted as belonging to the first Christian church erected by Gregory following the divine command in the vision.[58] A. Sahinian, the excavator, is also of the opinion that the Persians, during their incursions in the fourth and fifth centuries, destroyed the first church and transformed it into a fire-temple.[59] The stele, according to Sahinian, shows that in the Urartian period Ējmiacin and its surroundings were a cult-center.[60]

It seems to me, however, that things are more complicated, and I will indicate some problems to which I have no definite solution. For the interpretation of the archaeological findings I am only able to present hypotheses which I hope will stimulate further discussion.

The Armenian tradition as represented by the fifth-century historians certainly asserts that Gregory erected a church "in the middle of the city" of Vałaršapat. The principal witness to that is the text of Agat'angełos, especially the vision in §733-755 through which Gregory receives the divine command of building "the house of the Lord."[61] Łazar Parpec'i seems to reflect this tradition when stating that the "house of the Lord" in Vałaršapat had been erected by an angel.[62] In describing the vision seen by Sahak Part'ev at the "altar of the Lord" in the cathedral of Vałaršapat, Łazar clearly reveals his dependence on Agat'angełos.[63] It is generally believed that the cathedral of Gregory the Illuminator was destroyed or badly damaged by the Persians, under Shapur II, who invaded Armenia and ravaged the country.[64]   The evidence is the report of P'awstos Buzand of how the Persians destroyed the churches in many provinces and how they captured Vaɫaršapat and leveled the city without leaving a single building intact.[65] Using the same evidence of P'awstos, one could, however, argue in an opposite way. If the cathedral of Gregory, supposed to be renowned all over the country, existed at that time in Vaɫaršapat, it becomes difficult to understand why its destruction is not explicitly mentioned. Nor is it stated by P'awstos that churches were transformed into fire-temples.[66]

If the first and main textual witness of an early fourth-century cathedral in Ējmiacin is the book of Agat'angeɫos, and knowing that the actual Armenian text was not redacted before 460, how can we be sure that the remnants found below the fifth century level belong to a Christian building? In the materials to which I have had access, it is not obvious that the fire-altar was found in a layer distinct from the one belonging to the supposed early fourth-century cathedral. Moreover, it is peculiar that, according to Agat'angeɫos, a church is not immediately erected on the spot where the column of light appeared as is done on the places where the three lower columns were revealed. The place for the future cathedral, "the house of the Lord," is simply encircled and consecrated through the setting up of a cross (§769-770).[67]   Only at a later time is a church erected there by Gregory. Considering the compressed perspective of Agat'angeɫos' description of the conversion, this fact may be taken as an indication that, in reality, the cathedral was not constructed until a much later period, e. g. the fifth century.

If we look back to the imagery of the vision, Gregory sees an abundant fountain flowing forth which fills the plains. This, of course, may be an allusion to Christian baptism as explicated in the interpretation of the vision (§751). In fact, a basin with water conduits seems to have been part of the fourth century construction in Ējmiacin. This element has been taken to be the baptismal font of the first church;[68] however, the Iranian traditions which we have mentioned also speak about a fountain and ritual purifications. The shrines of western Mithraism are usually provided with a water basin and ducts, as is the rule in Zoroastrian fire-temples. Moreover, the fire-temples often have a dome-like structure resting on four corner-piers or pillars[69] and could easily be transformed into Christian churches or vice versa.[70] It must, however, be noted that the normal form of Iranian fire-temples, at least in the Sasanian period, had the fire-altar in the center of the dome.   In

Ējmiacin the fire-altar was found in an apse outside the square formed by the four bases.[71]   The fourth-century construction may then represent an Armenian pagan sanctuary dedicated to the cult of Mihr or perhaps Anahit. This sanctuary could have been reutilized, after some modifications, as a Christian church until the fifth-century cathedral was erected.   Another possibility is that the original, supposedly pagan building was demolished to give place to the fifth-century church.   In the vision, Gregory sees four columns from which wonderful vaults are stretching, and there is something like a dome above.   As A. Khatchatrian has pointed out,[72] these details suggest that the visionary is describing an actual building either completed or under construction.   In this case, however, it would have been the construction of the fifth century cathedral which, with respect to chronology, fits well with the final redaction of the Armenian text of Agat'angełos.[73]

The foregoing remarks are intended to illustrate the complexity of the data which we have to consider when interpreting the earliest history of the cathedral of Ējmiacin.   Whatever the implications drawn from the discovery of the fire-altar, I think that the imagery used by Agat'angełos, together with the discovery of the stele, point to the existence of a pre-Christian cult in the place where the present cathedral stands.

In conclusion, the vision of Gregory is in itself an eloquent witness to the change of religion in ancient Armenia.   In addition to the obvious Judeo-Christian background of our imagery, we find a continuity expressed in the preservation of certain pre-Christian symbols, figures, and ideas.   The materials taken over have been adapted and Christianized and we may see a concrete expression of this process in the emphasis put on the cross (xač'n terunakan) in the text of Agat'angełos.   On his campaign to uproot the pagan cults, Gregory sets up the Lord's cross, "the all-saving sign," everywhere, consecrating the ancient places of worship for the new faith.[74]   Just as the cross engraved on the pre-Christian stele found below the altar of the cathedral seems to have been a mark of Christianization, so too the crosses which appear above the column of light and the fiery altars in the vision may be seen as the visible mark of the Christianization of pagan symbols or ideas.

NOTES

I wish to express my thanks to Peter Cowe, Hebrew University of Jerusalem, for correcting the English of my manuscript.

[1]The basis for the study of Agat'angełos is the critical edition of the Armenian text by K. Ter Mkrtč'ian and S. Kanayeanc' (Tiflis, 1909). Furthermore, the recent edition and translation by R. W. Thomson, Agathangelos' History of the Armenians (Albany, NY: SUNY, 1976) is particularly useful for the commentaries and the references in the English text to Biblical passages alluded to by Agat'angełos. The Greek translation of the authoritative Armenian text (Aa) has recently been edited by G. Lafontaine, La version grecque ancienne du livre arménien d'Agathange, édition critique (Louvain, 1973). Another Greek text (Vg) of the life of Gregory contains the vision treated in the present study. It has been edited by G. Garitte, Documents pour l'étude du livre d'Agathange (Studi e Testi 127; Città del Vaticano, 1946). Garitte (246-260) shows that this Greek version is based on an Armenian text different from the one that has come down to us.

[2]See, for instance, Agat'angełos §§211-213, 221, 225, 243, 246, 728, and 832.

[3]Ibid., §§67, 232, 234, 241, 771, 787, and 799.

[4]Ibid., §§789, 797, 809, and 839.

[5]Ibid., §§789, 837, 839, and 865.

[6]The legends of Thaddeus and Bartholomeus preaching Christianity among the Armenians in the first century may contain an historical core in preserving the memory of an early mission in Armenia. The Roman church reveres a St. Acacius said to have been martyred in the year 110 in the region of Ararat together with many other Christians. Eusebius cites a letter from a Greek patriarch to an Armenian bishop. For this and other indications of Christianity in Armenian before the fourth century, see M. Ormanian, L'Eglise arménienne (2 ed., Antelias-Liban, 1954), 3-8.

[7]P'awstos Buzand 3.13.

[8]Armenian folklore has preserved fragments of the ancient pre-Christian faith, cf. the general statements of M. Abeghian (Abełyan), Der

armenische Volksglaube (Leipzig, 1899), 5-7, and of A. Aharonian, Les anciennes croyances arméniennes (d'après le folk-lore arménien) (Genève, 1913), 12. See note 42 below on the epic David of Sasun. A summary of pagan survivals in the Christian culture of Armenia is given in E. Bauer, Arménie son histoire et son présent (Bibliotheque des Arts: Lausanne-Paris, 1977), 78-79.

[9]It appears from §735 that this is the same place where the column of light is revealed.

[10]The Armenian text does not explicitly mention Vałaršapat but the context makes it clear that the words "in the middle of the city" refer to Vałaršapat. (Vg) reads "in the most central place of the city Artašat," which does not seem original. On the other hand, (Vg) may be right in stating that the column of light and the other columns had "a royal foundation" (§77: krēpida basilikēn, §78: treis krēpidas basileōn). The word krēpis is often used of altar-foundations (see H. G. Liddell and R. Scott: A Greek-English Lexicon (ed. H. S. Jones; Oxford, 1940), 994), and perhaps the royal cult-places in Vałaršapat are hinted at: cf. the pagan remnants below the church of St. Hřipsimē (see further note 56). The Armenian text (Aa) speaks about "a circular base" which is "near the royal palace" (§736). (Vg) translates the Armenian xarisx "base" with basis.

[11]The Armenian Bible uses the terms siwn ampoy and siwn hroy, and the words describing God's guidance during the night run as follows: lusatu linel noc'a i gnaln.

[12]It must, however, be noted that with regard to the wording Agat'angełos shows no direct dependence on the Armenian Bible. According to Ezek 1:26-27, the prophet sees something which resembles a throne (nmanut'iwn at'oroy) and above it the likeness of a human figure (nmanut'iwn kerparanac' mardoy) whose appearance is a radiant fire (ztesil hroy i nerk'oy). This is the kābōd of God which surrounds itself with light (ew loysn or šurǰ znovaw bak uner). In 10:4, the movement of the kābōd is described: the cloud filled the sanctuary and the courtyard was filled with the light of the glory of the Lord (ew srahn li ełew lusov p'arac'n teařn). The arrival of the kābōd in the new temple seen by Ezekiel makes the earth shine like luminaries around the "glory" (ew erkirn lusaworec'aw i nmanut'iwn lusaworac' i p'ařac'n šurǰanaki). Daniel 7:9 mentions the throne of God which

was like flames of fire (at'oł nora ibrew zboc' hroy). The passage under discussion in Agat'angełos §738 runs: tesanēi at'oł zarmanali astuacakert sk'anč'eli hrełēn ew zxač'n tērunakan i veray nora zorov p'areal xač'in ew maceal i noyn miacaw.

[13]Strabo in his Geography (11.14:16) states this influence with the following wording: "All sacred things (hapanta hiera) of the Persians, are also held in honour by both Medes and Armenians."

[14]Oratio 36:40.

[15]Dēnkart 7.2:56-58.

[16]The Pahlavi text runs: mart i rāyōmand.

[17]Selections of Zātspram 8:8-9. The most important words are: pat ātaxš aivēnak hač hān i asar rōšnēh frōt āmat.

[18]In Pahlavi: brāh ut payrōk dur giyāk payrokēnihist.

[19]See for this question A. Hultgard, "Das Judentum in der hellen-istisch- römischen Zeit und die iranische Religion, ein religionsgeschichtliches Problem," Aufstieg und Niedergang der Römischen Welt 2.19:1, 517-518, with reference to the works of G. Widengren and M. Molé.

[20]Justinianus 38.2:1-3.

[21]The tradition concerning the Magi and their cult is first utilized by the author of the Gospel of Matthew in the infancy narrative 2:1-12. Using new legendary material, partly of Iranian origin, the theme is further elaborated in the Protoevangelium of James which, however, splits the unity of the primitive narrative into two distinct parts. First, the birth of Christ in the cave (19:2), which is filled with an intense light and when that light withdraws the child appears. Only later (21:1-2) the Magi arrive guided by the great Star from which, in the original Iranian tradition, the light filling the cave emanated. Drawing on the Gospel of Matthew and the Proto-evangelium of James, the adoration of the Magi becomes a popular motif in Christian literature and art.

[22]This has been pointed out by U. Monneret de Villard, Le leggende orientali sui Magi evangelici (Città del Vaticano, 1952), 48-50 and in particular by G. Widengren, Les religions de l'Iran (Paris: Payot, 1968), 238-243.

[23]This is an anonymous commentary on the Gospel of Matthew probably redacted around the year 400. When commenting on Matt 2:1-12, the author asks, Qui sunt magi? Then he presents the information which was available to him about the Persian priests. The text with introduction and notes is found in J. Bidez and F. Cumont, Les mages hellénisés (Paris: Société d'édition "Les Belles Lettres," 1938), 2.118-120.

[24]This chronicle published under the title Incerti auctoris Chronicon Pseudo-Dionysianum vulgo dictum, by I.-B. Chabot, (CSCO, Script. Syri. 43; Paris, 1927), is found in a ninth century manuscript of the Vatican library. The final redaction of the Chronicle took place around the year 775, but it incorporates much older materials. At some passages, the Chronicle gives rather long excerpts from other writings. On pages 41-45 we find a passage from the History of Alexander introduced with the words: mn tš'yt' d'l 'lksndrws. Similarly, when arriving at the birth of Christ, the Chronicle gives a long extract from an earlier source, prefaced with the following headline: "On the revelation of the magi and on their arrival in Jerusalem and on the offerings which they brought to the Christ" ('l glyn' dmgwš' w'l mtythwn dl'wršlm w'l qwrbn' d'ytyw lmšyh'). The Opus imperfectum appears to draw on the same source as the Chronicle. The source is probably an early Jewish-Christian composition with gnostic tendencies which has incorporated authentic Iranian traditions in the description of the Magi and their cult.

[25]Chronicle of Zuqnin (ed. Chabot), 66.

[26]Ibid., 67.

[27]Corpus Inscriptionum et Monumentorum Religionis Mithriacae (CIMRM; ed. M. J. Vermaseren; Haag (M. Nijhoff, 1956), nos. 256, 353, 390, 428, and 860.

[28]CIMRM, no. 42.4 (Fig. 18).

[29]See M. J. Vermaseren, Mithras, Geschichte eines Kultus (Urbanbücher 83; Stuttgart, 1965), 51.

[30]Plutarchus, Alexander 30:4. Darius raises a question to his eunuch which begins: eipe moi sebomenos Mithrou te phōs mega kai dexian basileion.

[31]Alexander Romance of Pseudo-Kallisthenes 1.36 (Historia Alexandri Magni; ed. W. Kroll; Berlin, 1926). The passage quoted belongs to one of the older sources of the Romance, see R. Merkelbach, Die Quellen des

griechischen Alexander-romans (München, 1954), 1-5, 39, and 195-219.

[32]Porphyry, De antro nympharum, 5.

[33]As far as I have been able to ascertain, Agat'angełos is the first to make use of the originally Iranian image of divine light or fire descending from heaven to earth in the form of a "column" or "stele" (cf. the phloginēn stēlēn of (Vg) §82). Gregory the Thaumaturge writes (around 270) concerning the Adoration of the Magi that "a star with its torch guided them" (Second Homily on the Annunciation to the Holy Virgin Mary). Here a comet is meant, conceived as the star with its "torch" depicted on a coin of Augustus showing the caesaris astrum (H. Mattingly, Coins of the Roman Empire in the British Museum (London, 1923), (Plate VI, 6). In the Christian traditions of the Magi and the Star, the column of light appears in later compositions like the Syriac and the Armenian infancy gospels; see P. Peeters, Evangiles Apocryphes (Paris, 1914), 25 (the Syriac version) and 125 (the Armenian version).

[34]Agat'angełos §736: xarisx oski mecut'eamb ibrew zmec'mi blur.

[35]Movsēs Xorenac'i, Patmut'iwn Hayoc' 1.31.

[36]In this connection mention must also be made of the Gospel of Ējmiacin, showing the Adoration of the Magi who present crowns as gifts to the child, a feature which points to Iran. See G. Widengren, Iranische-semitische Kulturbegegnung in partischer Zeit (Köln-Opladen, 1960), 111.

[37]Cf. G. Widengren, Les Religions de l'Iran, 252-53, with references to earlier literature. This temple is mentioned in Agat'angelos §790.

[38]For this sanctuary, see the recent article by A. Sahinian: L'antico Tempio della forterezza di Garni (Actes du premier congrès international sur l'art arménien; Venice, 1979), 601-604.

[39]See, for this, the discussion in A. Meillet, "Sur les termes religieux iraniens en arménien," REArm 1 (1920-21), 233-34; G. Widengren, Les Religions de l'Iran, 214; and I. Gershevitch, "Die Sonne das Beste," Mithraic Studies (ed. J. Hinnells; Manchester, 1975), 87.

[40]Cf. also R. Frye, "Mithra in Iranian History," Mithraic Studies 1.66.

[41]A. Meillet, "Termes religieux iraniens," 234.

[42]Dio Cassius, 63.5.

[43]Pseudo-Plutarch, De Fluviis 26 §4.

[44]The relevant parts have been translated into English by J. A. Boyle, "Mher in the Carved Rock," Mithraic Studies 1 (1976), 107-118.   This translation is based upon the recension of D. Tchitouny, Sassounacan, épopée populaire arménienne (Paris, 1942), 1083-1097. For the connections of these popular traditions with western Mithraism, see I. Gershevitch, "Die sonne das beste," 81-89, and with the eschatological role of Mithra, see G. Widengren, Les Religions de l'Iran, 238.

[45]Tchitouny, Sassounacan §887 line 3.

[46]On the Mithridates and their royal ideology, see the summary in A. Hultgård, L'Eschatologie des Testaments des Douze Patriarches (Uppsala, 1977), 339-341.

[47]For the royal monuments and inscriptions of the dynasty of Commagene, see K. Humann and O. Puchstein, Reisen in Kleinasien und Nordsyrien: Textband und Atlas (Berlin, 1890); K. Dörner and Th. Goell, Arsameia am Nymphaios (Berlin, 1963), and H. Waldmann, Die kommagen-ischen Kultreformen unter König Mithradates I: Kallininkos und seinem Sohne Antiochus I (Leiden, 1973).

[48]CIMRM 19:   Sagarios Mag[aphe]rnou strategos Ariaramneias ema-geuse Mithrē.

[49]CIMRM 18, a dedication theō dikaiōi Mithrai.   CIMRM 23 is dedicated to Mithra, God of the sun (from Phrygia first century A. D.), CIMRM 17 from Caesarea in Cappadocia: Soli invicto Mythrae. CIMRM 22 records the celebration of Mithrakana in Phrygia.

[50]There is in Agat'angełos another passage which also seems to reflect the Iranian complex of light and fire symbolism.   When the king and the people go down to baptism in the river Euphrates, a marvelous sign is revealed by God: an intense light (loys sastik) appears in the form of a shining column and above it is the likeness of the Lord's cross (§833).

[51]See A. Khatchatrian, L'architecture arménienne du IVe au VIe siècle (Paris, 1971), 77.

[52]Ibid., 75 suggests deities like Jupiter or Vulcanus.

[53]Agat'angełos §809.

[54]Cf. B. Piotrovsky: The ancient civilization of Urartu (Geneva, 1969), 153, 174.

[55]Agat'angełos §812. P'awstos Buzand 30.3 states that this was the first church, mother of all other Armenian churches.

[56]See A. Sahinian, Recherches scientifiques sous les voûtes de la cathédrale d'Etchmiadzine, REArm 3 (1966), 69, 50.

[57]For the results of the excavations I rely on A. Sahinian, Recherches scientifiques, and his report, "Novye Dannye ob Arxitekturnom Oblike Ečmiacinskogo Sobora," (Orientalist Congress in Moscow, 1960), 575-578, and on Khatchatrian, L'architecture arménienne, 67-73.

[58]Sahinian, Recherches scientifiques, 41-42 and A. Khatchatrian, L'architecture arménienne, 73, 84.

[59]Sahinian, Recherches scientifiques, 42-43, 68.

[60]Ibid., 70.

[61]The completion of this command is related in Agat'angełos §770, cf. §841.

[62]Łazar P'arpec'i 8 in the description of Vałaršapat: Zhreštakac'oyc himnarkut'iwnn srboy tann astucoy.

[63]Łazar P'arpec'i 16-17. The opening of the heavens may be a traditional image, but the intense light which illuminates the earth and the appearance of a man resplendant of light is taken from Agat'angełos. The text states explicitly that the vision of Sahak is similar to the one Gregory had.

[64]So for instance J. Strzygowski, Die Baukunst der Armenier und Europa (Wien, 1918) I.334, and A. Sahinian, Recherches scientifiques, 42-43.

[65]P'awstos Buzand 4.55, 58.

[66]P'awstos 4.58 records only that Vahan and Meružan ordered fire-temples to be built on several localities as on their own domains.

[67]The reason for not building a church on this spot is not given. In §782 within the framework of a general description of Gregory's work, it is said that he did not build an altar anywhere because he was not a priest. This seems, however, an artificial explanation in view of the fact that there

were bishops and priests in Armenia before and during the period of Gregory.

[68]See Khatchatrian, L'architecture arménienne, 71.

[69]Cf. E. Herzfeld, Archaeological History of Iran (London, 1935), 66-67, 88-93.

[70]Cf. Widengren, Les Religions de l'Iran, 304.

[71]In Uruk-Warka there has been found a construction with an apse, in all probability a Mithra-sanctuary; cf. Ibid., 259 and Fig. C.

[72]Ibid., 73-86.

[73]The redaction of the authoritative Armenian text.   See for this R. W. Thomson, Agathangelos, xxv.

[74]Agat'angełos §§768-770, 782, 784, 785.

ETHNO-HISTORY AND THE ARMENIAN INFLUENCE UPON

THE CAUCASIAN ALBANIANS

Robert H. Hewsen

Glassboro State College (USA)

It is to be expected at a conference devoted to the reciprocal influences between Armenia and its neighbors that sooner or later our attention should be drawn to the relations betweenn the Armenians and the Caucasian Albanians.[1] Christianized by the Armenians,[2] with a church subordinate to that of Armenia,[3] and endowed with an alphabet invented by an Armenian (St. Mesrob Maštoc'),[4] the Albanians acquired several districts of eastern Armenia in the fourth century,[5] and after being largely Islamicized and Turkified in the seventh to twelfth centuries, most of the survivors apparently ended by being absorbed by the Armenians.[6]

If we were merely to restate these facts, however, there would be little need for us to do so here, for they are all well known. What draws our attention to the question of Armeno-Albanian relations is the fact that in recent years these have become the subject of a curious polemic between Azerbaidzhani and Armenian scholars in the Soviet Union. This polemic forces specialists in the West, where objectivity is more easily maintained, to re-examine what we know of these relations, in an attempt to resolve the issues which have been raised.

The controversy in question began in Baku in 1965 with the publication of a monograph entitled "Azerbaidzhan in the Seventh-Ninth Centuries" by the Azerbaidzhani scholar Z. Bunjatov.[7] Space does not permit a detailed analysis of the hypotheses set forth by Bunjatov in this work, but essentially they may be reduced to the following points:

1)   The Albanians in antiquity were one of the three major peoples of Caucasia, with a country which extended from Lake Sevan eastwards to the Caspian Sea, and from the Caucasus Range southwards to the River Arax.

2)   The influence of the Albanian Church upon its people was gradually reduced by the Armenian Church, which fostered a deliberate polity

27

of Armenicization upon it.[8]

3)   The Albanians had a rich national literature which the Armenian clergy, with the connivance and cooperation of the Arabs, translated into its own tongue and then destroyed.[9]

4)   The Azeri population of present-day Azerbaidzhan represents in large part the Islamicized and Turkified Albanians. The Armenian population of Azerbaidzhan similarly represents not the Armenian people per se but only the Christianized and Armenicized Albanians.[10]

5)   The Armenian population of the mountainous regions of Aran (Siwnik', Arc'ax, Xač'en, Šak'ē, Gardman, etc.) and elsewhere in Soviet Azerbaidzhan, as well as that of certain villages in the rajons (Russian: 'district') of Sisian, Basargeč'ar and elsewhere in Soviet Armenia, shows itself, by its customs and manners, to be identical to the Azeri population of Azerbaidzhan and hence must represent the descendants of Albanians belonging to the Armenian Church, who became assimilated to the Armenians.[11]

Stripped of its academic trappings, what Bunjatov is obviously implying is that the Armenian and Azerbaidzhani populations in both Karabagh and Azerbaidzhan proper are essentially one and the same people except for such details as language and religion. Since the Soviets openly speak of the coming together of the languages of the peoples of the U. S. S. R. (their "mutual enrichment" being the euphemism) and the Soviet attitude toward religion is well known, it is easy to see that neither of these factors would be regarded as being an insurmountable obstacle to the assimilation of peoples in such disputed areas as Karabagh. But beyond this easy equating of two such otherwise distinct ethnic entities as Karabaghi Armenians and Azeri Turks, Bunjatov's hypotheses have weightier implications. What he appears to be saying is that not only is Karabagh properly Azerbaidzhani territory but much of eastern Soviet Armenia too, if all were allowed their claim.

As bold, aggressive, and pregnant with implications as Bunjatov's hypotheses obviously are, it was only natural that Armenian academicians should have quickly geared themselves for a campaign in the scholarly journals as their ancestors had once done for battle in the field. The office of Armenian Commander-in-Chief and paramount strategist in this strange war of words was assumed by A. S. Mnac'akanyan, who in less than a year launched a counterattack against the Azeri invasion in the form of a little book with the disingenuous title <u>On Questions of Albanian Literature</u>,[12] a work speedily translated into Russian doubtless to increase its impact.[13] In this study, Mnac'akanyan rebuts the hypotheses of his Azeri antagonist along the following lines:

1)   Quoting Strabo (11.4.6; 8.4), Pliny (6.15.4; 16.2), and Ptolemy (5.11), as well as P'awstos Buzand (5.13), Movsēs Xorenac'i (2.44-45), Stephan of Byzantium, and the anonymous Ašxarhac'oyc', Mnac'akanyan demonstrates that prior to the end of the fourth century A. D. the Albanians inhabited only the regions lying between East Georgia and the Caspian Sea and between the Caucasus Mountains and the River Kur.[14]

2)   The regions lying south of the Kur between Lake Sevan and the Arax, i. e. the old Armenian lands of Arc'ax and Utik', belonged, he claims, to the Armenians from the earliest formation of the Armenian people, i. e. from the seventh century B. C. Taken from the Armenians by the Medes in the sixth century B. C., these lands were reunited with Armenia by King Artašēs in the second century B. C.[15]

3)   Eastern Armenia, according to Movsēs Xorenac'i (1.12), formed the hereditary domains of the Princes of Siwnik', a house of Armenian origin.[16]

4)   These eastern regions were lost to Armenia and passed under Albanian rule only in 387 A. D. Mnac'akanyan refers to this lost territory as "New Albania" to distinguish it from Albania proper, lying north of the Kur.[17]

5)   "New Albania" asserts Mnac'akanyan, was an Armenian entity in every way. Far from being assimilated by their Albanian rulers, the local Armenians reasserted their Armenian nationality, and being culturally more advanced than the Albanian tribes, who had no single language in common, they ultimately absorbed them.[18]

6)   All conflicts in regard to Albanian history, ethnicity, language, literature, etc., must be examined, and can only be understood, in the light of the existence of this dual Albania, i. e. Albania proper, north of the Kur, and New Albania, comprised of Armenian territories lying south of that river.[19]

7)   The Albanian kings, being Arsacids like the kings of Armenia, were pro-Armenian themselves, and the pro-Armenian element constituted the most advanced stratum of the Albanian population. For this reason Armenian soon became the official language of both the Albanian state and

the Albanian church.[20]

8)   St. Mesrob provided for the use of the Armenian alphabet among the Armenian population of "New Albania"; his Albanian script was devised only for the use of the Albanians of Albania proper.[21] The scriptures which he presented to the Albanian King Arsuał and to Eremia, the Chief Bishop of Albania, could only have been the already existing Armenian translation.   This shows both the high degree of Armenicization of the Albanians at this time, as well as the Armenian orientation of the Albanian church and court.[22]

9)   What has been called "Albanian" literature is really only the literature of the Armenians of "New Albania."   This is why, as might be expected, all that has survived of it is written in Armenian.   The seventh-century elegy for King Juanšer by the poet Davt'ak, for example, was written in Armenian, as was the History of Albania, by Movsēs Dasxuranc'i, and the numerous so-called "Albanian" documents which it contains.[23]

10)   The government of "New Albania" became increasingly Armenian in orientation and the suppression of the Arsacid monarchy of Albania by the Persians in c. 510 A. D. was intended to arrest this process.[24]

11)   The Arabs included "New Albania" in the jurisdiction which they called al-Armīniya and referred to the local princes in New Albania as "Armenians."[25]

12)   Finally, apart from the fact that the so-called "Albanian" lands south of the Kur were originally and always Armenian, the Armenians possessed certain territories north of the river as well.[26]   The district of Kambečan in original Albania, for example, is called Armenian by Strabo,[27] while the anonymous Ašxarhac'oyc' describes the Albanian River Seboj as flowing past the Albanian capital Kabala (Arm. Kabałak) across "Lesser Armenia."[28]   Plutarch, moreover, after describing Pompey's campaigns in Albania in the first century B. C., tells us that he wintered in "Lesser Armenia," a decision involving a march which is incomprehensible if we are to assume that the Lesser Armenia lying west of the Euphrates is intended.[29]

In short, what Mnac'akanyan seems to assert is that Azerbaidzhan between the Kur and the Arax is, and always has been, ethically Armenian, and, if all parties have their own, the Armenians could justifiably lay claim even to Azerbaidzhani territory north of the Kur.

Mnac'akanyan's counterattack is a valiant one and, on the surface of it, rather successful. So enthusiastic was the Soviet scholar H. S. Anassian about his colleague's work that he wrote an article on it for the Revue des études arméniennes in which he endorses Mnac'akanyan's book with unqualified praise.[30] Upon closer inspection, however, we find that despite his point-by-point rebuttal of Bunjatov's argument and the numerous novel and imaginative evidence he offers in support of his own, Mnac'akanyan is almost as reckless with his own forces when it comes to overstating his case, misusing his sources, and setting forth as facts what are only suppositions unsupported by the texts which he quotes.

It is not my purpose here to take issue directly with any of the points raised by Bunjatov or Mnac'akanyan. Rather, I would like to confine myself to the role of a third investigator entering the same thickets but unencumbered by the same concern as to the implications of my findings.

Let us take as a starting point the question of the ethnic composition of the population of Arc'ax and Utik', the regions between the Arax and the Kur which were Armenian territory until 387 and which lie in Azerbaidzhan today. To Mnac'akanyan, this territory was originally Armenian; to Bunjatov, it was Albanian. What do we actually know of its history? Our earliest information is to be found in the History of Herodotus. According to this author, the proto-Armenians were migrants who entered the Armenian plateau from Phrygia in the West, i. e. from Anatolia.[31] The general consensus today is that the Armenians, as we know them, represent a fusion between these incoming tribes—conventionally called "Armens"—and the diverse natives of the plateau who had previously formed a part of the Urartian federation.[32] For this fusion to have taken place, however, the so-called "Armens" would have had to have spread across the plateau from west to east and, though we know little of the circumstances attending this migration, we do catch glimpses of it taking place. Herodotus, writing ca. 450 B. C., makes it clear that in his time the Armenians inhabited only the western third of the plateau, and that to the east of them lay pre-Armenian peoples--Saspeirians and Alarodians.[33]--who had previously formed components of the Urartian state. Xenophon, who travelled through Armenia in the winter of 401-400 B. C., confirms the data of Herodotus, for when he entered the territory of the Phasians and Taokhians, in what was later called north-central Armenia, it is clear that he had left the Armenians behind.[34]

After the fall of the Persian Empire to Alexander in 330 B. C., the Orontids, who had been the Achaemenian governors of Armenia, were allowed to keep control of their province,[35] but, by the time they assumed the royal title in ca. 190 B. C., we find them residing at Armavir in the Ararat plain.[36] Obviously, the fall of the Persian Empire had provided an opportunity for continued Armenian expansion towards the east, so that in the century between Xenophon's journey and the establishment of the Orontid monarchy, the Armenians, under Orontid leadership, must have secured control over the central Armenian plateau.

From Strabo we learn that under King Artašēs (188–ca. 161 B. C.), the Armenians expanded in all directions at the expense of their neighbors. Specifically we are told that at this time they acquired Caspiane and "Phaunitis," the second of which can only be a copyist's error for Saunitis, i. e. the principality of Siwnik'.[37] Thus, it was only under Artašēs, in the second century B. C., that the Armenians conquered Siwnik' and Caspiane and, obviously, the lands of Arc'ax and Utik', which lay between them. These lands, we are told, were taken from the Medes. Mnac'akanyan's notion that these lands were already Armenian and were re-conquered by the Armenians at this time thus rests on no evidence at all and indeed contradicts what little we do know of Armenian expansion to the east. Since these eastern regions had formed part of the Persian province of Media before the time of Alexander, it seems likely that if they were seized by the Armenians from the Medes a century or so later, then they had probably remained a part of Media throughout that time. To attempt to demonstrate that these eastern territories were always Armenian by quoting Movsēs Xorenac'i, as Mnac'-akanyan does, is hazardous in the extreme. Whoever the enigmatic Xorenac'i may have been, whenever he may have lived, and however valuable his compilation of antiquities may be as the received tradition of the Armenian people, it has been amply demonstrated that his historical knowledge is highly defective even for the most recent periods with which he deals, and that as a source for early Armenian history his book must be used only with the greatest care.[38] The same is true for the other texts which Mnac'akanyan marshals to his cause; all are late and none of them can be used as sources for the extent of Armenian penetration to the east or the boundaries between Armenia and Albania prior to the time of Artašēs, let alone the time of Alexander. As for the Armenian origin of the House of Siwnik' asserted by Movsēs, this is highly dubious, and we have evidence of Siwnian separateness and ethnic particularlism as late as the sixth century A. D.[39]

What do we know of the native population of these regions—Arc'ax and

Utik'—prior to the Armenian conquest?   Unfortunately, not very much.
Greek, Roman, and Armenian authors together provide us with the names of
several peoples living there, however—Utians, in Otene,[40] Mycians,[41]
Capians,[42] Gargarians,[43] Sakasenians,[44] Gelians,[45] Sodians,[46] Lupenians,[47]
Balas[ak]anians,[48] Parsians,[49] Parrasians,[50]—and these names are sufficient
to tell us that, whatever their origin, they were certainly not Armenian.
Moreover, although certain Iranian peoples must have settled here during the
long period of Persian and Median rule, most of the natives were not even
Indo-Europeans.   Thus, the Utians and Mycians appear to have been migrants
from the south, the Yutiya and Maka of Achaemenian times, who at one time
had lived in southeastern Iran.[51]   The Caspians, on the other hand (if indeed
they gave their name to the sea and not the other way around) were probably
related to the proto-Georgians,[52] while the Gargarians and the people of
Gardman are almost certainly Georgian peoples as well.[53] The Sakasenians
of the region, we know, were surely a Scythian enclave;[54] the Gelians,
Sodians, Lupenians and Balasanians were possibly Caucasian tribes;[55] the
Parsians and Parrasians alone were probably Iranian.   These peoples, all
conquered by the Armenians in the second century B. C., must have been
subjected to a great deal of Armenicization over the next few centuries, but
most of them were still being cited as distinct ethnic entities when these
regions passed to Albania in 387, some 500 years later.[56]

But what do we know of the Albanians?   According to Strabo, they
were originally a group of twenty-six tribes, each with its own king and
language, who, sometime before the first century B. C., had federated and
had come to be ruled by a single king.[57]   From what little we know of the
Albanian language, these tribes must have been largely of autochthonous
Caucasian origin,[58] but we cannot be certain that this was true of all
twenty-six of them.   Thus, properly speaking, there was no Albanian people
per se but only a federation of Caucasian tribes among whom the Albanians
were possibly only one, paramount, tribe which had organized the federation
to begin with.

From all of this it appears that the population of southeast Caucasia,
whether under Armenian or Albanian rule, was highly mixed, and to label it
as being essentially one or the other or even to divide it simply into two
groups is well in advance of the evidence.

In 387 A. D., the various peoples of Arc'ax and Utik', whether
Armenians, Armenicized aborigines, or both, passed under Albanian rule,[59]

which, under these conditions, would have meant that to the various ethnic elements comprising the Albanians north of the Kur a number of others was added to the south. That these peoples were highly Armenicized and that many were actually Armenians per se cannot be doubted.[60]   That the Albanians north of the Kur were Armenicized to any great degree seems less certain.[61]   That the so-called "Christian" or "New" Albanian culture, which flourished after the transfer of the capital from Kabala, north of the Kur, to Partav, south of the river, in the fifth century, A. D., was essentially Armenian is also beyond question, and here the arguments of Mnac'akanyan are strongest.   No trace of an Albanian literature in the Albanian language has survived, and all of the so-called "Albanian" literature which has come down to us is certainly written in Armenian.[62]   Contrary to Bunjatov, there is no evidence that any of this literature was translated into Armenian from another language[63] and his assertion that the Armenian Church caused the Albanian literature to be translated into Armenian and then had the originals destroyed is a flight of fancy.   As for Mnac'akanyan's statements concerning Armenian settlement north of the Kur, all we can say at present is that from the evidence at hand it does seem likely that the Armenians at one time possessed the district of Kambečan, possibly granted to them by the Romans to serve as a wedge between Albania and the East Georgian kingdom of Iberia.   There is no evidence, however, that Armenians settled in this "Lesser Armenia" in any great numbers in early times or that it ever became ethnically Armenian.   The modern Armenian population of nearby Šak'ē and Nuxa probably derives from the dislocations caused by the Turko-Mongolian invasions of the eleventh to thirteenth centuries.

In sum, then, Bunjatov errs in assuming that the basic population of Azerbaidzhan and eastern Armenia is descended from the Caucasian Albanians.   He ignores the ethnic complexity of the Albanian Federation north of the Kur as well as that of the Armenian regions south of the river, and he is remarkably cavalier in regard to the extent and impact of Turkish immigration, which was sufficiently large to extinguish almost every other ethnic group in Azerbaidzhan and which must have brought about a major change in the ethnic composition of its lowlands.

Mnac'akanyan, on the other hand, oversimplifies as well.   He is certainly wrong in claiming that the lands between the Kur and the Arax were "originally" Armenian, and he, too, underestimates both the ethnic complexity of the region in question and how late the aborigines must have survived as distinct peoples, whether under Armenian or Albanian rule. As far as we can tell, then, the population of southeastern Caucasia, whether north of the River Kur or south of it, consisted of a great variety of peoples: Caucasian mountaineers (Including Albanians), proto-Georgian elements, Scythian enclaves, Iranian, Armenian, and Arab settlers, other miscellaneous interlopers (including some Hungarians)[64] and, above all, a veritable flood of Turkic tribesmen. Ultimately the Christian elements in this heterogenous mass must have been assimilated to the Armenians (and, in part, the Georgians),[65] while the Islamic population was absorbed by the Azeri Turks. The underlying substrata, however, were originally much too diversified to enable us to agree with either Bunjatov or Mnac'akanyan that the present day population represents a common ethnic entity, either Albanian or Armenian. Although the present population doubtless contains many true Armenians and many pure Turks, it also comprises many more elements neither Armenian nor Turkish, however totally Armenicized or Turkified they now may be.

On July 7, 1923, Karabagh, the mountainous core of far eastern Armenia, inhabited almost exclusively by Armenians,[66] was declared an autonomous oblast' within the Azerbaidzhani S.S.R., and so it has remained until the present day. Whether this is just or unjust need not detain us here, for this is a political question rather than an academic one and will doubtless be resolved, if it ever is, on the basis of political considerations. It will not be settled by scholars rummaging about in the fragments of data which have come down to us on the ethno-history of southeastern Caucasia two millenia ago. While scholars certainly have an important and useful role to play in political affairs, Bunjatov and Mnac'akanyan, both excellent scholars, have both erred in placing scholarship at the service of political concerns, which is another matter altogether, and we are reminded, once again, that when such tendentiousness enters the historical arena, scholarship quickly departs.

NOTES

[1]Caucasian Albania (Russian Kavkazkaja Albanija) is the term now conventionally used for classical Albania by both Soviet and Western scholars to distinguish it from the modern Albania in the Balkans with which it has

no connection. The French Aghovanie based on Armenian Ałuank' (Ag-
houank') is a monstrosity which has fortunately failed to gain currency. The
native name for the country is unknown to us.

[2]P'awstos Buzand, Patmut'iwn Hayoc' (Venice, 1933), French trans. J.
B. Emin in M. F. Brosset's Collection des historiens anciens et modernes de
l'Arménie (Paris, 1880), 1, 201-310; Movsēs Xorenac'i, Patmut'iwn Hayoc'
(Tiflis, 1913), English trans. R. W. Thomson, Moses Khorenats'i History of the
Armenians (Cambridge, Mass., 1978), 3.3; Movsēs Kałankatuac'i or Das-
xuranc'i, Patmut'iwn Ałuanic' Ašxarh (Tiflis, 1912), English trans. C. F. J.
Dowsett, Movsēs Dasxuranc'i, The History of the Caucasian Albanians
(London, 1961), 1.4.

[3]Movsēs Dasxuranc'i 3.8; M. Ormanian, The Church of Armenia
(London, 1912; revised ed. London, 1955), 117.

[4]Koriwn, ed. N. Akinean (Vienna, 1952), English trans. B. Norehad,
Koriun, the Life of Mashtots (New York, 1964).

[5]P'awstos Buzand 6.1; Ašxarhac'oyc' (ed. Soukey; Venice, 1881), 39.28-
29.

[6]C. Toumanoff, Studies in Christian Caucasian History (Washington,
1963), 58.

[7]Z. Bunjatov, Azerbaidžan v VII-IX vv (Baku, 1965).

[8]Ibid., 97.

[9]Ibid.

[10]Ibid., 100.

[11]Ibid.

[12]A. S. Mnac'akanyan, Ałuanic' ašxarhi grakanut'yan harc'eri šurjě
(Erevan, 1966).

[13]Mnac'akanyan, O literature kavkazkoj Albanii (Erevan, 1969). I have
used this Russian version in preparing this paper.

[14]Mnac'akanyan, Literatura, 18-29.

[15]Ibid., 19.

[16]Actually, all Movsēs Xorenac'i asserts is that the House of Siwnik'
was of Haykid origin which, as Toumanoff has shown (Studies, 108, 216, 218,

222, 469), should be taken as meaning only that it was of immemorial origin; i.e. that it had been sovereign in Siwnik' for so long that no one remembered its origin.

[17]P'awstos Buzand 6.1 describes these losses in a general way but the Ašxarhac'oyc' makes it clear that the lands which seceded were in fact the same as those which first fell away in the 360's (P'awstos Buzand 4.50) and recovered temporarily through the efforts of Mušeł Mamikonian a few years later (P'awstos Buzand 5.8-9, and especially 5.12-13).

[18]Mnac'akanyan, Literatura, 37-44.

[19]Ibid.

[20]Ibid., 51-52.

[21]Ibid., 68-72.

[22]Ibid.

[23]Ibid., 127.

[24]Ibid., 90-102.

[25]Ibid., 59-62.

[26]Ibid., 37-44, 48, 59, 64, 67, 85, 178, 192.

[27]Ibid., 38-41.

[28]Ašxarhac'oyc', 29, where the editor inserts a question mark.

[29]Plutarch, Lives (Pompey) LCL, 36.2.

[30]H. S. Anassian, "Mise au point relative à l'Albanie caucasienne," REArm 6 (1969), 299-330.

[31]Herodotus, LCL 7.73.

[32]Toumanoff, Studies, 52-67.

[33]Herodotus, 3.93-94.

[34]Xenophon, Anabasis LCL, 4.6.5-6.

[35]Toumanoff, Studies, 288-289.

[36]Ibid., 283, 286.

[37]Strabo, 11.14.5; Adontz, 307, 496 n. 72.

[38]R. Thomson, Moses Khorenats'i, "Introduction."

[39]Sebēos, Sebēosi episkoposi i Herakln (ed. Patkanian; St. Petersburg, 1879), 26.

[40]Herodotus 7.8; Strabo 11.7.1; Pliny 6.16.42, 11.7.1, 8.2; Ptolemy 5.12.4.

[41]Herodotus 7.68.

[42]Ibid., 3.93; Strabo 11.8.8.

[43]Strabo 11.5.1; Movsēs Xorenac'i 2.85, 3.54.

[44]Ibid., 11.8.4, 11.14.4; Ptolemy 5.13.9 (where the corrupt form Sakapene is found for the district).

[45]Pliny 7.18.48; Strabo 11.7.1, 11.8.1; Ełišē Patmut'iwn Vardananc' (Tiflis, 1913), French trans. by V. Langlois in CHAMA 2.178-251.5, p. 116; Sebeos 12-13; Movsēs Xorenac'i 2.54; Movsēs Dasxuranc'i 2.19.

[46]Ibid., 6.11.29; Ptolemy 5.12.

[47]Ibid., 6.12.30; Agat'angełos, Patmut'iwn Hayoc' (Tiflis, 1914), ed. and English trans. R. W. Thomson, Agathangelos' History of the Armenians (Albany, N.Y., 1976), 1.1; Ełišē passim.; Łazar P'arpec'i, Patmut'iwn Hayoc' (Tiflis, 1907), 30, French trans. by S. Ghesarian in CHAMA, 2.253-368.

[48]P'awstos Buzand 3.7; Koriwn 11.5, 34; Ełišē 6 p. 134; Ašxarhac'oyc' 33/34.

[49]Strabo 11.7.1

[50]Ibid.; Herodotus (7.68) has the Mycians and the Utians in Southern Iran; E. Herzfeld, The Persian Empire (Wiesbaden, 1968), 300-301, identifies them with the Maka and the Yutiya of the Achaemenian inscriptions.

[51]Herzfeld, Persian Empire, 300-301.

[52]Toumanoff, Studies, 60 n. 58, where through the mutation of the K-S root we find the relation Kashkai - Kaspioi - Qulḩa - Kolkhis - and possibly K'art'li (east Georgia).

[53]Supra n. 52.

[54]Strabo 11.7.1; Adontz, 324, 495 n. 70.

[55]Ibid.

[56]Agat'angełos, 1.1; Ełiśē 3.58 (both 5th cent.) cites the Lp'ink' who are the Lupenii of Pliny (6.11.29) writing half a millenium earlier (cf. also Movsēs Dasxuranc'i 2.2). This people has since disappeared but left its name in that of the Lop'nas River (now the Dzegam or Akstafa?).

[57]Strabo 11.4.6.

[58]A. Shanidze, "Novootkrytyj alfavit kavkazkix Albantsev i ego značenie dlja nauki," Bulletin de l'Institut Marr 4 (Tbilisi, 1938); G. Dumezil, "Une chrétienté disparue. Les Albaniens du Caucase," Journal Asiatique 232 (1940-41).

[59]Supra nn. 5, 17.

[60]The overwhelmingly widespread use of the Armenian language as shown in the pages of Movsēs Dasxuranc'i makes this absolutely clear.

[61]The Udi language appears to have been the Caucasian language prevalent north of the Kur until the nineteenth century, and the present Armenian population appears to be of relatively recent arrival. Many undoubtedly settled there fleeing the Turko-Mongolic invasions but many more entered the region with the coming of the Russians in the early nineteenth century. Cf. Don Juan van Halen, Narrative of Don Juan van Halen (London, 1827), II, 343; Hyde Clark, Memoire of the Comparative Grammar of Egyptian Coptic and Ude (London, 1873), 13.

[62]The nearest thing to an "Albanian literature" we possess in the corpus of documents and other antiquities compiled by Movsēs Dasxuranc'i in the tenth century and expanded as late as the eleventh.

[63]The meticulousness of early Armenian translators in their fidelity to the texts which they were rendering into Armenian precluded "loose" renderings into a "smooth" Armenian, and was such that the original language may almost always be detected in the style of the translation.

[64]Pseudo-Vardan, Aśxarhac'oyc' Vardanay Vardapeti (ed. H. Berberian; Paris, 1960), 34 line 129; J. Markwart, Osteuropäische und ostasiatische Streifzuge (Leipzig, 1903) 34-20, 428, 496; Markwart, Skizzen zur historischen Topographie und Geschichte von Kaukasien (Vienna, 1928), 35; J. Laurent, L'Arménie entre Byzance et l'Islam (Paris, 1919), 23-24.

[65]Toumanoff, Studies, 58-59.

[66]In the Soviet census of 1970 the Armenians formed 80.5% of the

population of the Nagarno-Karabaxskaja A.O.

EŁIŠĒ'S HISTORY OF VARDAN:
NEW LIGHT FROM OLD SOURCES

Robert W. Thomson

Harvard University (USA)

The History of Vardan and the Armenian War by Ełišē is one of the great classics of Armenian literature. In form it is unique, for no other work of Armenian historical writing deals with the events of so short a period or uses letters and speeches to such dramatic effect. Ełišē's History is unique in another respect also. Whatever the actual historical significance of the events of 450-451 that he purports to be describing, his History has become a classical exposition of moral attitudes. Fifteen hundred years later, Armenians still look to the protagonists in this work for idealized portraits of Armenian patriots and religious heroes, and still repeat with approval their aims and motives as expounded by Ełišē.

Since this History has taken such a strong hold on the Armenian imagination, it is not surprising that popular reaction to scholarly critique of the book has sometimes been extreme. Nersēs Akinian, at the beginning of his controversial three-volume study of Ełišē, notes the horrified reaction of members of the audience in Paris where he presented some of his ideas in 1931.[1] I am not here going to take issue with Akinian's theories about the date and authorship of this History. The question I wish to raise in this paper is not whether the book was written by an eye-witness of the events or is a composition of a later period; rather, I shall be concerned with the motivation of the author and the means he used to give his ideas effect. For Ełišē's History is not a random chronicle of happenings; it is a very carefully constructed piece of literary work. And we must remember that, as in the classical historians of Greece and Rome, so in Ełišē the speeches and letters play a dramatic role. They are not to be construed as documents extracted from archives or recorded verbatim by an eye-witness. They are the literary means whereby the author gives expression to his interpretation of events, whereby he points out certain moral issues and draws general conclusions from the individual events.

41

Like other early Armenian historians, Ełišē was a learned man, familiar with literatures other than his own--even if many of the Greek and Syriac texts he used were available in Armenian.[2]   And like most early Armenian writers he was deeply imbued with Christian ideals and thoroughly conversant with the Bible.   Here we should remind ourselves that his audience was also more familiar with the text of Scripture than are many modern scholars.   For I am sure that the many verbal allusions to Biblical texts in Ełišē and other Armenian writers would be immediately familiar to his audience or the reader, making the story more vivid for them and drawing out its significance—just as the text of Shakespeare is that much more meaningful to the hearer or reader who is versed in Scripture.

Ełišē draws on many sources to enrich his story and to give it wider perspective.   Naturally enough, his text is full of quotations from the Bible as well as Biblical allusions.   There are numerous reminiscences of the Liturgy and of common theological themes, especially in passages modelled on the Creed. Parallels with hagiographical texts abound.   Here we may especially note the verbal parallels with the Armenian of the Syriac Acts of Persian Martyrs which was traditionally ascribed to the Abraham mentioned in Ełišē's own History:[3]   the epithets there applied to the persecuting judges are in Ełišē applied to Yazdegerd; their threats and interrogations, their charges that Christians used magic and sorcery, the speeches of the martyrs with their refutations of idolatry and their prayers--all these are paralleled in Ełišē.   The types of torture, the eulogies over the dead martyrs and the cult of their bones—these too Ełišē describes in the vocabulary of the Armenian Vkayk' Arevelic'.

Ełišē knows the Armenian Text of Chrysostom's Biblical commentaries, at least he uses those on Matthew and on the Epistle to the Ephesians. He is acquainted with the Armenian version of Eusebius' Ecclesiastical History, and has Vasak die the death of Herod as there described (plus extra details from the death of Antiochus, as described in 2 Macc 9, thrown in for good measure).   Ełišē also uses an Armenian version of the Hermetic text known as "The Definitions of Hermes Trismegistus to Asclepius."[4]   More important is his debt to Philo, again used in the Armenian version.   There are extensive quotations, including the elaborate description of the sun (167) from the De Jona, the picture of the doctor treating a courtier unconcerned with the pomp and show around him (172) from the De Providentia, the picture of grasshoppers who exist without food merely by breathing air (202) from the De Vita Contemplativa, and various quotations from the Quaestiones in Genesin and in Exodum.[5]   Of Armenian authors, Ełišē most frequently alludes to passages in Agat'angełos, both the "historical" part and the Teaching of Gregory, and there are also parallels with P'awstos Buzand, Koriwn and Eznik. (I leave aside for the moment the complicated issue of the relationship between the Histories of Ełišē and Łazar.)   Needless to say, not a single one of his sources is identified. Though occasionally Ełišē will introduce a direct quotation with a comment such as "as someone said," usually there is no external clue that he is indebted to another source for an image or an idea.[6]

But there is one source in particular that has helped mold the whole attitude of Ełišē to his material. That is the story of the Maccabees. It is, of course, no recent discovery that there are quotations from or reflections of the Books of Maccabees in Ełišē. Bishop Kiuleserian's monograph on Ełišē, published in 1909, for example, drew attention to several passages where Ełišē borrows from those books.   Further study shows a far greater indebtedness than I had supposed possible, not merely verbal borrowings of a descriptive nature, but some very basic themes.   It seems, therefore, worthwhile to pursue the matter.[7]

Only once does Ełišē refer to the Maccabees explicitly by name. In Vardan's exhortation to the Armenian troops as they prepare for the battle of Avarayr, he mentions them as exemplifying two themes relevant to the Armenian struggle. In the first place, they fought against the Seleucid king in defense of their religion; and even though they died in battle, their fame survived both on earth and in heaven. Secondly, some of them had split away from the union, had offered impure sacrifices, and abandoned God, only to be killed by the holy covenanters.

Ełišē, of course, has chosen his words carefully (105): "the Maccabees fought for their God-given religion (astuacatur awrēnk̕)." This immediately recalls to mind the earlier phrase in Vardan's speech (102): "let us struggle against the impious prince for our ancestral and God-given religion," where the Armenian is a direct borrowing from 3 Macc 1:12 (i veray kargac'n naxneac' ew hayreni awrinac'n). Ełišē had earlier used a similar phrase (82, line 1) when one of the Persian captives was given a list of Armenian complaints to bring before the shah: "he had constrained them to abandon their ancestral religion." However, the translation of "religion" for awrēnk' may be misleading. After all, Armenia had not been a Christian country from time immemorial. Koriwn's biography of Mašt'oc' makes it clear that even in the early fifth century there were many in Armenia still unconverted. So by saying "ancestral" perhaps Ełišē was optimistically putting back to the time of Gregory the Illuminator the conversion of the whole country, which would allow several generations to elapse before the revolt of 450. But more importantly, the term awrēnk' also includes the sense of "customary way of life." So it is relevant to note that Ełišē also speaks of the Armenians being deprived of their ancestral liberty (22: hayreni azatut'iwn), and being forced to abandon their ancestral land (hayreni erkir) for foreign slavery.

It is therefore interesting that Ełišē does not compare the Armenians who are being persecuted to the early Christian martyrs who died for their faith—though as we shall see, the theme of personal salvation does play a role in his History. Nor does he draw attention to Armenia as a Christian land in order to compare it to other Christian lands. Although he draws attention to those other Christian nations in the Caucasus who were under the control of the Iranian shah, Ełišē does not write of Armenia as being but one small part of a larger Christian world. Rather, he emphasizes that the Armenians are alone, that they are fighting for their individuality as Armenians. The phrase hayreni awrēnk', then, means not only the practice of Christianity—which was relatively new in Armenia—but also a traditional way of life.

Ełišē then has Vardan go on to say tht the Maccabees died for their faith (katarec'an). Now the verb katarel in this sense is a calque on the Greek teleiousthai or the Syriac eštamli which carry the connotation of martyrdom. Much of the terminology in Ełišē is reminiscent of the vocabulary applied to Christian martyrs. But the main point here is that the dead heroes—that is, the Armenians who are about to be killed—will not be merely remembered for their valor as were the Maccabees; Vardan and his companions will immediately attain bliss in heaven. So there is a significant difference between the Maccabees and the Armenians, for the only passage in Maccabees that definitely associates eternal life with loyalty to the covenant (a theme I shall come back to later on) is 2 Macc 7:36: the youngest of the seven brothers to be martyred says to Antiochus: "My brothers have now fallen in loyalty to God's covenant, after brief pain leading to eternal life." But many of the protagonists in Ełišē's History seem more interested in their own heavenly rewards than in planning the most rational defense of their homeland. Our author has not fully resolved the tension between the cause of personal salvation and the welfare of one's people and nation. (Parenthetically, we may note here that the brief address of Vardan to his troops as reported in Łazar refers merely to the joys of heaven for the dead. Vardan urges his companions to hasten to the banquet of Christ and not to abandon the group like Judas Iscariot.)[8]

As a foil to those Maccabees who died for their cause, Vardan then refers to the relatives of Matathias who had split away from the union, abandoned God, and had received punishment of death. (105, line 9) Here, too, Ełišē's terminology is paralleled in the Books of Maccabees. But more especially, he draws attention to one of his main concerns throughout his History—the disunity of the Armenians. In his Preface he explains that chapter 4 will deal with the secession (erkpařakut'iwn) of those who abandoned the covenant. The noun erkpařakut'iwn and the cognate verb and adjective occur frequently in Ełišē and recall Macc 3:29, which refers to the discord that Antiochus had brought about by abolishing traditional laws and customs. On the other hand, Matathias himself and his companions had not weakened or slackened but became even firmer—all terms used elsewhere in Ełišē and reminiscent of numerous passages in the Books of Maccabees.

There were, naturally, heroes other than the Maccabees whose examples might inspire the Armenians. So on the eve of the fateful battle, claims Ełišē, the priest Łewond also addressed the assembled troops and reminded them of various Old Testament figures who vanquished the enemies of truth. It is not insignificant that these are the heroes of Israel—not the Christian martyrs of the previous centuries who had died for their faith, but men who fought for their country and their people.

Of more direct relevance to our theme than the individual heroes mentioned by Łewond is the fact that his speech as a whole is modelled on that of Matathias himself in 1 Macc 2. This is his dying speech, and like other figures of the Old Testament, in his final moments he recalls the earlier heroes of Israel. Matathias' list of famous men has close parallels with that in Sir 44ff., which in turn is echoed by Paul in Heb 11. It is perhaps worth noting that this passage from Paul forms part of the readings for the Christian festival of the Maccabees as celebrated in Armenia.[9] Interestingly enough, the heroes enumerated by Łewond in Ełišē's History are derived from all three lists, without following any one of them exclusively or in toto. Again, the contrast with the speech put into Łewond's mouth by Łazar is noteworthy. Łazar speaks of the advantages of a martyr's death and holds up Gregory the Illuminator as an example. But Ełišē has no reference to this national Armenian hero.

The Books of Maccabees, then, have provided Ełišē not only with explicit examples of heroism to be enumerated, they have also provided him with some important themes.

Let us now return to the theme of the unity of the covenanters, mentioned above with reference to the disunity of the Armenians. The theme of the union or covenant—uxt—is a key feature of the briefer account of the war in Łazar, who describes the alliance of soldiers, clergy and common people. But for Ełišē one could almost say that the covenant is the core theme, more important than that of the fatherland.

The covenant is, of course, also central to the Books of Maccabees. In Macc 1:15-16, for example, the renegade Jews who introduced non-Jewish customs, intermarried with Gentiles, and took up evil ways are described repudiating the holy covenant. This idea of a holy covenant, bĕrît qôdeš in Hebrew, does not appear in Judaism before the time of the Maccabees and the struggle against the Seleucids.[10] It is different from the older idea of a covenant between God and the Jews. For in 1 Macc, as just quoted, or in Dan 11:28-30, which describes the animosity of Antiochus towards the Jews, the "holy alliance" means the community of the faithful who have united to preserve from contamination the purity of their religion and way of life. And as we noted above, the concepts of religion and way of life, nomoi in the Greek text of Maccabees or awrēnk' in Armenian, are almost as indistinguishable in Ełišē as they were for the Maccabees. Those who break the holy covenant are both traitors to their fellow-countrymen and faithless to God, as Ełišē takes care to point out in the case of Vasak.

The term uxt is used in several senses by Ełišē. It can mean a straightforward pact between a group of people—as when the Armenian nobility and clergy swear together to resist the Persians (65). In this pact Vasak later joined, swearing on the book of the Gospel and sealing the written oath with his ring (66). Then uxt can refer to the clergy as a group or class, either the Armenians who gather as a synod, or the Greek clergy in Constantinople to whom they write a letter (81). In this sense uxt renders the Greek klēros. But most generally uxt refers to the group that has sworn to uphold Christianity. Hence the frequency of the expression "the unity of the covenant of the church" (e.g. 59, 62, 123) or simply "the unity of the covenant" (e. g. 75, 79, 90, 95, 127) which the Persians cannot break.

The concept of the holy covenant as the body of faithful, found in Maccabees or Daniel, does not appear in the New Testament. It is, however, a significant feature of Syrian Christianity, where the covenant (qyama) referred to the group of Christians par excellence, those who at baptism dedicated themselves to celibacy. This is not the place or time to study in detail the terms bnai qyama (members of the covenant) and the feminine bnat qyama, which have given rise to much controversy. But it is relevant for Ełišē's concept of the covenant to mention at least one Syriac author who deals with the qyama. I refer to Afrahat, whose homilies were translated into Armenian but were erroneously attributed to Jacob of Nisibis.[11] In his Homily 7, for example, an extended passage urges those who have joined the covenant (uxt in the Armenian version) to prepare for holy war. The theme of a holy, spiritual war also figures in hymns attributed to Ephrem Syrus. And this call to holy warfare was part of the early Syrian ritual of baptism, when the committed joined the qyama, the covenant.[12]

Now I am not attempting to suggest that Ełišē's History of Vardan is some kind of theological allegory in which the themes of the Armenian covenant and the holy war against the Persians are but symbols for spiritual perfection and the fight against sin. The History of Vardan is no mythic piece, such as the document composed by the community at Qumran and entitled The War of the Sons of Light and the Sons of Darkness, which was discovered with the Dead Sea Scrolls. What I would like to suggest, however, is that Ełišē would perhaps have been aware of traditions stemming from Syria that would strengthen, in Christian terms, his indebtedness to the Jewish themes he took from Maccabees.

But let us turn from the speculative to a question more easily verifiable. What correlation did Armenians after Ełišē see between the war of the Armenians against Persia and that of the Maccabees against the Seleucids?

The basic story of the Maccabees would have been familiar to Armenians, quite apart from the Armenian version of the Books of Maccabees themselves. On Hrotic' 26 (= August 1) was celebrated, as in the rest of Eastern Christendom, the feast of the Maccabees with appropriate readings.[13] In the collection of sermons or homilies known as Čařĕntirk' the Maccabees had their place, remembered by passages from the Armenian version of Gregory Nazianzenus' Homily on the Maccabees.[14] And the full version of that Homily had a wide circulation.[15] So the concept of the

Maccabees as heroes and martyrs was familiar to Armenians. P'awstos (3, 11) was the first author to mention them explicitly when he describes the festival of those Armenians who died fighting the Persians, since "they fell in combat like Judas and Matathias Maccabee and their brothers." Movsēs Xorenac'i has one reference to Matathias (III, 68) as he laments that no second-day Maccabee has arisen to deliver Armenia in his own time--although there are many more unacknowledged references to the text of the Books of Maccabees in his History. Yovhannēs Kat'oḷikos recalls the Old Testament heroes including Maccabaeus, and later echoes Movsēs' lament that no new Matathias has arisen to save the Armenians from Antiochus.[16] Likewise, T'ovma Arcruni (III, 13) compares the exploits of Gurgen Arcruni against the Tačiks to those of Judas Maccabaeus against Antiochus. Anania Širakac'i mentions the Maccabees in his Chronicle,[17] as does the later Vardan; while in his History Stephen Asoḷik adds a few more circumstantial details.

The story of Vardan and his companions was, of course, alluded to much more frequently by Armenian writers. It is not necessary here to rehearse one by one the numerous references in later literature to Eḷišē or Vardan Mamikonian. There are certain problems that arise, such as the confusion between the Vardan who died in 451 and the Vardan Mamikonian who rebelled in the 570's. But more relevant to the present discussion would be the desire of patriotic authors such as T'ovma Arcruni to elaborate on the received account by claiming that the ancestors of his own patron played a significant role at Avarayr. For this indicates that Vardan and his companions were regarded as national heroes. As Yovhannēs Kat'oḷikos says: "Vardan fought many brave battles for the Christian faith." Or Asoḷik: "Saint Vardan died for the holy covenant and the Christian faith."[18] A colophon in a gospel of 1232 explains the defeat of Vardan as due to the multiplication of our sins.[19]

But comparisons between the Vardanank' and persons of their own time are rare in later Armenian writers. The author of the History of the Archers (Grigor of Akanc') has king Het'um say: "The battle of the Vardanank' was for the Christians. Just as such a number of horsemen strove on behalf of the Christians and became worthy of heavenly crowns, so also did my sons. T'oros fought for the Christians and was martyred for the Christians. He has joined the band of the holy Vardanank' and has become worthy of the same crown."[20] A colophon of 1453 compares the treachery of Lucas Notaras at the fall of Constantinople to the treachery of the apostate Vasak, who was the cause of the ruin and destruction of Armenia.[21]   But such explicit comparisons are not at all common.

There is, however, one passage to which I wish to draw attention by way of conclusion. Nersēs Šnorhali, in his Lament on Edessa, connects the Vardanank' with the Maccabees. Writing of the inhabitants of Edessa in terminology very reminiscent of Ełišē (terms which in Ełišē go back to the Maccabees), he comments: "They died rather than be false to the covenant. They resembled the Maccabees and the war of the Vardanank'."[22]

This is to the best of my knowledge unique. It is surprising that despite the explicit comparison in Ełišē's History—which was of course well known and frequently cited—and despite frequent references in later writers to the Maccabees or to the Vardanank', the parallels between the two groups are not brought out. Not only is the literary indebtedness of Ełišē and other early Armenian historians to the Books of Maccabees passed over, the real influence of themes from Jewish history on Armenian historiography is ignored.

NOTES

[1]N. Akinian, Ełišē Vardapet ew iwr Patmut'iwnn Hayoc' Paterazmi (Vienna, 1932, 1936, 1960).

[2]In addition to Akinian's study see also B. Kiwleserian, Ełišē (Vienna, 1909).

[3]Abrahamu Xostovanołi Vkayk' Arewelic' (ed. G. Ter-Mkrtč'ian; Ēj-miacin, 1921).

[4]J. Mahé, "Les définitions d'Hermès Trismégiste à Asclépius," Revue des sciences religieuses 50 (1976), 193-214, and M.-G. de Durand, "Un traité hermétique conservé en arménien," Revue de l'histoire des religions 190 (1976), 55-72. The Armenian text was published by H. Manandyan in Banber Matenadarani, 3 (1956), 287-314.

[5]The page references are to the Armenian edition of Ełišē by E. Ter-Minasian (Erevan, 1957).

[6]A commentary to the literary sources used by Ełišē to accompany an English translation of the Armenian by R. W. Thomson is near completion.

[7]What follows is an expansion of the few paragraphs devoted to Ełišē in R. W. Thomson, "The Maccabees in Early Armenian Historiography," Journal of Theological Studies, 26 (1975), 329-341.

[8]Łazar P'arpec'i, Patmut'iwn Hayoc' (ed. G. Ter-Mkrtč'ian and S. Malxaseanc'; Tiflis, 1904), 71.

[9]See A. Renoux, Le Codex arménien Jérusalem 121 (Patrologia Orientalis 36.2; Brepols, 1971), 214-217.

[10]See A. Jaubert, La notion d'alliance dans le judaisme aux abords de l'ère chrétienne (Patristica Sorbonensia, 6; Paris, 1963), 82ff.

[11]The Armenian text was first published by N. M. Antonellus, Sancti Patris nostri Iacobi episcopi Nisibeni sermones (Rome, 1756). A new edition has been begun by G. Lafontaine, La Version arménienne des oeuvres d'Aphraate le syrien (CSCO 382, 383; Louvain, 1977).

[12]See R. Murray, Symbols of Church and Kingdom (Cambridge, 1975), 16.

[13]See note 9 above.

[14]See M. van Esbroeck and U. Zanetti, "Le manuscrit Érévan 993. Inventaire des pieces," REArm, 12 (1977), 123-167, esp. 156.

[15]For the Armenian version of the homilies of Gregory Nazianzenus see G. Lafontaine, "La tradition manuscrite de la version arménienne des Discours de Grégoire de Nazianze," Le Muséon 90 (1977), 281-340.

[16]Yovhannu Kat'ołikosi Drasxanakertac'woy Patmut'iwn Hayoc' (Tiflis, 1912), 258, 278.

[17]A. G. Abrahamyan, Anania Širakac'u Matenagrut'yunĕ (Erevan, 1944), 370.

[18]Step'anos Asołik, Patmut'iwn tiezerakan (ed. S. Malxaseanc'; St. Petersburg, 1885), 78; Yovhannēs Kat'ołikos, Patmut'iwn Hayoc', 60.

[19]Garegin Kat'ołikos, Yišatakarank' Jeragrac' (Ant'ilias, 1951), col. 882.

[20]History of the Nation of the Archers (ed. R. P. Blake and R. N. Frye), Harvard Journal of Asiatic Studies, 12 (1949), 363.

[21]Quoted in A. K. Sanjian, Colophons of Armenian Manuscripts, 1301-

1480 (Cambridge, Mass., 1969), 225.

[22]Nersēs Šnorhali, Ołb Edesioy (Erevan, 1963), 63.

SEBĒOS, HISTORIAN OF THE SEVENTH CENTURY

Mesrob K. Krikorian

Vienna (Austria)

Sebēos and his History; what do we know from mediaeval Sources?

The first time Bishop Sebēos was listed among the historians of Armenia as author of the History of Heraclius was by Step'anos Tarōnec'i in the late tenth or early eleventh century. After mentioning Agat'angełos; Movsēs the Rhetor, Xorenac'i; Ełišē, historian of Vardan Mamikonian and of his warriors; Łazar P'arpec'i and P'awstos Buzand, he continues as follows:

> and the History of Heraclius, recounted by Bishop Sebēos and the History of Łewond Erēc' (the priest), on the invasions of Arabs and the sufferings of Armenians because of their violent domination; and then histories of recent times of Šapuh Bagratuni and Tēr Yovhannēs, Catholicos of Armenians, who were in the days of first Bagratuni Kings—Ašot and Smbat . . .[1]

Later in the thirteenth century, Kirakos Ganjakec'i presents the Armenian historians Agat'angełos, Movsēs Xorenac'i, Ełišē, Łazar P'arpec'i, P'awstos Buzand in the same order:

> and Heraclius recounted by Bishop Sebēos; and the history of the marvellous man Koriwn and Xosrov, and the history of Łewond Erēc' on what Mahmet and his followers did in whole the world and moreover with the Armenian nation; and T'ovma Vardapet, historian of the house of Arcruni; and Šapuh Bagratuni and Tēr Yovhannēs Catholicos of Armenia etc.[2]

A few hundred years later, in 1784-86, Mik'aēl Č'amč'eanc' published his History of the Armenians counting more than ten ancient Armenian authors whose texts still were not known to him and to the public in general: Bishop Uxtanēs of Urfa (Edessa); Heraclius by Bishop Sebēos; Xosrov; Łewond; Smbat; T'ovma, historian of the attacks on Bułay; Šapuh Bagratuni.[3] About the same time, in 1795, Yakob Simonian Ayubeanc' in a list of the Armenian writers, cites Agat'angełos; Mesrob Erēc', biographer of St. Nersēs; Movsēs Xorenac'i; Koriwn, biographer of St. Mesrob; Xosrov, author of the History of St. Sahak; Ełišē Vardapet; Łazar P'arpec'i; P'awstos Buzand; Zenob, historian of Tarōn; and "10. Heraclius by Bishop Eusebius who has narrated the wars of Heraclius and Khosrow and other useful things" etc.[4] Apparently Ayubeanc' had seen or used the main MS of Sebēos which is now being kept in the Matenadaran (old. No. 611 = new No. 2639).

Among the above-quoted sources I have intentionally left out a secondary historian, namely Simēon Aparanec'i (1585),[5] just to emphasize the importance of his poetical History in which he includes many pages from Sebeos almost without any substantial changes.   Hence his book is of immense help for scholars in restoring the text of the History of Heraclius. In any case, in modern times it was Yovhannēs Šahxatunian of Ējmiacin who, about 1830-31, discovered the MS of Sebēos.

Manuscripts and Editions

In 1850/51 T'. M. Mihrdateanc' of Istanbul, after receiving a copy of the History of Heraclius from the Catholissate of St. Ējmiacin and having at his disposal a MS dated 1568, edited for the first time the text of Sebēos with the following title:

History of Bishop Sebēos on Heraclius.[6]

In 1862, K'. Patkanian published in St. Petersburg a Russian translation:

History of the Emperor Heraclius by Bishop Sebēos,

author of VIIth century.

Later, in 1879, he edited the Armenian text of Sebēos, based on Mihrdateanc''s copy and on a copy of the MS of St. Ějmiacin.[7] The last and best publication of the History of Heraclius was carried out by Malxaseanc'[8] who used all editions and the available manuscripts:

(1)   No. 2639 (old No. 611) at the Matenadaran, written in 1672 at the monastery of Amrdōl, by the scribes Pawłos Gawařc'i and Grigor Erēc' (the priest);

(2)   No. 2867, ibid., a nineteenth-century copy of No. 2639;

(3)   No. 3122, ibid., 1852, Erevan, copied by Oskan Tēr-Georgian Yovhanniseanc' for M. Émin;

(4)   No. 6454, ibid., nineteenth-century copy;

(5)   Copy of the Armenian Academy of Sciences, Erevan, nineteenth century. Is this MS the same as No. 9252 (nineteenth century) at the Matenadaran?

There are still two other manuscripts, although of no value for textual criticism, which are kept in the Mekhitarist Library of Vienna, Nos. 52 and 86, both copied from the MS of Mihradateanc'. All these manuscripts actually originate from the same "mother copy," i.e. No. 2639 of Erevan which in its turn was transcribed from an older MS (= "the copy of Vardapet Yunan").[9]   Therefore, in fact, we possess only one form of the text of Sebēos.   Certainly, it is understandable how difficult it is to restore a historical text based on a single manuscript.

New Studies and Discussions: Is Sebēos really the Author of the History of Heraclius?

A very lively interest in the person and History of Sebēos was aroused in 1965 when G. V. Abgaryan published his study:[10]

The History of Sebēos and the Enigma of

the Anonymous Author.

Here I summarize the main theses of his research:

(1)   The history book published in the name of Bishop Sebēos (Bagratuni?) in reality belongs to Xosrov, seventh-century author.

(2)   The History of Heraclius by Bishop Sebēos still remains unknown and might one day be discovered. The book of Xosrov is the history not only of the emperors Heraclius and Khosrow Parvīz, but also, in general, it narrates the relations and wars of the Byzantines, Persians, and Armenians in the sixth and seventh centuries.

(3)   The prologue of the History of Xosrov
(published in the name of Sebēos) relates the fall
of the Arsacid kingdom in Armenian and consequently has nothing to do with the antecedent two
chapters (2 x 2 = in 4 parts), known (!) as an
anonymous work.   In this sense and form Patkanian had already published the book under
discussion.

(4)   The chapters at the beginning of the History of Xosrov are for the most part collected or
extracted from the works of P'awstos Buzand,
Movsēs Xorenac'i, Step'anos   Tarōnec'i (Asołik)
etc.   Therefore they have been compiled earlier
than the eleventh century and probably belong to
the History of Bagratid Dynasty written by Yovhannēs Vardapet Tarōnec'i.

Numerous reviews on Abgaryan's 'sensational' book were published
both inside and outside Armenia.   P. Ananian from the Mekhitarist Fathers
of Venice initiated a series of articles which later were collected in a small
volume.[11]   Following the view of Malxaseanc',[12] detecting similarities of
language and style between the two writings, he tries to demonstrate that
the anonymous chapters under discussion really form coherent parts of the
History of Sebēos.   Thanks to the studies of Patkanian, Akinian and others,
we know that the second anonymous chapter has been taken from the History
of Step'anos Tarōnec'i (XIth century).   Replying to such a problem, the
Mekhitarist scholar presumes that these extracts are not original, but later
interpolations (!).

In Vienna, M. K. Krikorian also undertook a series of research articles
about Sebeos.   In a review, he evaluated the work of G. Abgaryan, especially
the 46 textual remarks or corrections,[13] and found "quite probable and
convincing"[14] the main conclusion of the study that Xosrov is the author of
the History ascribed to Sebēos.   As to the question of the two chapters, he
supported the view of Zarbhanalian, K'. Patkanian, M.-F. Brosset, F. Macler,
and N. Akinian--that they could not have been written earlier than the
eleventh century.   In a short excursus, he even pointed out differences
between the two anonymous chapters and inferred that, either they were
compiled by two different historians, or Yovhannēs Tarōnec'i was not the

proper author but an untalented collector who had not cared at all to achieve an internally consistent work.[15]

During the years 1967-1971 Krikorian[16] also edited about 72 remarks on and corrections to the text of Sebēos, and finally[17] he examined thoroughly the problem of the authorship—Sebēos or Xosrov?   In the meantime, X. T'orosyan from the Matenadaran in Erevan had published critical and polemic articles against Abgaryan, rejecting his thesis and declaring that first, Sebēos was indeed the author of the History of Heraclius and secondly, Xosrov the Historian lived in the fifth century (not the seventh century) and produced a biography of St. Sahak Part'ew.[18]   In a detailed textual and philological investigation Krikorian cleared up the misunderstandings, demonstrated that Xosrov the Historian could not have been the author of the Biography of St. Sahak and concluded:

> By refuting the hypothesis of T'orosyan, I have not
> necessarily confirmed the supposition of Abgaryan.
> The problem still remains uncertain; for that
> reason I have kept in my study the traditional
> name of the History of Heraclius.   In my modest
> opinion, as long as there is no new evidence, it is
> absurd to consider the question 'Sebēos' or 'Xos-
> rov,' since we know nothing about either of
> them.[19]

The Contents of the 'History' of Sebēos

Sebēos begins his History with a short prologue, first mentioning the fall of the Arsacid kingdom, the Persian domination of Armenia, and the rebellion of the Armenians against Yazdegerd II (439-457).   He then briefly presents his program which covers a period of about two hundred years (approx. 460-661/662), concentrating his attention on Byzantine- Armenian-Persian political relations and wars, which he correctly and reliably describes in 38 chapters.[20]   Although, since the eleventh century, his book has been referred to as the History of Heraclius, he in fact has devoted only six chapters to the famed emperor (chapters 24, 26, 27, 28, 29, and 30).[21] In connection with the Emperor Maurice (582-602), we find, interestingly enough, even more historical accounts (chapters 2, 3, 5, 6, 8, 9, 10, and 20); therefore, the traditional title does not really reflect the contents of the book. If, however, we bear in mind that very important events, such as the siege of Jerusalem, the capture of the Holy Cross by the Persians, the later liberation of the Holy City, and the return of the Cross, happened during the reign of Heraclius (610-641), we can understand, at least to a certain extent, why Sebēos named his book for this particular emperor. It is worthwhile to note the Sebēos provides us with much more material about Persian than Byzantine sovereigns.   Except Balāsh (484-488), all the other Iranian emperors of the period are recorded in a regular succession and their actions and wars are described in detail.   In particular, Khosrow II Parvīz, who reigned about 37 years (591-628), is the central figure of the History: the author devoted 16 to 18 chapters (2, 3, 4, 6, 11, 12, 14, 15, 17, 18, 19, 20, 21, 22, 23, 24, 26, and 27), i. e. almost half of the book, to him. One would rightly expect to find in the title the name of the Emperor Khosrow rather than that of Heraclius, and this appellation would certainly fit the prologue at the end of chapter 2. In an outline of the following chapters, Sebēos preludes, in a rhetorical tone, the heroic undertakings of Parvız vaunting him as a great conqueror who terrified the whole world. He speaks of his Book as Chronicles of Imperial History, the "heroic tale of Khosrow Parvīz, a struggler, a Sasanian plunderer who set fire and burned out the entire inside, shaking the sea and the land, in order to destroy the entire world . . ."

To this eulogy we can add the witness of Tabari, which certainly sounds more positive:

> Afterwards, Khosrow Parvīz, the son of Hormizd and the grandchild of Khosrov Anūshīr-van, became king. This was one of those Persian kings who with their courage, wisdom, and remote military expeditions distinguished themselves. As it is told, his strength, conquests, and victories, his richness of money and of other treasures, and his constant luck were so great that no other king on such a high grade possessed the same. For that reason he was called Parvīz i. e. "the Trium-phant."[22]

Speaking of Khosrow II, it is impossible, from an Armenian standpoint, to disregard one of the most talented and skillful commanders-in-chief of the Iranian army, namely Smbat Bagratuni the Victorious.[23] At that time, Persia was being continuously attacked and troubled by barbarous Turkic-Mongolian nomad tribes around the Caspian Sea.[24]   Actually, the Hephtalite Huns (the "Kushans" of Sebēos), raiding from their settlements in Balkh-Bactria, Tokharistan and Badakhshan, permanently were terrifying and oppressing the bordering provinces, especially Tabaristan and Gurgan.

In 591 Khosrow Parvīz assigned Smbat as marzpan (governor) of Hyrkania and gave him every power to combat the Hephtalites.   Smbat organized his own army corps of about 2000 soldiers, mainly Armenians which fought against the dangerous Turkic-Mongolian nomads and killed their king (609).   On this occasion (or earlier) he was made chief marzpan and honored with the title 'Khosrow Šum' (or Šnum) which means "the joy of Khosrow"'! Also his son Varaztiroc' was highly respected and had been appointed as imperial head butler.   In his continuing attacks and struggle against the Kushans, he was always successful and received more and more honors from the Shah.   In the end, he became the third minister of Khosrow and officiated as Ērān-dibīrbad (dipīrpat) or chairman of the Imperial Council.[25]

As a historian, Sebēos seems in general to sympathize more with the Persians than the Byzantines, but it would not be appropriate to call him an Iranophile.   Rather he is a supporter of a national orientation between the two superpowers, and occasionally, in connection with the Council of Chalcedon (451), he criticizes the Byzantines and those Armenians who expressed a tolerant attitude to the Chalcedonian Christology.   For instance, in chapter 35, he relates how the Emperor Constantine (641-668) came to Dvin, Armenia in order to bring about a Church reunion.   It was in the year 652, on a Sunday, that at St. Gregory's cathedral the Armenians and Byzantines together celebrated a Liturgy in the Greek language during which the Catholicos Nersēs Išxanc'i (641-661), the commander in chief Mušeł Mamikonian, and all the bishops, together with the most eminent guests, received communion.   The agreement was politically motivated, since the Arabs were growing in power and becoming challenging adversaries; and theologically, the christology of Chalcedon was interpreted afresh as a Monothelite doctrine.   However, one of the Armenian bishops publicly refused to take communion and went away, so that the Emperor was obliged to intervene in order to reconcile the Catholicos with the unknown Bishop! Nersēs was blamed as a "two-faced" person who acted and spoke once pro and once contra Chalcedon.   Surprisingly enough, the author of the History of Heraclius, who circumstantially relates this meeting as an important event, does not mention the name of the bishop who protested against the

Armenian-Byzantine communion. Ormanian is right in concluding that most probably Sebēos himself was the bishop who found it difficult to approve or pronounce the Council of Chalcedon.[26] Before closing this part of my study, I would like to append here a chronological table indicating in parallel columns all the Iranian and Byzantine emperors who are recorded in the History of Heraclius.

Fīrūz
(459-484)

Balāsh
(484-488) not mentioned by Sebēos
Kavadh
(488-531)
Khosrow I Anūshīrvan
(531-579)

Hormizd IV	Maurice
(579-590)	(582-602)
Khosrow II Parvīz	Phocas
(591-628)	(602-610)
Kavadh II	Heraclius
(Feb.-Sept. 628)	(610-)
Ardashīr III	
(628-629)	
Bor(an)	
(629-630)	
Khosrow III	
Azarmiduxt	
Hormizd V	
Yazdegerd III	
(632)	

Arab-Byzantine	Constantine II
hostilities and wars	(641) and
	Heraclonas
	(641)
Yazdegert III killed	Constans-Constantine
(651)	(641-668)
Muawiya	
triumphant Caliph	
(661-662)	

_ The Byzantine Policy towards Armenia

The cultural "Hellenization" and hence "Westernization" of Armenia, which had begun under Tigran the Great (95/94-56/54 B. C.), reached its fulfillment and zenith in about 301 or 314 when Christianity was officially proclaimed the state religion. At that time, the Arsacid dynasty was reigning in Armenia. In 384-387, at a critical moment, the emperors Theodosios and Shapur III divided the country; Persia received a larger part of Armenia, whereas Theodosioupolis (Erzurum) and some cantons in Western Armenia were left within the share of Byzantium. After the fall of the Arsacid kingdom in 428, "Eastern" Armenia was totally controlled by the Iranians. The rivalry between the two Empires became stronger and more intense; both sides were convinced that whoever could possess Armenia would also in general gain the game. In approximately 450, Yazdegerd II (439-457) even tried to subjugate Armenia culturally in order to facilitate a definitive integration of the Armenians in his dominion. Fortunately, this Persian plan failed completely, and at the end the Emperor Balāsh (484-488) was obliged to recognize the religious-spiritual freedom of Armenia. The rest of the history has been told us by Bishop Sebēos. It is interesting to note that after harsh treatment in the fifth century, Iran was very cautious and rather followed a policy of gaining the sympathy of the Armenians. This is very clear in the History of Heraclius. In contrast, the Byzantines followed a short-sighted political and religious policy which resulted in catastrophic consequences for both Byzantium and Armenia.

Armenia, because of its natural geography and strategic location, was an attractive country and a buffer state between East (Iran) and West

(Byzantium and, later, the Ottoman Empire).   Another factor which continuously created rivalry and tension between the Armenians and the Greeks was that both were talented in trade and war.   Particularly, under the Emperors Tiberius II (578-582) and Maurice (582-602), the Byzantines persistently pursued a method of dividing and deporting Armenians in order to achieve peace, order, and unity in the eastern borders of the Empire.   As early as 571-72, after a failed revolt against the Persians, Vardan Mamikonian and his companions had fled to Constantinople.   Such Armenian emigrations continued also under Arab and Seljuk pressures and oppression.   The Emperor Maurice, however, systematically organized the exchange and transportation of Armenians.

Sebēos, in his History, preserves a copy or a summary of a remarkable letter of Maurice addressed to Shah Khosrow Parvīz in which the Emperor proposes to expel Armenians to remote regions:

They are an undiciplined and disobedient nation,
[he says] who live between us and disturb us.   But
come, let us gather and concentrate mine in
Thrace and you assemble and order yours to the
East.   If they die, enemies die, and if they kill,
they kill adversaries and we shall live in peace.
Because if they remain in their country, there will
never be any calm for us [c. 6].

In fact the policy of Maurice had several aspects and advantages: on one hand, he would have removed "undisciplined and disobedient" elements, and on the other hand, he could combat his dangerous enemies; on one hand, he would have secured the pacification of Armenia and on the other, he could enrich the industrious elements of his empire.   In about 590-591, just before or after the new partition of Armenia between Byzantium and Iran, Maurice really started to gather Armenians and send them to Thrace, where the Avars were growing in power and becoming aggressive.   Many soldiers and naxarars fled from the Byzantine part into the Persian, seeking protection and security under Shah Khosrow.   It is interesting to know that the Iranian court received the Armenians with great hospitality and honors.   Probably encouraged by this attitude of Persia, some princes in Byzantine Armenia, like Samuēl and Sargis Vahevuni, Varaz Nerseh, Nersēs, Vstam and T'ēodoros Trpatuni, revolted and waged war against the Emperor.   In Thrace too, the "enemies" attacked the Byzantine army and caused many casualties.   Maurice immediately enlisted thousands of Armenians and under the command of Mušeł Mamikonian directed them to "western regions on the bank of the great river Danube." After the defeat of Mušeł, once again an elite Armenian cavalry 2,000 strong, led by Sahak Mamikonian and Smbat Bagratuni, son of Manuēl, was sent against the Avars and Slavs. This is the Smbat who later was exiled to Africa and whom some authors identify with Sumbat "Khosrow-Šnum"! It is worthwhile noting, however, that Thrace was not the only region where Armenians were concentrated; during the reign of Tiberius and Maurice, thousands of them were uprooted from their homeland and deported to western provinces of Asia Minor and also to the island of Cyprus.[27]

In ecclesiastical policy too, the Byzantines acted from a position of strength to exert pressure upon Armenia in order to suppress the independence and national identity of the Armenian Church. In 590, the Emperor Maurice, wishing to force the Council of Chalcedon on the Armenians, assigned Bishop Yovhannēs of Bagaran as anti-patriarch under his dominion.[28] At that time the regular Catholicos was Movsēs Ełivardec'i (574-604). In 633, Heraclius arranged a reunion of Churches in Theodosioupolis on the basis of the Monothelite doctrine, in the days of the Catholicos Ezr P'aražnakertc'i.[29] In 648, the Emperor Constans-Constantine and the Patriarch of Constantinople commissioned the Armenian Chalcedonian philosopher Davit' Bagavanc'i to go to Dvin in order to convince the authorities of the Armenian Church to acknowledge the Council of Chalcedon. The Catholicos Nersēs Išxanc'i and the commander in chief T'ēodoros Řštuni assembled a synod together with all the bishops and naxarars and politely refused the Byzantine proposal of ecclesiastical union, "defending the foundation of the orthodox Faith which our fathers have received from true apostolic teachers." Sebēos includes the text of a long letter[30] which the Armenians addressed to the Emperor, and Ormanian rightly thinks that Sebēos himself worked with some others in the composition of the reply.[31] Although the Byzantines could not accomplish their plan to gain the Church of Armenia for their direction and tradition, in Caucasia they succeeded in separating the Georgian Church from the Armenian and Albanian. Ever since the days of Gregory the Illuminator, the Georgians had been on very friendly terms with Armenia on doctrinal questions and cultural activities, but as the political and ecclesiastical influence of Byzantium grew in Georgia, the bonds of friendship which united the local Church with that of Armenia became loose and were finally, in 608, officially dissolved. The Catholicos Abraham Ałbat'anec'i (607-615) repeatedly invited the Georgian Patriarch Kyrion to continue in the com mon way, but he was flatly refused.

The Byzantine policy of "dividing and deporting" Armenians continued throughout the centuries. Although every empire is naturally condemned to fall at a certain moment of history, the Byzantine state would probably have lasted longer, if the leaders had pursued a realistic policy. In fact, Armenia was a firm and solid barrier against Persians, Arabs, and various Turkic-Mongolian tribes; but instead of supporting and strengthening Armenia, Byzantium undertook every effort to weaken it. On August 26, 1071, the Seljuks, led by Alp Arslan, won the decisive battle of Malazgirt (Manzikert) and captured the Emperor Romanus IV Diogenes (1067-1071). This was actually "one of the blackest days in the long history of Byzantium."[32] The corridor to the capital city was open: the conquest of Constantinople was only a matter of time.

The Tragedy of the Armenians

The geo-political position and the feudal social system of Armenia were the main factors shaping the destiny of the people. The Armenian principalities, divided between Byzantium and Iran, separated by mountains, and lacking a cohesive spirit, failed to secure the unity and sovereignty of the country. Surely and naturally they wished to have national independence, but the socio-political and economic forces and powers both inside and outside their homeland were too strong to be controlled by them; and this was their tragedy. Turning the pages of Sebēos' History the reader can easily perceive how the naxarars were desperately striving on one hand to survive and on the other hand to obtain a certain freedom and autonomy. Not only were the leading houses divided into two main groups, but the same feudal commanders were sometimes allied with the Byzantines and other times with the Persians; they were caught up in an endless swing between Byzantium and Iran. However, one may clearly trace the orientation of the Mamikonian House, which was traditionally more for the Byzantines, whereas the Bagratuni dynasty was more for the Persians. It was the latter principality which, after experiencing a bitter destiny, concluded that semi-independence could only be realized by active or silent support of the eastern superpower. Among Bagratunis, Smbat 'Khosrow-Šnum' proved himself to be a great military and political personality whose memory undoubtedly influenced the policy of his descendants, who succeeded in 885 in re-establishing the national independence of Armenia. A parallel figure was T'ēodoros Řštuni (ch. 28, 29, 30, 32, 33, 35, 36, and 38) who, according to the account of Sebeos, played an important role in forming the new orientation of Armenia, that is, reconciliation and co-operation with the Arabs!

Cultural Achievements

Sebēos was primarily interested in the political history of his time, and, for that reason, he paid very little attention to the cultural life of his country. He makes no mention of the intellectuals and writers of the seventh century, among whom were the particularly illustrious Anania Širakac'i, Vrt'anēs Tełapah, Yovhannēs Mayragomec'i, T'ēodoros K'rt'enawor, Grigoris Aršaruneac', etc. As a bishop of the Armenian Church, he recorded the names and activities of the successive catholicoi of the seventh century:

Movsēs Ełivardec'i (574-604)

(Vrt'anēs Tełapah) (604-607)

Abraham Řštuni Ałbat'anec'i (607-615)

Komitas Ałc'ec'i (615-628)

K'ristap'or Apahuni (628-630)

Ezr P'aražnakertc'i (630-641)

Nersēs Išxanc'i (641-661)

Sebēos considered it important to describe not only the doctrinal position of these patriarchs, but also the churches they built. Abraham Řštuni[33] initiated the erection of St. Gregory of Dvin, which was finished in the days of Komitas. Komitas not only restored, with shaped stones, the wooden dome of St. Ējmiacin, but he also fundamentally reconstructed the beautiful church of St. Hřipsimē.[34] Last, but not least, Nersēs built the renowned church of Zuart'noc'[35] on a round plan and in three external floors. Interestingly these three buildings represent three different typical church forms, and it is worth remembering that ecclesiastical architecture in Armenia, according to T'oros T'oramanian, flourished and experienced its "Golden Age" in the seventh century. Although this traditional architectural style had naturally assimilated Syrian, Iranian, and Roman-Byzantine elements, it was, in fact, an original achievement which, in its turn, provided some new architectural forms for Byzantium and Europe, in spite of the political misfortunes which were the Armenians' lot.

Concluding Remarks

It is amazing how correct and exact Sebēos' data are. Most probably he collected his first-hand information directly from the Armenian troops and naxarars who were immediate participants in the wars and events of the time. Since there are not many contemporary Byzantine or Persian- Arab historians, the History of Heraclius is a very valuable, almost indispensable source book on seventh-century political life and Byzantine, Armenian and Iranian relations.

NOTES

[1]Step'anos Tarōnec'i, Patmut'iwn tiezerakan (St. Petersburg, 1885), 6-7.

[2]Kirakos Ganjakec'i, Patmut'iwn Hayoc' (Erevan, 1961), 6-7.

[3]Mik'aēl Č'amč'eanc', Patmut'iwn Hayoc' (3 vols.; Venice, 1784-6), 1.18-19.

[4]Azdarar (Madras, 1795), 188-89.

[5]Simēon Aparanec'i, Vipasanut'iwn saks Pahlawuneac'n zarmi ew Mamikoneanc' seri (Vałaršapat (Ējmiacin), 1870).

[6]T'. Mihrdateanc', Patmut'iwn Sebēosi Episkoposi i Herakln (Istanbul, 1851).

[7]K'. R. Patkanian, Patmut'iwn Sebēosi Episkoposi i Herakln (St. Petersburg, 1879). A very bad re-impression of this was published at Tiflis in 1912 in the series of 'Lukasean Matenadaran' (No. 7).

[8]S. Malxaseanc', Sebēosi Episcoposi Patmut'iwn (Erevan, 1939). [After this paper was written, G. Abgaryan's critical edition of the History of Sebēos was released (Dec. 1979).]

[9]N. Akinian, Matenagrakan hetazotut'iwnner (Vienna, 1924), 2.8-15.

[10]G. V. Abgaryan, Sebēosi Patmut'yunĕ ew Ananuni ałełcuacĕ (Erevan,

1965). Prior to this, he had published parts of his research in Banber Matenadarani 4 (1958), 61-72; 6 (1962), 25-56; 7 (1964), 239-71; and in Patmabanasirakan Handes (1962), 1.210-25.

[11]P. Ananian, Sebēosi Patmut'ean grk'i masin k'ani mĕ lusabanut'-iwnner ('Bibliotheque d'Armenologie Bazmavēb 1; Venice, 1972).

[12]Malxaseanc', Sebēosi Patmut'iwn, Introduction.

[13]Abgaryan, Sebēosi Patmut'yun, 134-205.

[14]M. K. Krikorian, Handēs Amsoreay (Oct.-Dec. 1965), 546.

[15]Ibid., 547-48.

[16]Krikorian, Handēs Amsoreay, 1967-1971; and Ditołut'iwnner ew srbagrut'iwnner Sebiosi Patmagroc' bnagrin veray (Azgayin Matenadaran 214; Vienna, 1972/1973), 1-189.

[17]Ibid., 190-228.

[18]X. Thorosyan, Banber Erevani Hamalsarani (1967), 2.201-211, and Banber Matenadarani 9 (1969), 59-99.

[19]Krikorian, Ditołut'iwnner, 227-28.

[20]Being personally convinced that the first two (anonymous) chapters do not belong to the History of Sebēos, I have totally disregarded them in my presentation (!). All references to chapters follow the edition of Patkanian.

[21]Naturally our reckoning provides only an approximate idea, since the present division of chapters has been done by Mihrdateanc' and accepted by Patkanian. It seems that originally MS 2639 was divided into 50 chapters, but in the course of time, some of the chapter numbers were damaged (see Akinian, Hetazotut'iwnner, 25-28, and Malxaseanc', Sebēosi Patmut'iwn, Introduction, 77).

[22]I have rendered into English the German translation of Th. Nöldeke, Geschichte der Perser und Araber sur Zeit der Sasaniden, aus der arabischen Chronik des Tabari (1879; repr. Leyden, 1973), 275.

[23]In the History of Sebēos there are two distinct Smbats: (a) Smbat Bagratuni, son of Manuēl, who was in the service of the Byzantines and at the end was exiled to Africa (ch. 10); and (b) Smbat Bagratuni, marzpan of Hyrkania (ch. 14 ff). Two medieval authors, Mxit'ar Anec'i and Simēon

Aparanec'i, and some modern scholars, such as Ferdinand Justi, Iranisches Namenbuch (Marburg, 1895), 314b, identify the two, but Sebēos, who is the earliest historian, does not support this identification.

[24]Edmond Schütz, "T'etal in chapter 50 of the Chronicle of Sebēos," Indiana University Uralic and Altaic Series 134, "Aspects of Altaic Civilization," II (Bloomington, 1978), 155–169.

[25]Krikorian, Ditołut'iwner, 42–46.

[26]M. Ormanian, Azgapatum (1st ed.; vols. 1–2, Istanbul, 1912–3; vol. 3, Jerusalem, 1927), 1.724–26.

[27]Peter Charanis, The Armenians in the Byzantine Empire (Lisbon, 1963), 14 ff., and Andreas S. Stratos, Byzantium in the Seventh Century, I (602–634) (Amsterdam, 1968), 21–22.

[28]Sebēos, ch. 9; Ormanian, Azgapatum, 1.577–80.

[29]Sebēos, ch. 29; Ormanian, Azgapatum, 1.687, 695.

[30]Sebēos, ch. 33.

[31]Ormanian, Azgapatum, 1.717–720.

[32]H. St. L. B. Moss, "The History of the Byzantine Empire: an Outline," Byzantium (ed. N. H. Baynes and H. St. L. B. Moss; Oxford Paperbacks No. 16, 1961), 28.

[33]Sebēos, ch. 17 and 23.

[34]Ibid., ch. 25.

[35]Ibid., ch. 33 and 38.

A CRITIQUE OF SEBĒOS AND HIS

HISTORY OF HERACLIUS, A SEVENTH-CENTURY ARMENIAN

DOCUMENT

Zaven Arzoumanian

Columbia University (USA)

During the seventh century, a series of major political events marked the turning point in the medieval history of eastern Anatolia: the Byzantine and Persian wars, the capture of Jerusalem by Sasanid Persia in 614, the rise and the rapid invasions of the Arabs, the fall of Sasanid Persia in 642, and the creation of the Umayyad dynasty of the Arab Caliphate in Damascus in 661. Since no specific contemporary source is available in any of the related languages—Persian, Greek, or Arabic—the Armenian historiography of Bishop Sebēos, known as the History of Heraclius, becomes indispensable for the political history of the century. For this reason Sebēos' History was given immediate attention and evaluation both by Armenian and Western scholars since the discovery of its manuscript text in Ējmiacin by Yovhannēs vardapet Šahxatunian in 1831.[1]

At first the Arab invasions in Sebēos drew the attention of Hübschmann,[2] and the Byzantino-Persian wars of the text served as material for Gerland's[3] doctoral dissertation during the last quarter of the nineteenth century. Leading scholars, such as N. Marr, J. Markwart, A. Gutschmid, E. Dulaurier, and F. Macler, have either dealt with the problem of the integrity of the text or have rendered partial translations of it. The best available translation of Sebēos with annotations is the French translation of 1904 by Macler.[4]   Among Armenian scholars, Mihrdateanc', Patkanian, and Malxaseanc', have published the text,[5] the last of which, by S. Malxaseanc', is the best critical edition available, published in Erevan, 1939, with the peculiar title: History of Bishop Sebēos, (Sebēosi Episkoposi Patmut'iwn),

68

without Heraclius' name. Other historians, like Adontz, Akinian, Sargisian and Abgaryan, have examined the textual interrelationship of this document with other Armenian historical texts.

Despite the importance of this source, and perhaps because of it, students of history have found Sebēos' work a controversial one. In view of both its content and sources, the common problem which prompted extensive research on the part of the leading scholars is twofold:

(a) The basic question is whether the book we now have is really the History of Heraclius referred to by later historians. Or is it, as Abgaryan has argued, that Sebēos' real work is lost and instead the one we know is labelled as Sebēos'?

(b) The integrity of the text has also been questioned. Scholars are in disagreement as to the authenticity of the first two chapters of Sebēos' History, which are believed to have been written at entirely different times, the first chapter much earlier and the second chapter much later than the seventh century.

To deal with these problems we should first address ourselves to some of the references made by later Armenian historians and then turn to the examination of the manuscript text, a task which was thoroughly undertaken by Abgaryan in 1965. From historical evidence we know that the medieval Armenian historians, Step'an Tarōnac'i Asołik (tenth century), Samuēl Anec'i (twelfth century), Mxit'ar Anec'i (twelfth century), Kirakos Ganjakec'i (thirteenth century), and Mxitar Ayrivanec'i (thirteenth century), include Sebēos' name in their listings of the historians preceding them. In addition, they identified Sebēos as the author of the History of Heraclius. A tenth-century historian, Uxtanēs, mentions the work without Sebēos' name, but instead he adds a valuable remark on the History of Heraclius when speking about Smbat Bagratuni (d. 617), the Iranian viceroy of Vrkan (Hyrcania) from 595 to 602.[6] Uxtanēs says:

> Smbat Bagratuni waged many wars in Armenia, in
> Byzantium, and in Persia, as can be demonstrated
> to you by the History of Heraclius.[7]

This allusion is justified by the lengthy description of Smbat by Sebēos, who devotes chapters 10 and 14 through 19 of his History to the same marzpan of Vrkan.

Other historians, Łewond (eighth century), T'ovma Arcruni (tenth century), Yovhannēs Kat'ołikos (tenth century), Vardan Arewelc'i (thirteenth century), quote Sebēos almost verbatim, but none of them mention his name.[8] It is observed by Abgaryan that the indications in this case are such that the title of Sebēos' work was lost at a much earlier time, and that the text was copied by subsequent scribes both with neither title nor author's name. For example, Samuēl Anec'i is among those later historians who lists Sebēos and the title of Sebēos' work in his book. When drawing on Sebēos' History for an account of the invasion of Dvin by the Arabs, however, he writes: "During the days of Constans, son of Heraclius, Dvin was taken by the Arabs, as says the historian" (emphasis added).[9] It must be concluded that he does not mention the author of the account he is using because he does not know it, for with the exception of material from Sebēos he always indicates his sources by their author's names. Asoɫik deals with Sebēos in the same way.

It is my contention that historians differ in their evaluation of Sebēos' History simply because the texts available to them were not identifiable. The primary problem is, therefore, identification. If, however, Sebēos' History was not identifiable then, ten centuries ago, how can we expect a final word on it today? According to internal evidence, the History of Heraclius, particularly the third chapter, the "contemporary history" (matean žamanakean), is the closest conceivable document that can be ascribed to Sebēos.

Now for the manuscript text of Sēbeos' History. As mentioned above, the main manuscript of the work, copied in 1672, bearing neither the title nor the author's name, was accidentally found in Ējmiacin by H. Šahxatunian in 1831. Based upon the evidence of later Armenian historians, Šahxatunian assumed that this must have been the lost work of Sebēos and marked the manuscript accordingly. It is important, therefore, to bear in mind that the title of the book, Patmut'iwn Sebēosi Episkoposi i Herakln (Bishop Sebēos' History of Heraclius), is simply Šahxatunian's own designation. From this main manuscript of 1672 others were soon copied, some of which, together with the original, are preserved in the Matenadaran of Erevan.[10]

The 1672 manuscript text of Sebēos is a part of a collection of different texts, catalogued under number 2639 in the Matenadaran, presumably written at two different times. The collection contains Łazar P'arpec'i's History and Letter; an untitled text (Sebēos' present History of Heraclius); Koriwn's Life of Mašt'oc'; Agat'angeɫos' History; Eɫišē's History; Movsēs Xorenac'i's Armenian History; and the Mesrop Vayac'jorec'i's History. The 1672 collection was copied in Bitlis, at the school of Amrdōl, by Pawɫos

Gavṙc'i and by Grigor Erēc' from an older text which is now lost. Abgaryan, after careful study of the history of the manuscript, brings to our attention that in 1675, or a little after, Vardan vardapet of Bitlis, the renowned teacher of Amrdōl, had prepared the catalog of the manuscripts kept at his school, in which catalog the manuscript of 1672 is identified and described differently.[11] According to Vardan's description, the collection of 1672 had a different arrangement of contents than number 2639 of the Matenadaran.[12] Moreover, not only does Vardan's catalog not include Sebēos' name, but it also adds the name of a certain Xosrov as a bona fide historian along with the rest.

G. Tēr Mkrtč'ian first studied the seventeenth century collection,[13] and in 1965 Abgaryan examined it and concluded that the History of Sebēos we now have was erroneously ascribed to Bishop Sebēos, its true author being the Xosrov whose name Vardan of Bitlis had included in his catalog.[14] Abgaryan links Xosrov's name with the listings of the Armenian historians who, as a rule, name their predecessors chronologically. Kirakos Ganjakec'i, for example, knows of a certain Xosrov, a historian, who is classified as the one preceding Łewond, the 8th century historian of the Arab domination. Kirakos Ganjakec'i mentions Xosrov's name immediately before Łewond, after having mentioned Sebēos' name already:

> . . . and on Heraclius by Bishop Sebēos. And the
> wonderful history of Koriwn.   And Xosrov. And
> the history of Łewond the priest.[15]

Kirakos does not solve the problem completely, for although he mentions Xosrov's name as a historian, he places Sebēos before Koriwn, and Koriwn is definitely a fifth-century biographer of Mesrob Maštoc'. Advocating Xosrov's authorship, Abgaryan produces an unpublished list of Armenian historians found on folio 2556 of manuscript 126 of the Matenadaran. It reads:

> Xosrov Korovi (Brave) and his history. Łewond
> who tells thoroughly about the advent of Muham-
> mad.[16]

What Abgaryan is actually demonstrating is not so much the authorship of our present text of Sebēos as the existence of a certain historian Xosrov, whose name is placed immediately before Łewond. There is no question that the name of a certain Xosrov is revealed as a potential author of an unidentified text based solely on scattered listings of much later date.

Certainly this cannot be regarded as enough evidence to ascribe Sebēos' History to an otherwise unknown historian Xosrov. Besides a more recent bibliographic study (1979) has revealed that Abgaryan has rescinded his own views regarding Xosrov's authorship.[17]

Another way of evaluating the authenticity of our present text is to deal with the structure and content of the History of Heraclius. In 1851, Mihrdateanc', the first editor, arbitrarily divided Sebēos' History into three chapters, according to its chronological content, and called them tprut'iwnk'.[18] Whereas the last chapter of the text represents a contemporary history of the late sixth century through the year 661 A. D., the first chapter contains the legendary history of the origin of the Armenian people. The second chapter deals with the revolt of the Parthians against the Seleucids, as well as with the Armenian and Parthian Arsacid kings and their chronology. At the end it also carries a chronological list of both the Persian and Greek monarchs to the fall of Sasanid Persia.

Following the second Armenian edition (1879) of Sebēos by Patkanian, the first two chapters of the work were separated from the 'contemporary history' (matean žamanakean) and were considered to be anonymously written. The problem soon evolved into an argument on textual interrelationship, particularly because scholars were confronted with two different chapters, each based upon sources of its own. The problem of their authorship was thus further complicated by questions of chronology, source material, and content.

Gutschmid argued that Movsēs Xorenac'i was responsible for the first anonymous chapter, which he later used as a synopsis for his famous History.[19] Obviously, considerable attention was given to the first chapter as the Armenische Urgeschichte, or the Primary History of Armenia, as it is called by Toumanoff. According to Toumanoff, the so-called Primary History of Armenia belonged to the group of ancient sources, compiled probably during the fourth and fifth centuries.[20] It contains information on the Greek inscription found at the entrance of the Armenian Arsacid king Sanatruk's palace in Mcurk'.[21] The anonymous author copied this inscription from the book of Marab the Philosopher of Mcurk', which contained the chronology and the names of the first five kings of the Arsacids, Armenians, and Parthians. The Greek inscription was written by Agat'angełos and by order of king Trdat of Armenia.[22] It is understood by Toumanoff that the Primary History in Sebēos purports to be the translation of the original Greek arjanagir ("inscription") work by Agat'angełos, found in Marab's book as well. Toumanoff substantiates Gutschmid's argument and refers to Movsēs Xorenac'i's claim that the text of his History corresponded to an extract made by one Marabas Katina from a Greek translation of a Chaldaean book.[23] Toumanoff concludes that the two texts are thus associated with one and the same text of a Syrian author, Mār Abbās. They simply represent two parallel versions of one historical tradition, the longer of which, expanded and recast, is the one found in Xorenac'i.[24]

The Xorenac'i-Sebēos relationship has led other leading scholars, including Adontz, Akinian, and Manandyan, to the conclusion that the problematic portion of Sebēos is an integral part of the text and that it was used by Movsēs Xorenac'i who himself lived after the seventh century.[25] A textual relationship was also sought between the anonymous chapters and the History of P'awstos Buzand on the hypothesis that the latter's missing first two chapters, also known as tprut'iwnk', are actually the ones in the present text of Sebēos.[26]

As for the second chapter, the names of Movsēs Xorenac'i and Step'an Tarōnac'i are distinctly marked as its sources. The Armenian historiography recognizes only one historian by the name of Step'an Tarōnac'i, known also as Asołik, who wrote his Universal History in the tenth century. It has been very difficult to discover another Step'an Tarōnac'i who lived prior to the seventh century, whom either the anonymous chapters or Sebēos could have mentioned by name. Moreover, a whole page in the anonymous chapters is a verbatim copy of the corresponding text found in Step'an Tarōnac'i's Universal History.[27] Obviously one of the two has served as a source for the other. Abgaryan, who has done substantial research on the origin of the anonymous chapters, has come up with an altogether different solution. He states that the chapters in question belong neither to Sebēos, nor are they related to Xorenac'i; rather, they bear the sign of a much later composition, the author of which was Yovhan Tarōnac'i, who lived in the eleventh century and whose work, the history of the house of the Bagratids, is lost, only its title being preserved in one of the manuscripts (#1775) in the Matenadaran.[28]

Presently S. Malxaseanc''s views in favor of the integrity of Sebēos' History are predominant and seem to be accepted as satisfactory by the historians in Erevan since his first study of the History of Sebēos and Movsēs Xorenats'i in 1899.[29] Malxaseanc' confirmed his position in 1939 when he edited Sebēos' History and established the integrity of the text in its entirety, claiming that the Sebēos of the seventh century was also the author of the two anonymous chapters. Malxaseanc' confirms the integrity of the text from the point of view of a single author, basing his arguments on the locigal structure and consistency of the entire text. For Malxaseanc', the anonymous chapters are the integral and necessary parts of Sebēos' History because they represent coherence of plan and conformity with the third chapter, particularly if we realize that the original text included neither divisions nor chapters of any kind. Malxaseanc' remarks, "astonishing similarities between the anonymous and the main section of Sebēos' History are clear indications that the anonymous chapters and the History are written by the same author, Sebēos."[30] Malxaseanc''s conclusion is that by accepting the single authorship of Sebēos' History we can have a consistent and complete history of the Armenians from the most ancient legendary periods down to his own days, including the lists of the Persian and Armenian Arsacid kings.[31]

This seemingly simple approach is not readily acceptable primarily because of the problem of Step'an Tarōnac'i as a source for the second anonymous chapter, whose author is strongly believed to be the tenth century historian Step'an Asołik.[32] Malxaseanc''s basic position on the authorship of Sebēos for the third tprut'iwn of the History of Heraclius that is, the rest of the book is, however, acceptable without serious complications. It is also important to know that the preface of the main history of Sebēos ends with these words:

> I wanted to tell you about all these events through
> my present book.[33]

Sebēos, whose identity is hardly known, becomes a contemporary author if we recognize in his History the many first-hand and extremely valuable documents which, most importantly, do not occur incidentally. They are written by the author as the integral parts of the related events. This strongly supports the placement of Sebēos, or the author of this book, among the events as they occurred. Among such diplomatic and ecclesiastical documents is the correspondence between the Persian rebel Bahrām Chūbīn and Mushel, the Armenian prince of Tarōn, in which Chubin seeks help from the Armenians in overthrowing the Sasanid king and promises to restore the Armenian kingship with its Arsacid borders.[34] Emperor Maurice's (582-602) letter of accusation against the Armenian naxarars, addressed to king Khosrow II Parvīz of Persia, is an important historical document whereby the two monarchs agree to deport the Armenians to Thrace and to the East, respectively, because "if they [the Armenians] live in their homeland we shall find no rest."[35]   The document of the peace treaty of 652 between Mu'awiyah, the Arab governor of Syria, and T'ēodoros Řštuni, prince of Armenia, is unique in the annals of the Armenian diplomatic history.[36] Although believed to be a draft of an official declaration of the Armenian faith, composed at the Council of Dvin in 648 and addressed to Emperor Constans II (641-668), this document is preserved only by Sebēos and carries the endorsement of Catholicos Nersēs III (641-661), Prince T'ēodoros Řštuni, the Armenian bishops, and the naxarars.[37]   These are but some of the many documents scattered throughout the History of Heraclius.

Sebeos is a contemporary author because his History ends with the first year of the reign of Mu'awiyah (661-680), the first Caliph of the Umayyad dynasty.   The author further designates that his work is meant to be a "contemporary history," starting from king Hormizd of Persia (579-590), who is succeeded by his son Khosrow II Parvīz (590-628).   Khosrow II Parvīz seeks Emperor Maurice's help and restores his kingship by defeating the royal rebels.   Sebēos reports that Khosrow Parvīz returned the Armenian territories to Emperor Maurice for the favor that the Emperor had shown to him.[38]   Sebēos relates in detail the lengthy wars between the two empires after Maurice's assassination, and the repeated victories of Khosrow II over the Greeks.   The Persians had reached the Bosphorus, and it was not until Heraclius (610-641) succeeded to the throne that the war swung into the east. The Persians were defeated, and the Greeks headed to Ctesiphon.   At the end of his work, Sebēos describes the Arab invasions of Palestine, Syria, Mesopotamia, Persia, and Armenia, as well as the end of Sasanid Persia.

What do we know about Sebēos himself? Two things: (a) his name has been mentioned by the historians; (b) a certain Bishop Sebēos of the house of the Bagratunis attended the Council of Dvin in 645. Bishop Sebēos' signature as "Lord Sebēos, bishop of the Bagratunis," is the eighth among the sixteen bishops attending the Council, according to the Canons of the Holy Council of Dvin.[39]   Despite the fact that no mention is made in this work of the Council of Dvin which was convened by Catholicos Nersēs III, Ormanian was the first to identify the historian Sebēos with the bishop of the Bagratunis.[40] Other evidence supporting Ormanian's view are the combination of the general religious tendency of this work, the anti-Chalcedonian convictions of the author, and the one curious instance at the Armenian Cathedral of Dvin, where Catholicos Nersēs and his bishops, except for one, were forced to receive communion with Emperor Constans, thus accepting Chalcedon. Sebēos describes the incident with the knowledge and dignity of a churchman who is also disturbed by the abandonment of the true faith on the part of the Catholicos. The Armenian faith had been preserved "up to this day," as the eyewitness Sebēos specifies, by the previous Catholicoi since the Illuminator. He finally adds that one of the bishops present at the religious ceremonies whose name is not given, refused to receive the communion at first.   It is again Ormanian who sees the connections among the unnamed bishop, the bishop attending the Council of Dvin, and the author of this work.[41]   In his opinion, all three stand for Bishop Sebēos of the Bagratuni naxarars.

NOTES:

[1]Cf. G. Abgaryan, Sebēosi patmut'yunĕ ew ananuni atełcvacĕ (Erevan, 1965), 15, n. 1.

[2]H. Hübschmann, Zur Geschichte Armeniens und der ersten Kriege der Araber.   Aus dem Armenischen des Sebeos (Leipzig, 1875).

[3]E. Gerland, Die Persischen Feldzuge des Kaisers Herakleios (Leipzig, 1894).

[4]F. Macler, Histoire d'Heraclius par l'eveque Sebeos.   Traduit de l'arménienne et annotée (Paris, 1904).   This translation does not include the first two anonymous chapters found in the 1851 edition.

[5]Patmut'iwn Sebēosi Episkoposi i Herakln (ed. T'. Mihrdateanc'; Constantinople, 1851).   In view of the fact that this edition only was available to me I have used it throughout the present study.   The best edition available is that of S. Malxaseanc' (Erevan, 1939).   Patmut'iwn Sebēosi Episkoposi i Herakln (ed. K'. Patkanian, Tiflis, 1912).   Also first edition by same (St. Petersburg, 1879); translation into Russian (Patkanian, St. Petersburg, 1862).   Sebēosi Episkoposi Patmut'iwn (ed. Step'an Malxaseanc'; Erevan, 1939).

[6]Cf. C. Toumanoff, Studies in Christian Caucasian History (Washington: Georgetown University, 1963), 340.

[7]Uxtanēs, Patmut'iwn Hayoc', (Vałaršapat, 1871), 56.

[8]G. Abgaryan, Sebēosi patmut'yun, 19 f. M. Krikorian, Ditołut'iwnner ew srbagrut'iwnner Sebēosi patmagroc' bnagrin veray (Vienna, 1973), 81-83.

[9]Samuēl Anec'i, Hawak'umn i groc' patmagrac' (Valarsapat, 1893), 80.

[10]S. Malxasenc', Matenagitakan Ditołut'yunner (Erevan, 1961), 181.

[11]G. Abgaryan, Sebēosi Patmut'yun, 22f. and n. 17.

[12]Ibid., 21-23.

[13]Ararat (1891), 147-155; (1901), 542-549.

[14]G. Abgaryan, Sebēosi Patmut'yun, 23-25. Also Banber Matenadarani (1958), 68 n. 1; 69-70.

[15]Kirakos Ganjakec'i, History (ed. Melik-Ohanjanyan; Erevan, 1961), 7.

[16]G. Abgaryan, Sebēosi Patmut'yun, 27.

[17]S. Melik-Baxšyan, Hayoc' patmut'yan ałburagitut'yun (Erevan, 1979), 107, n. 20.

[18]Sebēos, History of Heraclius (ed. Mihrdateanc'), 1, 27, 45 (footnotes).

[19]A. Gutschmid, "Über die Glaubwurdigkeit der armenische Geschichte des Moses von Khoren," Berichte d. Kon. Sachs. Gesell. d. Wissensch. zu Leipzig philol. list Klasse (Bd. XXIII, 1876).

[20]Cf. J. Markwart, Armenische Urgeschichte des Sebeos (Rome: Pontificio Instituto Biblico (unpublished)). Also Toumanoff, Studies in Christian Caucasian History, 18.

[21]The text (Sebēos) (ed. Mihrdateanc'), 1) has Mcbin (Nisibis) which should be corrected to read Mcurk'. See H. Manandyan, K'nnakan Tesut'yun Hay Žolovrdi patmut'yan 2.1.16-17. Cf. also P'awstos Buzand, History of the Armenians (trans. S. Malxaseanc'; Cairo, 1954), 4.14 (233). N. Akinian, Handēs Amsoreay (1923), 407-409.

[22]Sebēos, History of Heraclius (1851), 1-2.

[23]Movsēs Xorenac'i, Patmut'iwn Hayoc' (ed. S. Malxaseanc'; Erevan, 1968), 1.8-9; 2.9.

[24]Toumanoff, Studies, 307.

[25]Malxaseanc', Matenagitakan Ditoɫot'yunner (Erevan, 1961), 192.

[26]Ibid., 186-187.

[27]G. Abgaryan, Sebēosi Patmut'yun, 57-58.

[28]Cf. Ibid., 13, 53ff.   Also Patmabanasirakan Handes (1962), 1.210-225 and Banber Matenadarani 6 (1962), 25-56.

[29]S. Malxaseanc', Sebēosi Patmut'iwně ew Movsēs Xorenac'i (Tiflis, 1899).

[30]S. Malxaseanc', Matenagitakan Ditoɫot'yunner 191.

[31]Ibid., 192.

[32]Before Malxaseanc', three scholars, Mihrdateanc', Norayr Biwzandac'i and Aršak Ter-Mik'elian, had argued that Step'an Tarōnac'i, mentioned in the second chapter of the Anonymous was not the eleventh-century historian Asoɫik.   Rather, he was a disciple of Mesrob Maštoc' and lived in the fifth century.   He was the author of an article entitled "Apostolic Succession and its Uninterrupted Continuation of the Armenian Orthodox Holy Church," published in Ararat (1868), 104-105.   Cf. Abgaryan, Sebēosi Patmut'yun 53 n. 51.   Abgaryan finds this thesis erroneous and states that both Tarōnac'is are the same historian Step'an Asoɫik, the author of the eleventh-century Universal History.   Cf. Ibid., 53-71.

[33]Sebēos, History of Heraclius (ed. Mihrdateanc'), 44.

[34]Ibid., 63-64.

[35]Ibid., 79-80.

[36]Ibid., 215-216.

[37]Ibid., 188-211.

[38]Ibid., 75-76.

[39]Canons of Dvin, 200-202 (Canons of the Holy Council of Dvin) Ararat (1905).   Cf. N. Adontz, Armenia in the Period of Justinian, appendix III L, 100.

[40]M. Ormanian, Agzapatum (Constantinople, 1912), 1.713.

[41]Ibid., 725.

LEGENDS ABOUT CONSTANTINE IN ARMENIAN

Michael van Esbroeck

Bollandist Fathers, Brussels (Belgium)

At the end of the last century, such prominent historians as Louis Duchesne, A. L. Frothingham and F. Conybeare were convinced that Movsēs Xorenac'i's History was written in the middle of the fifth century.[1] Consequently, the legends about Constantine's conversion and the Inventio (recovery) of the Holy Cross, and that of the baptism of the Emperor by Saint Sylvester, Bishop of Rome, were sometimes dated or situated in the early fifth century, simply because Movsēs Xorenac'i's History was the only one available. Since Movsēs quoted the "Doctrine of Addai" and the reports of Agat'angełos concerning the conversion of King Trdat, both books were themselves viewed as reliable sources dating from the fourth century.

The work of A. von Gutschmid, P. Vetter, H. Gelzer and A. Carrière already showed how difficult it was to prove that Movsēs' account was really an ancient one.[2] In 1913, F. Dölger issued a statement on Constantine's baptism in which Agat'angełos is reduced to an echo of a basically Greco-Roman tale.[3] Far more complete is the analysis made by W. Levison in 1923, which checks the Latin manuscripts of the Sylvester legend.[4] The oriental part of that study seems to remain unchallenged by further publications. It was composed by Levison with the acknowledged aid of A. Ehrhard for Greek sources and A. Baumstark for oriental reports.

The articles of Dölger and Levison throw no light upon the means by which the legends of Constantine grew up in the East. They do not explain the reasons which led Armenian historians to express the experience of the new official religion in the emblematic terms already familiar in the traditions of the Roman Empire. In converting the Roman world, theocratic symbols played a role analogous to those used by pagan forerunners in establishing the eminence of any one Roman emperor over his predecessor. In the pagan Tetrarchy, we know that Galen was proclaimed as offspring of Jupiter, and Constans, Constantine's father, that of Hercules. After Maximian's death, Constantine claimed to be the protégé of Sol Invictus and

Apollo, and he attributed his right to victory to the supreme divinity. That symbol of victory, as everybody knows, was to be superseded by the monogram of the Cross with the words en toutōi nika.

Not even that new Christian sign stopped the search for a more imposing guarantee of legitimacy. In his letter to Constans II, Cyril of Jerusalem claimed for the semi-Arian emperor a higher symbol of victory than that of Constantine himself. In the holy city of Jerusalem, Constantine alone succeeded in digging the Cross up from the earth, but Constans II was honored by seeing a burning Cross of light in the sky over Jerusalem![5] Such a rivalry among the symbols of the conversion of the Emperor not only continues the pagan habit of invoking higher divinities, it also gives us the key to the interpretation of use of symbols in the story of the conversion of Trdat and the Armenian kingdom.

Since the formulation of the claim is not expressed with the same words in every Greek source, the description of the Vision of Constantine has to be observed with the greatest care in Armenian as well. With this in mind, it seems possible to draw the chronological limits within which the Armenian reports were written. On one hand, the Greek and Roman stories ought to be read in a definite order, and on the other, it is clear that the Armenian Agat'angełos was compiled from several distinct redactional levels long before Movsēs Xorenac'i made his own Chronicle at the beginning of the eighth century.

Such are the general grounds for wishing to attempt to understand better the relationship of Armenia to the Roman Empire from the fourth to the seventh centuries. For simplicity, I shall first treat the Vision of Constantine, the major symbol of the Empire's conversion. In a second phase, our attention will be concentrated upon the records of the Inventio of the Cross, with special reference to the Armenian position in relation to the general diffusion of that legend in the Middle East. Finally, we shall consider the Legend of Sylvester and its influence on the various stages of Agat'angełos.

*   *   *

The most ancient testimony of Constantine's Vision is Lactantius' record ca. 318 A. D. Before the battle against Maxentius in Rome, the Emperor is asked in his sleep to engrave the caeleste signum upon the shields of the warriors.[6] In his Ecclesiastical History, Eusebius speaks only of this same sign, sōterion sēmeion, which was held in the hand of Constantine's statue at the Milvian bridge in Rome.[7]   Yet Lactantius already knew of celestial aid granted to Licinius: an angel gave him the victory over Maximianus Daia in 313, at Campus Ergenus, where the enemy was certainly a real persecutor of Christians.[8]   The report of Eusebius' Vita Constantini, which was left unfinished ca. 337, gives a description of that signum which matches Lactantius' description very well: tropaion ek phōtos sunistamenon, graphēn te autō sunephthai legousan: toutōi nika![9]

In the beginning of the fifth century, Rufinus gives a parallel story: Constantine dreams that he sees in the East in caelo signum crucis igneo fulgore rutilare, and the angels come and say to him: toutōi nika![10] These angels seem to have been borrowed from Licinius' campaign of 313. Otherwise, the statement of Rufinus does not improve the vision of the Vita Coinstantini.   Socrates, however, uses an original wording: eiden en tōi ouranōi stulon phōtos stauroeidē en ōi grammata ēn legonta: en toutōi nika![11] This expression is very carefully translated by Philo Tirakac'i in the seventh century, ca. 696 A. D.:   Etes yerknis xač'ajew siwn lusoy yorum ĕnt'ernoyr aŕeal: aysu yałt'ea.[12] This revelation, like that of Rufinus, is placed before the battle with Maxentius at the Milvian Bridge.

The Vita Constantini, however, considers that the victory occurred in Gaul, clearly in order to avoid the mention of a pagan guarantor, the god Apollo in Treves.   Medals were struck linking the monogram and the military success in Gaul in 313.   There is a good chance that Socrates is not drawing in this passage, on Eusebius' Vita, even though he quotes Eusebius several times in his first book.   A comparison of the Vita Metrophani et Alexandri with the Syntagma of Gelasius of Cyzicus, written ca. 475 A. D., shows that the words of Socrates may depend on the lost History of Gelasius of Caesarea,[13] the nephew of Cyril of Jerusalem, who was working about 380 A. D.   Both are speaking of Maxentius' battle with to sōterion tou staurou sumbolon phōtoeidē en ouranōi.[14] Sozomenos, although a contemporary of Socrates, juxtaposes the reports of Rufinus with that of the Vita of Eusebius.[15]

Before these major historians, another form of the Vision appeared in the History written by Philostorgius, the Eunomian philosopher and the personal enemy of Basil of Caesarea.   The passage of his Chronicle is only available in the brief resume given by Photius, together with quotations from the History, both to be found in the Vita Constantini edited by I. Guidi and in the Passio Artemii.[16] Three differences affect the structure of the Vision:

(1) the Cross appears like lightning, brighter thn the sun; (2) the inscription is made of stars in the form of a rainbow; (3) it is written in Roman letters: to tou staurou sēmeion uper ton ēlion exastrapton, kai asterōn auton kuklōi peritheontōn iridos tropōi.[17]   This new form is connected with that of Constans II which appeared twice simultaneously, one in Pannonia at Mursa in the battle against Magnentius in the year 351 A. D., and the other at Golgotha, from the high point in the sky, extending towards the summit of the Mount of Olives in Jerusalem.   In Mursa, as in Jerusalem, according to Philostorgius, the rainbow, the symbol of reconciliation, and the crown, the symbol of victory, stand shining in the sky.[18]   The Eunomian historian wrote about 430, but he was basing his accounts on an older source, the so-called "homoean-anonymous" chronicle, whose story intended to glorify Constans II during the reign of Valens, about 380.[19]

The first and the best source for the Vision in Jerusalem is naturally Cyril's Letter to the Emperor Constans II.   The words toutōi nika are never mentioned in Jerusalem.[20]   There we find the allusion to the lightning whose radiance is greater than that of the sun, and the description could suggest the form of a rainbow, of which no mention is made at all.   The Jerusalem vision is followed by the conversion of a number of people.

The last and most widespread legend in Greek is the prologue to the story of the Inventio of the Cross, whose first words read: "The seventh year of the reign on Constantine the great king, in the month of January, innumerable crowds of barbarians gathered together at the river Danube, seeking to cross the river and to destroy all the country to the East . . ."[21] The Emperor sees at night starou sebas ieron uperanōthen lampon echon epigraphēn di' asterōn . . ." the sacred wonder of the Cross shining from above, having an inscription made of stars." This very short text is already found at the head of the Inventio, in the Greek MS of Sinai, written in the eighth century. It is followed by the Letter of Cyril and a series of other old texts concerning the Cross and Saint Stephen.[22] Many copies of the prologue existed, not only in Greek, but in other langauges. We naturally find it in Armenian too. The translation of the vision sounds less accurate than that of Philo: zawrinag astuacełēn xač'in i verust p'ayleal, or unēr vernagir astełeay: aynu yałt'ea[23] "the divinely modeled sign of the Cross, shining from above and having the inscription of stars: by that sign you shall vanquish!"

This résumé exists in a parallel Georgian version which dates back to their oldest translations.[24] It is found in Syriac in two different versions, if not in very old manuscripts, at least in valuable collections.[25] One of these texts is even inserted between the two legends of the Inventio of the Cross, the first one under Emperor Claudius, the second one by Helen, Constantine's wife. A fragment of the Syriac version was found in Sogdian.[26] Lastly this legend exists in a genuine form in the Latin palimpsest MS of the sixth or seventh century, the Paris. Lat. 2769.[27] If the vision is placed in the sixth year of Constantine, this following description itself is the oldest version: vidit signum crucis Christi ex lumine claro constitutum et super litteris scriptum titulum.[28] That formula is closer to that of Eusebius' Vita. The existence of a Greek model for this Latin statement is beyond any doubt. Its oriental origin is clear because it claims Constantine's baptism by "Eusebius" of Rome, in the form which was bound to provoke the Roman reaction by producing the legend of Sylvester, the only true pope at the time of Constantine's conversion.

The role of the Latin legend is crucial in finding the structure of the Inventio, but before going further, let us consider the two traditions concerning the narration of Agat'angełos. First, the stars outshining the sun come from the anonymous homoean source ca. 380 A. D., under the influence of the Letter of Cyril, ca. 351 A. D., and Philostorgius claims a Latin origin, speaking of Roman characters. This form is perpetuated in the prologue to the Inventio by Helena which considers Eusebius bishop of Rome. Secondly, Rufinus invokes the titulum written in Greek characters, relying on an oriental tradition. The pillar of light, mentioned only by Socrates, is, however, nearer to Gelasius' and Eusebius' accounts. The baptism of the Emperor is mentioned only by Eusebius of Caesarea, and the bishop was, indeed, Eusebius of Nicomedia, the Arian favorite of Constantine.[29]

The earliest form of Agat'angełos' History gives the Vision according to the earliest form: stēlē de purinos ephanē en mesōi tōn udatōn staurou tupon ekhousa.[30] The stele of fire appears in the middle of the water, having the form of the Cross. But the Arabic text of Marr reads: the "pillar," stulon[31] and not stēlē, and it is probable that such a confusion occurred in Socrates' text. This vision is the main feature of the baptism of Trdat by Gregory in Bagavan. The way in which the different shrines are destroyed fits well with the oldest Latin document. The Cross brings about the conversion of the people and the destruction of the shrines. As soon as Constantine hears of that event, he sends priests to congratulate the new

Christian king and invites him to Rome, where Sylvester formerly gave him the baptism. During his journey to Rome, Constantine gives Trdat as the details of the vision of the Cross and of the victory.[32]

In the official text of the sixth century, the vision of the baptism at Bagavan runs as follows: ew loys sastik ereweal i nmanut'iwn sean lusawori, ew ekac' i veray ĵurc' getoyn ew i veray nora nmanut'iwn Tērunakan xač'in ew aynčap' cageac' loysn minč'ew argeloyr zčaɫagayt's aregakann ew nuaɫec'uc'anēr; kai phōsphodrotaton phanen kath'omoiōma stulou photoeidous estē epi tōn udatōn kai epano tou stulou to despotikon sēmeion. Epi tosouton de uperelampsen oste kai tas aktīnas tou ēliou kataluptein kai meiōsai "And a bright light appeared in the likeness of a shining pillar, and it stood over the waters of the river; and above it was the likeness of the Lord's cross. And the light shone out so brightly that it obscured and weakened the rays of the sun."[33] This second account uses the structure of the symbols in the Letter of Cyril in order to give prominence to the pillar already present in the first text. After Trdat hears of Constantine's conversion by Sylvester, Trdat and Gregory travel to Rome where Eusebius of Rome receives them with the greatest joy.[34]

In order to follow the various stages of Sylvester's becoming Eusebius of Rome, we first have to go back to the structure of the stories of the Inventio, and how the Armenian versions of them spread.

*   *   *

According to the official historiography, Queen Helena built the church of the Anastasis, and that of Golgotha on the site of the temple of Aphrodite, which was erected by Hadrian when Aelia Capitolina was founded. The churches were inaugurated under Bishop Macarius in 355, during the thirtieth year of the reign of Constantine.[35] Ten years later, Cyril speaks of the fragments of the Cross dispersed all over the world.[36] Ca. 390 A. D., John Chrysostom knew that three crosses had been found. Without the aid of the inscription at the top of Christ's Cross, it would have been impossible to decide which of the three was the true one.[37] Already in 395, Ambrose refers to Queen Helena as the leading figure in the Inventio, but the titulum again made it possible to find the true Cross. The nails were already mentioned as being inserted in the bridle of the imperial horse.[38]

Rufinus, ca. 405 A. D., was the first to speak of a woman who was desperately ill. The titulum fell away from the Cross, and it was necessary to touch the sick woman with each of the three crosses to see which of them

would heal her.[39] This would be the true Cross. Before 402, Paulinus of
Nola had given a longer report: the Queen inquires among the chief Jewish
authorities of Jerusalem, and receives from them the information she wants.
The true wood is revealed by the resurrection of a recens mortuus, a man
who died not long before.[40]

Socrates and Theodoret give the history of bishop Macarius of
Jerusalem and the old woman.[41] Sozomenus says a Jew was asked to show
the place they ought to dig up when Macarius was still the bishop of
Jerusalem.[42] The next form we have to analyze is the old Latin legend of
Helena, the contents of which would have been known to Paulinus of Nola and
Sulpicius Severus, ca. 400 A. D. As we have seen, the oldest Latin form
places at its head Constantine's Vision on the bank of the Danube. This
certainly avoided having to mention Licinius the Apostate in Pannonia, and
helped to represent all the enemies of Christianity as being on the side of
the barbarians. It was also an opportunity to recover the symbols of the
vision which Constans II had on the bank of the Danube. Lastly, it was not
too farfetched to identify Constantine's victory over the Goths in 332-333
with the statements of Eusebius' Vita, saying he was fighting against the
Gauls at the moment of the vision.

According to Eusebius, Christ himself gives instructions to Constantine
to engrave the monogram on the warriors' arms. Only the Latin text speaks
of a Vir splendidissimus,[43] coming with the same instructions, perhaps as a
substitute for the role of the angels in Licinius' campaign. The few
Christians in the army explain the teaching of Christ to Constantine. The
Emperor summons Eusebius of Rome and receives baptism, destroys pagan
shrines, and builds churches. The account of the baptism of Trdat by Gregory
the Illuminator in Bagavan follows this pattern exactly.

Later, the Latin text presents Helena's journey to Jerusalem and the
Inventio of the Cross as occurring on the 28th of the second month that is,
according to the Syriac version, the month of Iyyar (May) 28th. Then follows
a theological controversy. The Queen expounds the doctrine of Christ to the
Jews. Fifty Jewish doctors are listening, and one of them, Judas, explains
that his grandfather Zacchaeus transmitted to his father Simeon, and later
Simeon to himself, the secret of the truth of Jesus as the Messiah. Judas
is summoned to answer the Queen's questions. Since Judas does not know
where the Cross is, he is thrown into a well where he remains for seven days.
Afterwards, he agrees to find the place and makes a prayer in Hebrew to

obtain God's aid. An earthquake then takes place; sweet smells are emitted, and the digging begins. They find three crosses. A young man who died recently is brought back to life by the true Cross. Then, since Judas acquiesced to the orders of the Queen, Satan accuses him of treacherous behavior, and says that he will die a martyr under a future Emperor. Not long after, the bishop of Jerusalem dies, and the Queen appoints Eusebius, who was bishop of Rome, to annoint Judas bishop of Jerusalem, with the Christian name of Cyriacus, that is, "Dominicus." The finding of the nails follows that of the Cross. This story practically denies the presence of Macarius, whose name is found elsewhere. It represents the tradition best known to Paulinus ca. 402 in Western Europe.

The Inventio of the Cross by Cyriacus supposes the existence of two complementary statements: the martyrdom of Judas Cyriacus under Julian the Apostate, and the first Inventio by Protonikè, the wife of Claudius. Before reading these complements, let us glance at some of the documents which stress the antiquity of these legendary accounts.

In Greek, the vision which introduces Helena's legend is better adapted to the forms taken by Constans II's apparition, with the stars forming the letters en toutōi nika.[44]   That Greek account lies behind the versions in Georgian, Armenian, Sogdian, and Syriac. The oldest form, in Syriac, is well preserved in the unedited MS of Leningrad, N. S. 4, fol. 74-76,[45] of the sixth century, followed by Helena's legend in a text which corresponds very inexactly to that of the later MS Add. 14644, also of the sixth century, which was published by Nestlé.[46]   Both Syriac texts reproduce an old version of that combined legend. Another copy of Helena's legend was published by Bedjan from an unchecked manuscript.[47]   The two old Syriac codices are interesting because of the similarity of their content. It is worth remarking that Queen Helena found the Cross on Iyyar 28th, so that the second month mentioned in the Greek source depends on a Latin form of computation.

Some details are better described in the Syriac version: for instance, Saint Stephen is explicitly referred to as the brother of Judas' grandfather Zacchaeus. The parallel contents of the two sixth century manuscripts is striking. They include the Doctrine of Addai, the Doctrine of Saint Peter, Helena's legend and the Martyrdom of Judas Cyriacus. We also find the Doctrine of the Twelve Apostles in the London MS. In the Leningrad Codex we find the Life of the Apostle John, the Story of the Seven Sleepers of Ephesus, and an original composition about Gregory Thaumaturgus.[48]   The common source of both collections is certainly to be traced back to the fifth century. The story of the first Inventio of the Cross is included in the Doctrine of Addai,[49] and the second Inventio with its corollary on the nails announces the marytyrdom of Cyriacus. The three legends are already together. Reading the Doctrine of the Twelve Apostles, we can understand that the prominent figure here is Saint James, first bishop of Jerusalem,[50] just as Saint Peter is considered as the prominent figure in the Doctrine of Saint Peter which follows.

The London MS, which lacks the prologue on the Danube, inserts a special title before the Inventio: "Inventio of the Cross for the second time." Indeed, in the Doctrine of Addai, the first finding prepares for the second time in some details. In a more recent Syriac MS, Add. 12174, from 1196 A. D., both legends are brought together with a new title given to the second Inventio, and without the prologue on Constantine's vision on the Danube: its second part is an exact reproduction of the wording of the Leningrad Codex, which preserved the sixth-century prologue This old one only relates both legends in a single history.[51] An abstract of the Doctrine of Addai existed also in an isolated form in the Paris MS Syriac 234, published by Nestle, and in the Sachau MS 222, edited by Bedjan.[52] They are late derivations with new considerations at the end of the story.

Summing up, we may say that the Protonikē legend exists first in the Doctrine of Addai, which was translated by Leroubna into Armenian, It was made independent by the connection with Helena's Inventio. Let us proceed to the Protonikē legend.

The circumstances related by the legend are as follows: Protonikē, the wife of the emperor Claudius, sees the miracles of the Simon Peter in Rome and believes in Christ. She goes from Rome to Jerusalem with her two sons and her only daughter. She dwells in Herod's palace. James, the bishop of the church, visits her, and she asks him to show her Golgotha and where the Cross is. These are known to Onias ben Hanna, Gedalia ben Kaiapha and Juda ben Ebedshalom. The Queen orders them to reveal the secret to James. When she enters the tomb in which Christ is believed to have been buried, her daughter suddenly dies. Saying a prayer, she takes each of the three crosses and touches her daughter with them. The third one, the true Cross, brings her daughter back to life. She commands that a great building be erected on Golgotha. The Jews and the Gentiles become very sad. When Protonike comes back to Rome, Emperor Claudius commands that all the

Jews leave Italy. A short account of the event is sent by James to all the apostles.

In a somewhat abridged version of the first Inventio, this story, borrowed from the Doctrine, is extended by several episodes. With the persecutions against Christians in full force under Trajan's rule, the Jews see their opportunity and martyr Simeon ben Kleophas, bishop of Jerusalem. A certain Niketas then takes the Cross and gives it to the Jews, who conceal it in the earth at the depth of the height of twenty men. It was to be recovered a second time by the fifteenth bishop of Jerusalem, Judas, the last Jewish bishop of Jerusalem.[53] This episode is further elaborated in Bedjan's version: Simeon has to be judged by Nicetas' tribunal in a way similar to that in which Jesus was judged by Pilate. The author refers explicitly to the reports of Josepos, that is, Hegesippus, as quoted by Eusebius' Ecclesiastical History, III, 32.[54]

A testimony of Cyril of Alexandria shows that, ca. 430, the two legends of the Inventio were already known.[55] We may admit without difficulty that the Latin legend about the young man who dies is the one which inspired Paulinus of Nola in 402.

As all of Helena's legends refer to the Martyrdom of Cyriacus, we have to examine what made that third part of the triptych so popular a legend. It exists in Greek—but in a single very old MS, Sinaiticus 493—and in Armenian, Syriac, Coptic, and Latin.[56] A bad Greek derivation, also unique, was published by Papadopoulos-Kerameus.[57] The original Sinaitic Greek text remains unpublished, even though it is obviously the exact model of the oriental versions. There are only two Greek manuscripts which contain the Cyriacus martyrdom. This throws additional light on the complete absence of any version in Georgian, especially as Georgia was known for its orthodoxy. This scarcity must be connected with the appearance of Alexander's Treatise about the Cross, which was written between 543 and 553,[58] and remained the official orthodox history of the Cross. That text exists only in Greek and Georgian, in a very old translation, and the Greek copies are numerous. It clearly contains an attack upon those stories which introduced false names of bishops and Emperors into the story of the Inventio of the Cross, and it mentions Macarius of Jerusalem and the prologue to Helena's legend, with Constantine on the Danube.

The Danube legend, along with the Inventio, though very common in all these languages, does not occur very often in Armenian. This needs an

explanation. The spread of the Doctrine of Addai in Armenian explains why
the MSS which contain Helena's legend are relatively rare. Moreover, the
Armenians were the only ones who explicited identified Cyriacus with Cyril.
Cyril was obviously bishop of Jerusalem at the time of Julian's persecution.
For other reasons, the similarity between the names Cyriacus and Cyril,
already noted by N. Akinian,[59] cannot explain in itself the mention of Cyril,
martyred by Julian. The martyrdom of Cyriacus is paralleled by the way in
which Simeon was executed by Trajan.   The reason for this substitution
becomes clear if we look at the inclusion of the whole threefold cycle in the
legends about James, the head of the church in Jerusalem, whom, as we
already noted, was involved in the sixth-century Syriac MSS. The tradition
of James' autocephalic church was inserted in the Chronicon Paschale,
written about 532,[60] although lists of consuls into the next century were
later added.

    The Chronicle begins by stating that Simeon or Simon was the
fifteenth patriarch of Jerusalem after James; somewhat further on, it gives
the following additional information: Simon the Canaanite, whose surname
was Judas, son of Jacob and who was made bishop after James, the Lord's
brother, was crucified at the age of 120. A few lines later, the Chronicle
gives the names of Simeon, son of Kleopas, who also lived 120 years, as a
bishop of Jerusalem according to Eusebius' History. Clearly, the compiler
has confounded two different and contradictory traditions. Finally, he speaks
about Iustus Barsabbaeus as the third bishop of Jerusalem. This bishop is
quoted in an Armenian excerpt attributed to Yostos, fourth bishop of
Jerusalem.[61] The quotation was found in a treatise, "On Christ and the
Churches," which has been preserved only in Georgian. According to this
version, the author is Barsabbaeus, bishop of Jerusalem.[62] Lastly, this
Barsabbaeus is quoted in the Teaching of Saint Gregory the Illuminator, in
the final Armenian recension of Agat'angełos. The sequence of the Apostles
Eight to Twelve is: Jacob and Simeon, Thaddaeus and Barsabbas.[63]
Thaddaeus is included among the Twelve according to the later versions of
his legend in Artaz,[64] and Barsabbaeus becomes Justus according to the
Chronicon Paschale, which considers that Iustus Barsabbaeus was the apostle
who was not elected when at the command of the Spirit, an election was
made in order to fill the place left by Judas, the traitor, in Acts 1:23.[65]

    Now, ca. 561 A. D., at the time of Grigor Arcruni's letter to Yostos,
bishop of Jerusalem, we find the identification of the two bishops: Yostos

Barsabbaeus, third bishop of Jerusalem, is represented by the autocephalic claims of his late successor Eustochius, who was deposed by Justinian in the middle of the sixth century.[66] Eustochius borrows the name of Yostos just as Cyril used Judas' appellation Cyriacus. The whole claim is found in this consideration: the autocephaly of Armenia in the middle of the sixth century is founded on a complementary justification already rooted in Jerusalem's ecclesiastical autonomy as being Sion, mother of all the churches,[67] and the see of James, the Lord's brother, who was the first bishop. This seems the reason for which the identification of Cyriacus and Cyril was made explicitly only by the Armenians, under Julian the Apostate. On the other hand, Leroubna had spoken enough about the first Inventio to pay less attention to Helena's Inventio of the Cross. The text was less frequently copied in comparison to the wide diffusion of Helena's legend in Greek and the other languages.

If we consider the spread of the Inventio of the Cross, we must draw the conclusion that, already about 540, political changes affected the diffusion of Helena's legend in Armenian Christianity. In a complementary manner, the legend about Cyriacus is transformed into a Passion of Cyril of Jerusalem under Julian the Apostate. At this time, the legend about Cyriacus is omitted only from the Greek and Georgian accounts. In the middle of the sixth century, Jerusalem's claims were adapted to suit previous reflexes of autonomy: they identified Eustochius with Yostos, third bishop of Jerusalem, just as Cyril was made Judas or Simeon, second bishop after James, the founder of the church of Jerusalem. These identifications are to be found only in Armenian documents. The adaptations occurred at least in Jerusalem, when the opposition to Chalcedon provided new reasons for asking for independence. It can easily be guessed that, while the Pascal Chronicle speaks of James as Patriarch of Jerusalem, the claim would have been made after Juvenal came back from Chalcedon, having gained the new dignity of Patriarchate for the See of Jerusalem.

The connection of the martyrdom of Cyriacus with the cycle of the legends about Constantine is not so clear. Without the previous introduction which stresses the identification of Cyriacus with Judas who found the Cross, it would be possible to view the whole martyrdom as an example of an epic martyrdom among many others in the time of Julian. Cyriacus is the son of Anna, and, with a third notable, Admon, he is tortured for his faith and killed by the sword. It seems probable that some story of the martyrdom had already existed before some hagiographer for some political purpose thought it useful to conflate the martyr Cyriacus with Cyriacus who found the Cross. One must take into account another hagiographical novel which presents in a similar manner the perseverance of Christianity in Rome in the face of Julian's apostasy. The very old Bishop Eusebius of Rome is portrayed as the main figure in the maintenance of the faith, in the so-called Romance of Julian, as its editor Hoffmann named it.[68] Cyriacus plays the same role in the church of Jerusalem. Both legends magnify the heads of the original churches, that of Rome and that of Jerusalem. What claim could Constantinople, and even Alexandria or Antioch, present in opposition to such arguments based on unshakable faith?

*   *   *

Let us now look at the third Constantinian legend, that of his baptism by Sylvester, bishop of Rome. The Roman legend is not independent of its oriental parallel in which Constantine is always said to have been baptized by Eusebius of Rome, from the prologue of Helena's Inventio onwards. There is a sort of missing link which can give us an idea of the fluctuation in the connection between both legends: that is, the Coptic homily on the Cross, attributed to Cyril of Jerusalem.[69]

Preserved in three Coptic MSS, this legend is attributed to Cyril of Jerusalem at the time when controversy was going on about some Samaritan hereitics in the region of Gaza. The text itself cannot be more recent than the time of the controversy in it, probably in the seventh century. The legend gives a stage of development similar to that given by John Chrysostom and Ambrose on the Inventio of the Cross. It was only because of an inscription on a piece of leather inserted in the tomb by Joseph of Arimatheia and Nicodemus that it was possible to identify the true Cross. No mention is made of a young man who died suddenly, nor of a sick woman who was healed. The Inventio, however, was only possible through the help of Judas Cyriacus; in the wide-ranging discussion with the Jewish doctors, Constantine has to contend with seven leading specialists in Jewish tradition: Judas, Amin, Abiton, Adoth, Naasson, Yeshoua and Selôm.[70] There is a parallel in the manner in which the Emperor is involved in the discussion. In the Latin B form of the legend about Sylvester, Constantine argues with twelve Jewish specialists whose names are Abiathar, Ionas, Godolias, Aunan, Doedh, Chobec, Benoin, Ariel, Tharra, Sileom and Zambres. One can guess that Abiathar appears as Abiton and Selôm as Sileom; on the other hand,

Godolias is most probably one of the six names included in the Doctrine of Addai for the three main chiefs of the Jewish community under Claudius.

The Coptic legend places the very general controversy in the immediate context of the Inventio of the Cross. In the Latin legend Helena appears in danger of converting to Judaism as she wrote to Constantine a letter sent from Bythinia: the context of that letter gives a clear resume of Arian doctrine on the humanity of Christ. The letter results in the meeting of Constantine with the Jews in Rome in the presence of Sylvester, the protagonist.[71] The primary Roman aim behind the legend is obviously to reject the attribution of the baptism of Constantine to Eusebius of Nicomedia, the Arian bishop who, as a matter of history, baptized Constantine just at the end of the latter's life. That is the reason Helena is said to have come under Judaizing influence in Bythinia, in the region of Nicomedia. On the other hand, as is shown in Paulinus' version of the Inventio of the Cross, and in its Latin model, Rome was already in a position to reject the confusion between Eusebius of Rome and Eusebius of Nicomedia prevalent in the East. This oriental confusion was espoused in order to play down the Arian tendencies of Constantine, but, as we have seen, it was connected with Jerusalem's rivalry with Rome, as well.

The form taken by Sylvester's legend is no less complicated than that of the Inventio. Of the two Latin recensions which he has analyzed, Levison considers genuine the one which gives the full names of Bythinia and those of the two Roman philosophers, Craton and Zenophilus, appointed by Constantine to face the Jewish objections.[72] The second version of the legend does not mention these two philosophers representing the emperor, nor does it specify Bythinia as the place where Helena was in danger of being converted to Judaism. I think the influence of that version may be connected with the Coptic versions of the Inventio, where Constantine himself takes part in the controversy.

The origin of the Sylvester reports has already been dated to approximately 420 A. D.[73] It begins with some Roman questions about fasting on Saturday and about the new names given by Sylvester to the days of the week in order to eradicate the pagan divinities whose names were still in use., These typically Roman elements are found in the Greek version of the Sylvester legend as well as in the Syriac, which is preserved in a somewhat shorter form as part of the compilation attributed to Zacharias the Rhetor, completed ca. 565 A. D.[74]

The only way we could analyze in what milieu the Sylvester legend was received and translated in the East is by consulting the first book of Zacharias. It contains the following presentation of ancient facts in a MS, the Add. 17202, dated ca. 600 A. D. The legend is inserted between the tale of Joseph and Aseneth and the Inventio of Saint Stephen, dated 415 A. D. The second book opens with documents from the council of Ephesus and the acts of the Seven Sleepers.[75] It is noteworthy that the Latin and Greek texts introduce the Sylvester legend referring not only to the principal churches of that time, that is, Antioch, Alexandria and Rome, but also to Jerusalem and Ephesus.[76] The omission of Constantinople is surely a point of archaic interest. Ephesus was the center of Christian preoccupation thanks to the 431 council and the 449 "Robbery." In later times, it would have been unlikely for Ephesus to have such importance as to figure in the prologue of the Sylvester legend. It is most likely that Zacharias, in his Syriac version, used Greek compiler who quite adequately made the connection between the legend of Saint Stephen in 415 and that of Sylvester. The spread of Sylvester's legend in the Orient may have begun as early as the 430s. The theological arguments in the discussion with the Jews could have been brought out after Chalcedon, as Levison remarked, but they do not disprove the Apollinarist discussions of about 400 A. D.[77] Levison's intuition concerning the Latin style of the legend as a compilation of Arnobius Iunior, who died in 450,[78] confirms its diffusion in the fourth decade of the fifth century.

The central event in the Sylvester legend is the healing of Constantine's leprosy by holy baptism from Sylvester himself. One might wonder why this Roman legend specifies that Sylvester received the colobium--ancestor of the pallium--from Saint James the Apostle, through the kindness of Bishop Euphrosynus of Pamphylia.[79] Here seems to me to be an insight into the relationship between Rome and Jerusalem. It is not yet James, the brother of the Lord, who is meant by that text, but the Apostle who was thrown from the pinnacle of the temple. The other miracles in the Sylvester legend are the purification of various pagan shrines by exorcism: likewise the dragon of the Tarpeia Rock, and the episode of the magic death of the Bull of Zambres and its resurrection by Sylvester's prayer.

Abridged at many points but enlarged with passages of the Passio Eusignii, the Sylvester legend occurs twice in Armenian as an appendix to the translation of the Ecclesiastical History of Socrates, by Philo Tirakac'i.[80]

Certainly earlier, the influence of this legend was as important as that of the Inventio stories on the structure of Agat'angełos.

The earliest form of Agat'angełos, with its very strong Byzantine orientation, cannot be understood without some appreciation of the fact, that Trdat had no less rich an experience in personal conversion and penance than Constantine himself in his being healed of leprosy. Major exorcisms can be found in every legend: King Trdat, for example, is transformed into a wild pig. This is in no way inferior to the leprosy which covers Constantine. On the other hand, it is quite certain that Agat'angełos, in his first edition, already knew of the threefold Inventio of the Cross. At one stage of its development, the legend presents the conversion of the whole of the Caucasus. This version, with its strong Greek affinities, could not have been completed before Zenon's reign, before which the official Greek church was oriented along the Henotikon lines, even in Georgia and Albania.[81] At this time, as we saw at the beginning of this paper, Sylvester appears as bishop of Rome before Eusebius. This type of commingling of two different legends into a single pseudohistory also appears in the Latin Inventio of the Cross, where a bishop, most probably Macarius, is said to have died before Judas Cyriacus was made bishop in his place. It is an innovation of the Greco-Arabic version of Agat'angełos to have Constantine being converted before Trdat: in the letter he sent to the Armenian king, the Roman emperor invites Trdat, after hearing of the latter's conversion;[82] The chronology presupposed by that legend is as follows: the torture of Gregory by Trdat coincides with Diocletian's persecutions; that is, about 303 A. D. Afterwards, the old Emperor, at the end of his life, about 311 A. D., searches for the most beautiful girl in the Empire to become his wife. The messengers who discover the virgin Hṙipsimē in a convent in Rome announce this news to the Emperor, but the nuns have already escaped to Armenia when the Emperor's guards come back to Rome. Trdat would have found Hṙipsimē in Armenia about 313, and the martyrdom of St. Hṙipsimē would have occurred in 315. According to this version, Gregory remained in the well for 13 years. Theoretically, there is no contradiction in admitting the conversion of the Armenian king about 316, because 13 or 14 years are the oldest figures given in the versions of Agat'angełos. If Constantine was baptized by Sylvester in 313, Trdat could have been invited ca. 320 to Rome, when the pseudo-historic Eusebius was bishop of Rome. So, the coherence of the apparently contradictory legends is preserved.

Later, in the definitive edition of Agat'angełos, the chronology is completely changed. There is record of the virgins of Rome at the beginning of Diocletian's attacks upon Christianity, that is, in 303. Accordingly, the author has to find other reasons for placing Gregory in the well for 15 years, that is from 288 onwards. In that year, Trdat hears that Anak had killed Xosrov by treachery and learns that Gregory is his cousin, and he decides to throw Gregory into the well. The author could have found some aid as well in the fact that the Roman See really had a pope named Eusebius in 309. In this last development of Agat'angełos, of course, we do not find any mention of Sylvester. It is now Trdat who learns of Constantine's conversion ten years after he, the Armenian king, had converted to Christianity. The roles are reversed, and inasmuch as Armenia was under Sasanian rule, it was indeed safer to claim Iranian origin for both Gregory and Trdat, and conversion to Christianity independent of Greek hegemony. The version which was used by Yovhannēs Kat'ołikos of Bagaran[83] is the last stage in the growth of Agat'angełos' story.

At this time, an alliance with Maurice in Constantine appears imminent, the names of Sylvester and Eusebius disappear. When referring to the representation of the consecration of Gregory by Leontios of Caesarea,[84] the rearranger of the legend makes the ingenious discovery of a direct dependence on Leontius of Rome [sic!] in the ecclesiastical sphere, and an immediate dependence of Constantinople and Constantine in the political sphere.   This very clever transformation could have had two main motivations.

The first is the coincidence of the name of Leontios of Caesarea with the champion of Chalcedonism, Pope Leo the First; at the same time, this operation avoided the objection of two different people for the bishop of Rome at the time of Constantine's conversion. There was also some reason to imagine Constantine in Constantinople rather than in Rome if we consider that the Armenian version of Sylvester's account uses the Passio Eusignii, in which the founding of Constantinople is described as occurring very soon after the conversion of the Emperor. This is an addition reason for putting Constantine's conversion after that of Trdat. The result of this kind of interaction by which Church and Empire are substituted serves the interests of the independence of the Armenian ecclesiastical tradition, far removed from Byzantine ecclesiatical power but included in the sphere of the Greek Empire for mutual aid against Persian aggression.

At the end of this brief review we may conclude that a symbolic story is no less useful for writing history than an official report by a good historian is. The inherited symbols were adapted with truly remarkable sensitivity to the changes in political and religious trends. The manner in which the Armenians received the Greek symbol of the conversion of Emperor and Empire shows how adequately they understood to what end those emblematic representations were used.

NOTES

[1] F. J. Doelger, "Die Taufe Konstantine und ihre Probleme," Konstantin der Grosse und seine Zeit (Freiburg i. Br., 1913), 377-447, 403-404

[2] Ibid., 405-406.

[3] Ibid., 401-407.

[4] W. Levison, "Konstantinische Schenkung und Silvester-Legende," Miscellanea Francesco Ehrle (Vatican, 1923), 2.159-247.

[5] E. Bihain, "L'épître de Cyrille de Jérusalem à Constance sur la Vision de la Croix (BHG 413)," Byzantion (1973), 43.264-296. For the connection between both visions, see J. Vogt, "Berichte über Kreuzercheinungen aus dem 4. Jahrhundert n. Chr.," Annuaire de l'Institut de Philologie et d'Histoire orientales et slaves (1949), 9.593-606.

[6] Lactantius, De mortibus persecutorum 44.6 (ed. J. Moreau, Sources Chretiennes; Paris, 1954), 127, 433-436.

[7] Eusebius, Ecclesiastica historia 10.8.18-19 (ed. Schwartz; Leipzig, 1908), 898, and the interpretation of H. Gregoire, "Eusèbe n'est pas l'auteur de la 'Vita Constantini'," Byzantion (1938), 13.574ff.

[8] Cf. J. Moreau, "Sur la vision de Constantin (312)," Revue des Etudes Anciennes (1953), 55.308-310.

[9] Eusebius, Vita Constantini 1.28-30 (ed. F. Winkelmann; Berlin, 1975), 30.

[10] Rufinus, Historia Ecclesiastica 9.1-3 (ed. Schwartz), Eusebius'

Historia, 827-835.

[11]Socrates, Ecclesiatical History 1.2 (ed. R. Hussey, Oxford, 1853), 1.11.

[12]Sokratay Sk'olastikosi Ekelec'akan Patmut'iwn (ed. M. Tĕr-Movsessian, Vałaršapat, 1897), 4.

[13]Gelasius, Kirchengeschichte 1.5 (ed. G. Loeschke and M. Heinemann; Leipzig, 1908), 10. M. Gedeon, Anekdota Byzantina fasc. 1, 32, Ekklesiastike Aletheia (Constantinople, 1884), 4. Against F. Scheidweiler's position in favor of the posteriority of Constantine's Vita in "Die Kirchengeschichte des Gelasios von Kaisareia," Byzantinische Zeitschrift (1953), 46.277-301, see M. van Esbroeck, "L'opuscule 'Sur la Croix' d'Alexandre de Chypre et sa version géorgienne," Bedi Kartlisa (1979), 37.102-132, esp. 125.

[14]Gelasius, Kirchengeschichte, 10.

[15]Sozomenus, Ecclesiastical History 1.3.1-5 (ed. J. Bidez and G. C. Hansen; Berlin, 1960), 11.

[16]Philostorgius, Kirchengeschichte 1.6. (ed. J. Bidez; Leipzig, 1913), 7.

[17]Ibid., 7, quoted from Photius and the Vita.

[18]Ibid., 3.26.51-52.

[19]P. Batiffol, "Un historiographe anonyme arien di IVe siecle," Romische Quartalschrift (1895), 9.57-97.

[20]It is therefore quite normal that coins may have been struck in 350 with hoc signo victor eris: cf. H. Gregoire and P. Orgels, "S. Gallicanus, consul et martyr, dans la Passion des SS. Jean et Paul et sa vision 'constantinienne du crucifié'," Byzantion (1954), 579-605, esp. 596-599.

[21]E. Nestlé, "Die Kreuzauffindungslegende," Byzantinische Zeitschrift (1895), 4.324.

[22]R. Devreesse, "Une collection hiérosolymitaine au Sinai," Revue Biblique (1938), 47.555-558.

[23]Cl. Sanspeur, "La version arménienne de Uisio Constantini BHG 396," Handĕs Amsoreay 88 (1974) 316.

[24]References to the editions in M. van Esbroeck, Les plus anciens homéliaires géorgiens (Louvain-la-neuve, 1975), 99-100.

[25]E. Nestlé, De sancta Cruce (Berlin, 1889), 11 (1196 A. D.) and P. Bedjan, Acta Martyrum et Sanctorum (Paris, 1890), 1.326-343.

[26]F. W. K. Mueller and W. Lentz, "Sogdishe Texte II," Sitzungsberichte der Preussischen Akademie der Wissenschaften (1934), 19.504-520.

[27]A. Holder, Inventio sanctae Crucis (Lipsiae, 1889), 1-13.

[28]Ibid., 1, ll. 17-18.

[29]Dölger, Die Taufe, 381-385.

[30]G. Garitte, Documents pour l'étude du livre d'Agathange (Vatican, 1946), 100, "Vita graeca," par. 167.

[31]Cf. Garitte, Documents, p. 328.

[32]Ibid., "Vita Graeca," p. 113, par. 189.

[33]Patmut'iwn Agat'angełosi, 833. (Ed. Tēr Mkrtč'ian; Tbilisi, 1909), 434, 2-3. G. Lafontaine, La version grecque ancienne du livre arménien d'Agathange (Louvain-la-Neuve, 1973), 320. Translation by R. W. Thomson, Agathangelos' History of the Armenians (Albany, 1976), 367-369.

[34]Garitte, "Vita Graeca," Documents, 169 gives the name of Sylvester, and 182 that of Eusebius.

[35]Eusebius, Vita Constantini, 3.24-41. (Ed. F. Winkelmann; Berlin, 1975) 94-102.

[36]Cyril of Jerusalem. Catechesis 4.10 and 13.4, Patrologia Graeca, 35, cols. 467 and 686.

[37]Johannes Chrysostomus, In Iohannen 85, PG 59, col. 461, 9-18.

[38]Ambrosius, De obitu Theodosii, 45-48 (ed. O. Faller; Wien, 1955), 394-397.

[39]Rufinus, Historia ecclesiastica, 10.7 (ed. Th. Mommsen, Eusebius Werke, 2.2 (Leipzig, 1908), 969-970.

[40]"Sancti pontii meropii Paulini Nolani," Epistolae 23.5 (ed. G. de Hartel; Wien, 1894), 272-273.

[41]Socrates, Ecclesiastical History, 1.17 (ed. R. Hussey), 104-107. Theodoret, Historia Ecclesiastica 1.17 (ed. L. Parmentier and F. Scheidweiler Berlin, 1954), 64-69.

[42]Sozomenus, Historia Ecclesiastica (ed. J. Bidez and G. C. Hansen; Berlin, 1960), 47-49.

[43]A. Holder, Inventio, 1.14.

[44]For instance in Nestlé, Die Kreuzauffindung, 11-12, 324.

[45]N. Pigulevsky, "Katalog sirijskix rukopisej Leningrada," Palestinskij Sbornik 69 (1960), 140-143.

[46]Nestlé, De sancta Cruce, 25-36.

[47]Bedjan, Acta Martyrum (Paris, 1890), 326-343.

[48]The texts of the London MS were published by W. Cureton, Ancient Syriac Documents (London, 1864), 5-23 for the Doctrine; 24-35 for the Doctrine of the Apostles; 36-41 for that of S. Peter (all in Syriac). The Leningrad Codex is used for the Doctrina Addai by G. Phillips, The Doctrine of Addai the Apostle (London, 1876), 1-53.

[49]N. Pigulevsky, Le martyre de Saint Cyriaque de Jersalem, in Revue de l'Orient Chretien, 7.26 (1927-1928), 306.

[50]Cureton, Ancient Syriac, 32-33 (Syr.).

[51]Nestlé, De sancta Cruce, 7-20. The prologue of Leningrad is perhaps older than the Latin one from Paris. It remains unpublished and relates the Vision with the stars.

[52]Nestlé, De sancta Cruce, 21-25. P. Bedjan, Acta Martyrum (Paris, 1892), 3.175-187.

[53]Nestlé, De sancta Cruce, 9-11.

[54]Bedjan, Acta Martyrum, 3.183-187.

[55]Cyril of Alexandria, Commentarium in Zaccharia, 114 in PG, vol. 72, col. 272, quoted by L.-J. Tixeront, Les origines de l'Eglise d'Edesse (Paris, 1888), 169, note 3.

[56]The references to the editions in the Bibliotheca Hagiographica Orientalis (Brussels, 1910), no. 233 Syr., 234 (Coptic), 235 (Ethiopic), 236 (Armenian). The Syriac version of Leningrad is published by N. Pigulevsky, Le martyre de S. Cyriaque, 332-349, and completes Guidi's edition of the London MS. The Armenian version was published by N. Akinian, "Die Passio S. Cyrilli (Judae Cyriaci) in altarmenischen Ueberstzung," in Handēs

Amsoreay, 62 (1948), 145-155. The Greek model of the eighth century is unpublished. A Latin version is Acta Sanctorum Maii (Antwerp, 1680), 1.439-451, by Daniel Papebroch.

[57]F. Halkin, Bibliotheca Hagiographica Graeca (Brussels, 1957), no. 465.

[58]Cf. M. van Esbroeck, "L'opuscule 'Sur la croix'," 106-109.

[59]N. Akinian, "Die Passios Cyrilli," col. 130-131.

[60]Cf. K. Krumbacher, Geschichte der byzantinische Litteratur von Justinian bis zum Ende des oströmischen Reiches (Munich, 1897), 337-339.

[61]Chronicon Paschale (ed. L. Dindorf; Bonn, 1832), 1.460, 470-472. The Armenian text of Yostos is edited by N. Akinian, Untersuchungen zu den sogennanten Kanones des Hl. Sahak und das armenische Kirchenjahr am Anfang des 7. Jahrhunderts (Wien, 1955), 191-193.

[62]M. van Esbroeck, Les plus anciens homéliaires, 338-340.

[63]Patmut'iwn Agat'angełosi, par. 686, p. 355.

[64]M. van Esbroeck, "Le roi Sanatrouk et l'apôtre Thaddée," REArm 9 (1972), 279-283.

[65]Chronicon Pascale, 472.

[66]Cf. F. Diekamp, Die origenistischen Streitigkeiten im sechsten Jahrhundert und das funfte allgemeine Concil (Münster, 1899), 29-32.

[67]F. Diekamp, Hippolytos von Theben (Münster, 1898), 96-113.

[68]J. G. E. Hoffmann, Iulianos der Abtrunnige. Syrische erzahlungen (Leiden, 1880). Eusebius and Constantininus and his sons are mentioned in the title, 5.

[69]E. A. Wallis Budge, Miscellaneous Coptic Texts (London, 1915), 183-230 on the Brit. Mus. Or. 6799. Two other MSS are preserved in the Pierpont Morgan Library, no. 600 and 599.

[70]I found these names in Pierpont Morgan 600, 67, line 7.

[71]B. Mombritius, Sanctuarium seu Vitae sanctorum (Paris, 1910), 2.508-531, esp. 515.

[72]For the differences between the versions, see Levison, Kon-

stantinische Schenkung, 166-200.

[73]Dölger, Die Tauffe, 415-416 where the discussion on the fastdays is connected with a letter of Innocentius I in March 416.

[74]E. W. Brooks, Historia Ecclesiastica Zachariae Rhetori vulgo adscripta (Paris, 1919), 1.i-iv.

[75]Ibid., vii.

[76]F. Combefis, Illustrium Christi Martyrum lecti triumphi (Paris, 1660), 259. Levison, Konstantinische Schenkung, 230. Mombritius, 508.

[77]Dölger, Die Tauffe, 409-414.

[78]Levison, Konstantinische Schenkung, 205-206.

[79]Mombritius, Sanctuarium, 509, l. 50.

[80]The demonstration was made by B. Sarkissean, Tesut'iwn Selbestrosi Patmut'ean (Venice, 1893), 15-27. M. Ter Movsessian, ed., Sokratay Sk'olastikosi 691-799.

[81]Cf. M. van Esbroeck, "Le résumé syriaque de l'Agathange et sa portée pour l'Histoire du développement de la légende," Handēs Amsoreay 90 (1976), col. 497-506.

[82]Garitte, Documents 328.

[83]Esbroeck, "Le résumé syriaque de l'Agathange," Analecta Bollandiana 95 (1977), 293-357.

[84]Garitte, Documents, 222, 314-317. Some doubt has been cast on the existence of a council at Caesaria attended by twenty bishops. These doubts arise from a study of the manuscript tradition of the collections of Canons in Syriac. Garitte, 131, quotes a Syriac synod indicated by Lebon. The nonexistence is proved by H. Kaufhold, Die Rechtssamlung des Gabriel von Basra und ihr Verhältnis zu den anderen juristischen Sammelwerken der Nestorianer (Berlin, 1976), 10-14.

FOREIGN INFLUENCES ON THE ARMENIAN APOCRYPHAL

ADAM BOOKS

W. Lowndes Lipscomb

Columbia University (USA)

Speculation about Adam and other antediluvian figures known from the Bible occupied a prominent position in the literature of post-Biblical Judaism and early Christianity. Outside of the Biblical accounts themselves, this speculation is first attested within the Jewish apocryphal literature, where such works as The Book of Jubilees, Pseudo-Philo, the Life of Adam and Eve, and The Apocalypse of Moses supplemented the legends of Genesis with additional information about the lives of these figures such as the names of the many sons and daughters of Adam and Eve, the ways in which Adam and Eve repented for their disobedience to God, etc. Legendary expansion of Genesis was also widespread in the later Midrashic literature of the rabbis, where it frequently served homiletical purposes. In the New Testament and early Christian Fathers, Adam became the focal point for extended theological discussions of the origin of sin and the nature of Christ. The interest in Adam legends characteristic of Judaism was also fostered in early Christian communities, which were responsible for the translation and preservation of most of the surviving Jewish apocryphal books, and which produced their own apocryphal works while drawing heavily on Jewish sources.[1] Among these communities, the Armenian church preserved a version of The Apocalypse of Moses which has also survived in Greek and Slavonic, a related collection of short Adam books, and homiletical and poetic compositions.

A collection of these short Armenian Adam books was first published by S. Yovsēp'eanc',[2] based on a single copy of each work preserved among the MSS of the Mekhitarist monastery of San Lazzaro in Venice. The books, which have since been translated into English and German,[3] include The History of the Creation and Transgression of Adam, The History of the Expulsion of Adam from the Garden, The History of Cain and Abel,

Concerning the Good Tidings of Seth, The History of the Repentance of Adam and Eve, The Words of Adam to Seth, and The Death of Adam. Since Yovsēp'eanc', additional copies of all of these works, as well as hitherto unknown Adam books, have been discovered in various MS collections of the Soviet Union, Europe, the United States, and the Middle East.[4] A study of W. Lüdtke[5] suggests the existence of some of these works in Georgian MSS, but the precise relationship between the Armenian and Georgian Adam materials has not been established. None of the MSS thus far discovered has any claim to great antiquity.

Although these works have received some attention since their initial publication by Yovsēp'eanc',[6] many fundamental problems remain to be solved. First, previous studies have been based on the MSS published by Yovsēp'eanc' which contain corruptions and lacunae; other known MSS have not been consulted,[7] and no critical text has yet been produced.[8] Second, a thorough examination of the literary relationships between the various documents has not been carried out, although initial probings have indicated the importance of such a study.[9] Third, the role of this literature in the Armenian church has not been addressed. Such questions as how the transmission of these books in the Armenian church influenced their present form, why the Armenian church chose to preserve them, and how this literature and works of the same genre functioned within the Armenian church remain to be answered. A fourth problem, to which the present paper is addressed, concerns the sources of the traditions contained within the Armenian Adam books. A preliminary examination of these traditions indicates they bear significant affinities with earlier Jewish and Christian Adam materials, but the antiquity of these traditions and their precise relationship to older parallel sources has not been ascertained. A study of selected passages from the Armenian Adam books reveals dependency upon or close relationship to the following literatures:

1.   Bible. We have noted that the Armenian Adam books may be best characterized as legendary expansions of the Biblical stories about figures from Adam to Noah. This point may be illustrated by the story of the annunciation of the birth of Seth in Concerning the Good Tidings of Seth and the story of Abel's murder in The History of Cain and Abel.

a.   The Hebrew Bible devotes only one verse to the birth of Seth. Following the story of Abel's murder and God's punishment of Cain, we read in Gen 4:25, "And Adam knew his wife again, and she bore a son and called his name Seth, for she said, 'God has appointed to me another child instead of Abel, for Cain slew him'." The Armenian Adam books contain four more lengthy accounts of the birth of Seth, the longest of which appears in Concerning the Good Tidings of Seth.[10] According to this account, an angel comes to Adam and commands him to know his wife so that she may bear a son to replace Abel. Adam objects for fear of having a son even more wicked than Cain. The angel then reassures Adam, promising that Seth will be a consolation to him, foremost among the patriarchs, and that the lands will be filled with Seth's progeny. Here, the Biblical idea that Seth was a replacement for Abel serves as the point of departure for an elaborate annunciation story incorporating numerous themes not suggested by the Biblical text.

b.   Similarly, the Hebrew text of Genesis treats the murder of Abel in a single verse. We are told only that Cain and Abel were in the field together, and that Cain rose up against his brother and killed him.[11] In The History of Cain and Abel, this brief report is expanded into a full account of the manner in which the murder took place.[12] Knowing that his brother is the stronger of the two, Cain must resort to deceitful means to accomplish the murder. While the brothers are playing together in the field, Cain suggests that Abel allow him to bind him to a tree with a vinebranch to see if Abel is strong enough to break it. Abel agrees, and recognizes his brother's wicked intent only after he is securely bound. With the help of Satan, Cain finds a small sharp stone, and cuts his brother's throat slowly as Abel continually begs for mercy. Again, the Biblical notion that Cain killed Abel in a field serves as the point of departure for an elaborate story, many of whose elements have no foundation in the Biblical text. This type of entertaining expansion of Biblical stories is closely akin to and undoubtedly has its roots in Jewish haggadah, a form of narrative scriptural interpretation which employed legendary material for purposes of religious instruction.[13]

At points where the Armenian Adam traditions are rooted in the Biblical text, they employ Biblical quotations and paraphrases. In discussing the punishments of Cain,[14] for example, The History of the Repentance of Adam and Eve follows closely the Armenian text of Gen 4:11-15, a factor which suggests that the work was composed in Armenian.

Some of the features of these legends not found in the Hebrew Bible appear to be derived from the early versions of the Bible. This point may be illustrated with reference to the descriptions of the seven punishments of

Cain in The History of the Repentance of Adam and Eve[15] and The History
of Cain and Abel.[16]   The Hebrew text of Gen 4:11-14 describes the
punishments which Cain receives from God after killing his brother, but
neither enumerates these punishments nor refers to seven punishments. In
4:15, however, God announces that he who kills Cain will receive sevenfold
vengeance, an idea which is echoed in 4:24. Although the meaning of Gen
4:15 is unambiguous, the Septuagint may be understood in two ways:[17]

> i.   "He who kills Cain will pay seven penalties."

or

> ii.   "He who kills Cain will loose seven penalties."

The latter interpretation also appears in the Armenian Bible.[18] Similarly,
the reference to the sevenfold vengeance exacted on Cain's behalf in Hebrew
Gen 4:24[19] is rendered ambiguously by the Septuagint, which may also be
read, "seven times vengeance has been exacted from Cain."[20] This latter
meaning is again retained in the Armenian Bible,[21] and serves as the basis
for the two lists of the seven punishments of Cain in the Armenian Adam
books. While the list in The History of the Repentance of Adam and Eve is
obtained by dividing the Biblical account of Cain's punishment into seven
parts and is dependent upon the Armenian Bible,[22] the list in The History of
Cain and Abel is distinct from the former list and shows no signs of
dependence on the Armenian text of Genesis.

2.   Apocryphal literature. Other non-Biblical legendary materials
in these books are attested in Jewish apocryphal literature and may not be
viewed as the original creations of Armenian authors. Although the lack of
any explicit quotations or other clear indications of borrowing does not allow
us to identify the sources of the Armenian Adam traditions examined, the
existence of numerous parallels in Jewish apocryphal works attests the
antiquity of these traditions and is suggestive of their provenance. This point
may be illustrated with reference to two of the traditions referred to above.

a.   We have already mentioned the story of the annunciation
of the birth of Seth which appears in differeing forms in four loci in the
Armenian Adam books. An angel comes to console Adam and Eve who,
according to The History of Cain and Abel, mourn because they must look
upon Abel's blood-smeared corpse. Abel's body does not decay, and returns
to the surface of the ground whenever buried because Adam, the first man,
must first return to dust. As part of their mourning, Adam and Eve
discontinue having sexual relations. According to The History of Cain and

Abel, this period of abstinence lasts for two hundred years,[23] while The History of the Repentance of Adam and Eve gives the figure of one hundred and twenty years.[24]

The only other surviving account of an annunciation of the birth of Seth occurs in the perhaps first century A. D.[25] Apoc Mos (3:2-3)[26] in which God, in response to Adam's grief, sends an angel who tells him not to grieve and promises him another son to replace Abel. None of the more specific elements of the four Armenian accounts is paralleled here, but some are echoed in other Jewish apocryphal texts. In the second-century B. C. Book of Jubilees (4:7), for example, we are told that Adam and Eve abstained from sexual relations for "four weeks of years" while mourning Abel's murder. Some MSS of 2 Enoch[27] record the tradition that Adam buried Abel after Abel lay unburied for three years. In Apoc Mos 40:3-5, the earth does not receive Abel's body until Adam is buried. This idea is also implied in the perhaps first century A. D. Life of Adam and Eve 48:4-7, where Adam and Abel are buried simultaneously, and in Jub 4:29, where Adam is called the first to be buried in the ground.

b.   The two discussions of the seven punishments of Cain found in The History of Cain and Abel and The History of the Repentance of Adam and Eve[28] also contain traditions which are paralleled in Jewish apocryphal sources. In addition to the evidence cited above from the Septuagint, the perhaps pre-Christian T. Benj 7:3-5 notes that Cain received seven punishments, being allotted one punishment every hundred years for seven hundred years. The tradition found in both Armenian lists that Cain was made to tremble continually as one of his punishments is also found in Pseudo-Philo 2:1,[29] a work which may date from the first two centuries A. D. or earlier. Finally, the notion found in the History of Cain and Abel that Cain continued to live for 860 years is paralleled in Jub 4:1, 31, where the same figure is given.

3.   Other sources. Most of the traditions referred to above, as well as many others found in the Armenian Adam books, are widely attested in later Jewish and Christian sources. While again the absence of quotations or other indications of borrowing prohibits identification of the specific sources of the Armenian traditions, the wide currency of many elements of these traditions in Philo, the literature of the rabbis, the church fathers, Christian apocryphal works, and Byzantine chronographic writings is highly significant. These parallels may be illustrated with reference to the story of Abel's

murder in The History of Cain and Abel described above.

According to this account, Cain first tries to overcome his brother by wrestling with him, and resorts to deceitful means only after discovering that Abel is stronger. This idea is found in such rabbinic works[30] as BR 22:8, Midr Tan (ed. Wilna, 1833; Beresit 9), and Aggadat Šir (ed. S. Schechter, 1896, 43), which state that Abel was stronger than Cain and outwrestled him, but that he had mercy on Cain and allowed him to get up, after which Abel was killed. The statement in Philo, De Migr Abr 13[31] that Cain was a clever wrestler who overcame Abel by skill rather than strength also merits mention. The idea that Cain murdered Abel with a stone is first attested in Jub. 4:31, and later became widespread. The Christian apocryphal Syriac Cave of Treasures (fol. 8a, col. 1),[32] in closer agreement with our Armenian text, specifies the weapon was a flintstone; other suggestions include a sharp stone (Arabic Cave of Treasures fol. 97a),[33] large stone (Christian apocryphal Ethiopic Adam and Eve I:79),[34] stones (ninth century chronographer George the Syncellus, Chronographia, p. 19), [35] or merely a stone (several rabbinic works, including BR 22.8, Tg Ps-J to Gen 4:8; Pirqe R. el. 21; Midr Tan, Wilna ed. 1833, Berešit 9). Similarly, the story in Midr Tan (Wilna ed., 1833, Berešit 9) that Cain hit Abel on the hands and feet with a stone several times before discovering that breath came from the neck should be compared with the ideas in our text that Cain "did not know which is the place of killing" and that he killed Abel by cutting his throat. Finally, the notion that Satan incited Cain to murder Abel is paralleled in the Ethiopic Adam and Eve I.76, Syriac (fol. 8, col. 1) and Arabic (fol. 97b) Cave of Treasures, and in the Annals of Eutychius.[36] It is noteworthy that all the elements of tradition in this story which are elsewhere attested occur in rabbinic and/or eastern Christian sources, a fact which may suggest a Semitic source for the story.

Some traditions in the Armenian Adam books contain no known parallels, but can be shown on other grounds not to have originated in Armenian. Two features of the story of the annunciation of the birth of Seth are significant in this regard. First, in the form of the story found in Concerning the Good Tidings of Seth, the angel promises Adam another son, and adds: "you shall call his name Seth which, when translated, means 'consolations'."[37] This etymology is also found in The Death of Adam,[38] and is implied in The History of the Repentance of Adam and Eve[39] and The Words of Adam to Seth,[40] where Seth is called "son of consolation." In each case the name Set' is derived from the root mxit'ar, a derivation which cannot have originated in Armenian. Second, a comparison of parallel forms of the annunciation story found in Concerning the Good Tidings of Seth and The History of the Repentance of Adam and Eve suggests a common literary source for the two accounts which was not written in Armenian.[41]

In summary, we have shown that the Armenian apocryphal Adam books bear significant affinities with a large body of Jewish and Christian works containing traditions about Adam and other antediluvian figures beginning with pre-Christian Jewish materials and extending into medieval times. These affinities are manifest in the genre of narrative scriptural interpretation as well as in the more specific realm of parallel elements of tradition. If these works cannot be shown to belong to the large body of Armenian translation literature, it can at least be demonstrated that they draw heavily on foreign sources. That the attested traditions occur most consistently in Jewish and eastern Christian sources may suggest a Jewish or Semitic origin,[42] but no recognizable pattern of borrowing was discernible in the passages examined. More precise identification of the sources of these materials and an investigation of how they came to Armenia remain subjects for further exploration.

NOTES

[1]The recent interest in traditions about antediluvian figures is reflected in the work of the Society of Biblical Literature's Pseudepigrapha group, which devoted itself to a study of traditions about Seth and Enoch in 1977-78. For the results of their work on Seth traditions, see Society of Biblical Literature 1977 Seminar Papers (ed. P. Achtemeier; Missoula, Montana: Scholars Press, 1977), 2.1-43, and for their work on Enoch, see Society of Biblical Literature 1978 Seminar Papers (ed. P. Achtemeier, Missoula, Montana: Scholars Press, 1978), 1. Other important recent studies of Seth traditions include A. F. J. Klijn, Seth in Jewish, Christian, and Gnostic Literature (Leiden: Brill, 1977), the materials relating to the Sethian gnostics in The Rediscovery of Gnosticism (ed. B. Layton; Leiden: Brill, 1981), vol. 2, and the works of W. Adler, "Materials Relating to Seth in an

Anonymous Chronographer ('Pseudo-Malalas') and in the Chronography of George Syncellus," and D. Berman, "Seth in Rabbinic Literature: Translations and Notes" (Philadelphia: Dept. of Religious Studies, Univ. of Pa., 1977). These materials should be supplemented by E. C. Quinn, The Quest of Seth for the Oil of Life (Chicago: Univ. of Chicago, 1962), which includes a thorough treatment of medieval sources. V. Aptowitzer, Kain und Abel in der Agada, den Apokryphen, der hellenistischen, christlichen, und muhammedanischer Literatur (Wien und Leipzig: R. Löwit, 1922), remains the definitive study of traditions about Cain and Abel. For an extensive survey of legends about all the antediluvian figures in Jewish and early Christian sources, see L. Ginzberg, The Legends of the Jews (Philadelphia: Jewish Publication Society of America, 1909, 1939), vols. 1 and 5. On the role of Adam in early Christian theological speculation, see esp. G. T. Armstrong, Die Genesis in der Alten Kirche (Tübingen: J. C. B. Mohr, 1962), and J. Gross, Enstehungsgeschichte des Erbsündendogmas (2 vols.; München: Ernst Reinhardt, 1960).

[2]S. Yovsēp'eanc', Ankanon Girk' Hin Ktakaranac' (Venice: Armenian Monastery of St. Lazarus, 1896), 24-26, 307-332.

[3]For the English, see J. Issaverdens, The Uncanonical Writings of the Old Testament (2d ed.; Venice: Armenian Monastery of St. Lazarus, 1934), 43-78. An additional English translation of The Death of Adam with a commentary is found in M. E. Stone, "The Death of Adam--An Armenian Adam Book," HTR 59 (1966), 283-291. The German translation of these works is found in E. Preuschen, "Die apocryphen gnostischen Adamschriften aus dem armenischen übersetzt und untersucht," Festgruss Bernhard Stade (ed. W. Diehl et al.; Giessen: J. Richersche, 1900), 186-209.

[4]For a list of the MSS, see H. Anasyan, Haykakan Matenagitut'yun (Erevan: HSSH GA, 1956), 1.236-250, and M. E. Stone, "Report on Seth Traditions in the Armenian Adam Books," Rediscovery 9 (ed. B. Layton), 460-464. I am indebted to Prof. Stone for the identification of two additional MSS containing some of these works, one in the British Museum (BM Harl. Or. 5459, fols. 2-12b) and the other in the hands of a rare book dealer H. P. Kraus in New York.

[5]W. Lüdtke, "Georgische Adam-Bücher," ZAW 38 (1919), 155-168.

[6]In addition to the studies of Stone and Lüdtke cited above, Preuschen,

"Adamschriften," attributed these works to an early Christian gnostic sect called the Sethians. G. R. Cardona, "Sur le gnosticisme in Arménie: les livre d'Adam," Le origini dello gnosticismo: Colloquio di Messina. 13-18 aprile 1966 (ed. U. Bianchi; Leiden: Brill, 1967), 645-48, finds no clear gnostic elements in these works but claims these elements may have been stripped away in an attempt to make the texts conform to orthodoxy. Other brief mentions of these works are referred to in Stone, "Seth Traditions," 456.

[7]Some additional MS readings of The History of Cain and Abel, and The Death of Adam are available in M. Stone, Armenian Apocrypha Relating to Patriarchs and Prophets (Jerusalem: Israel Academy of Sciences and Humanities, 1981).

[8]The writer is currently preparing a critical edition.

[9]M. Stone, "Seth Traditions," 464-465. For example, has argued that The History of the Creation and Transgression of Adam, The History of the Expulsion of Adam from the Garden, The History of Cain and Abel, and Concerning the Good Tidings of Seth are consecutive portions of a single literary work, each portion commencing with a section designed to overlap with the end of the preceding section.

[10]Yovsēp'eanc', Ankanon Girk', 319, 17; 320, 7: (page number, line number). The three shorter accounts are found in The History of Cain and Abel (Yovsēp'eanc', 319,7-16) and The History of the Repentance of Adam and Eve (ibid., 326, 14-20; and ibid., 327, 11-16).

[11]Gen 4:8.

[12]Yovsēp'eanc', 316, 13 - 317, 26. A shorter account is found in The History of the Repentance of Adam and Eve (ibid., 326, 34 - 327, 3).

[13]For a discussion of rabbinic Haggadic method and literature, see J. Theodore, "Midrash Haggadah," The Jewish Encyclopedia (New York: Funk & Wagnalls, 1904), vol. 8.550-569, and G. F. Moore, Judaism (Cambridge: Harvard, 1927), vol. 1.161-173. For a more general and inclusive treatment of Midrash and an up-to-date bibliography, see M. P. Miller, "Midrash," The Interpreter's Dictionary of the Bible Supplementary Volume (ed. K. Crim; Nashville: Abingdon, 1976), 593-597.

[14]Yovsēp'eanc', 327, 28-36.

[15]Ibid., 327, 17 - 328, 4.

[16]Ibid., 317, 27 - 318, 21.

[17]Hebrew: kl hrg qyn šb'tym yqm. Septuagint: o apokteinas kain epta ekdonmena paralusei.

[18]Eōt'n vrēžs lucc'e.

[19]Ky šb'tym yqm qyn wlmk šb'tym wšb'h.

[20]Oti eptakis ekdedikētai ek kain. Ek may be rendered either "on behalf of" or "from."

[21]Zi t'ē eōt'n angam vrēžk' xndric'in i Kayenē.

[22]At least three other lists of the seven punishments of Cain obtained by dividing the Biblical account into seven parts are preserved in Greek sources. The lists in Ephraem Syrus, In Sanctam Parasceven (Ephraem Syri Opera Omnia (ed. P. Benedictus and S. Assemanus; Opera Graece-Latine; Rome, 1737-43), 3.477f.), Procopius of Gaza, Commentary on Genesis (Patrologia Cursus Completus (ed. J.-P. Migne; Series Graeca; Paris: Garnier, 1863), 87,1 col. 248), and Pseudo-Malalas, Anonymous Chronicle (Corpus Scriptorum Historiae Byzantinae (ed. W. Dindorf; Bonn: Weber, 1828), 8.), are closely related, but the differences between the Armenian and Greek lists indicate they were derived independently.   According to the description of Lüdtke, "Adam-Bücher," a list found in the Georgian Adam materials appears to be related to the Armenian lists and not to the Greek.

[23]Yovsēp'eanc', 319, 12.

[24]Ibid., 327, 14.

[25]The dates given for apocryphal works in this paper follow the consensus as reported in J. H. Charlesworth, The Pseudepigrapha and Modern Research (Missoula, Montana: Scholars Press, 1976).

[26]Apocryphal works not otherwise noted may be found in The Apocrypha and Pseudepigrapha of the Old Testament (ed. R. H. Charles; Oxford: Clarendon, 1913, 2 vols.).

[27]See the Melchizedek fragment 3:36 in W. R. Morfill, The Book of the Secrets of Enoch (Oxford: Clarendon, 1896), 85-93.

[28]For the references in Yovsēp'eanc', see notes 15 and 16 above.

[29]M. R. James, The Biblical Antiquities of Philo (New York:

Macmillan, 1917), rev. L. H. Feldman (New York: Ktav, 1971).

[30]For a recent survey of editions and translations of rabbinic texts through the sixth century, see J. T. Townsend, "Rabbinic Sources," The Study of Judaism (New York: Ktav, 1972), 35-80. Ginzberg, The Legend of the Jews, contains references to the older editions and the later rabbinic works mentioned in this paper.

[31]For a text and translation of the works of Philo, see F. H. Colson and G. H. Whitaker, Philo (10 vols.; Cambridge: Harvard, 1962), and the two supplementary volumes to the same series edited by R. Marcus.

[32]C. Bezold, Die Schatzhöhle (Leipzig: Hinrich's, 1833).

[33]M. D. Gibson, "Kitāb al Magāll, or the Book of the Rolls," Apocrypha Arabica (London: J. C. Clay, 1901).

[34]S. C. Malan, The Book of Adam and Eve (London: Williams and Northgate, 1882).

[35]W. Dindorf, Corpus Scriptorum Historiae Byzantinae, vol. 6.

[36]Migne, Patrologie Graeca, vol. 111, col. 910.

[37]Yovsēp'eanc', 320, 2-3.

[38]Ibid., 24, 20-21.

[39]Ibid., 327, 15-16.

[40]Ibid., 331, 9.

[41]The distinct elements and unique traditions found in the annunciation account in Concerning the Good Tidings of Seth and in the two accounts in The History of the Repentance of Adam and Eve make it unlikely that any one of these accounts serves as a source for the others. The similarities of structure, detail, and wording between the three accounts suggest a common literary source, while the differences in the Armenian vocabulary employed imply the source was not written in Armenian.

[42]A statement in Samuēl Anec'i's Chronology is suggestive in this regard. He notes that in ca. 590 A. D., a band of Syrian Nestorians entered Armenia attempting to propagate their doctrine and translated their books for their disciples. Included in a list of these works is a document called The Repentance of Adam.

SEVERIAN OF GABALA: NEW IDENTIFICATIONS OF

TEXTS IN ARMENIAN TRANSLATION

Henning J. Lehmann

University of Aarhus (Denmark)

Severian of Gabala is one of the authors of the Old Church for whom the Armenian transmission has been of greatest importance for the determination of questions of authenticity, integrity of texts, etc. The Armenian translations of homilies published so far can be summed up under four headings:

    (a)   The Aucher Collection,[1]

    (b)   The Akinian Collection,[2]

    (c)   Pseudo-Irenaeus,[3] and

    (d)   Pseudo-Chrysostom.[4]

Before turning to the question of new identifications it might be useful to bear in mind a few data concerning the transmission of the homilies known already. First, it should be noted that the collection of ten homilies, which form the core of Aucher's edition, has a very broad attestation in Armenian MSS. In contrast to that, the Akinian Collection as such is only found in one MS, New Julfa No. 110 (Cat. No. 395), a twelfth-century MS; for Akinian's homily No. XIII, however, it should be noted that there exists an excerpt or a shorter version, identical with Aucher's homily No. XI.[5] The one homily edited under the name of Irenaeus was also published from one single MS (MS Vienna Mech. No. 2, fifteenth century), whereas the Pseudo-Chrysostomic group has a broader attestation—together with the genuine Chrysostomic homilies in connection with which they have been transmitted. Both the Pseudo-Irenaeus and the Pseudo-Chrysostom belong to a later stage in the history of the Armenian translators' work than do the two first mentioned groups, the language of which is pure and classical.

Before leaving the well-known editions of texts, it should be recollected that homily No. X of Aucher's edition belongs to Basil of Caesarea, that homilies Nos. I, XIV, and XV of the same edition are attributable to Eusebius of Emesa, and that Severian's authorship of homilies Nos. XII and XIII in the Aucher Collection has been questioned.[6]

Turning now to homilies that have not been published so far, it is natural to begin with two homilies for which the main authorities are two MSS in the Armenian Patriarchate in Jerusalem, MSS No. 1, dated A. D. 1417, and No. 154, dated A. D. 1737, to which should be added two further nineteenth-century MSS of the Mekhitarist library of San Lazarro, MSS No. 680/294, dated 1824-25, and No. 1075/302, dated 1839-42.

The first of these homilies in the Jerusalem MSS bears the title: By Sewerianos, the Priest. Discourse on the Birth of Christ in Bethlehem in Judaea and on the Adoration of the Wise Men. This homily is rather closely related to the Greek homily In natale Domini nostri Iesu Christi (CPG 4657, PG 61, 763-768). The relationship between the two versions will appear from the following survey:[7]

MS Jer. arm 1 col., line	Number of lines	PG 61 col., line	Number of lines
(a) 41a, 48-42a, 35	84	763, 1-765, 3	69
(b) 42a, 36-42b, 19	12	deest	
(c) 42b, 20-43a, 2	31	765, 4-26	23
(d) 43a, 3-45	43	deest	
(e) 43a, 46-43b, 16	19	765, 27-44	18
(f) 43b, 17-44b, 3	83	deest	
(g) deest		765, 45-768, 12	141

Quantitatively the correspondence can be expressed in the following way: 134 out of a total of 292 lines of the Armenian homily find their parallel in 110 lines out of a total of 241 in the Greek "original," or in other words: a little less than half of the Armenian homily is identical with a little less than half of the Greek text. Whether this fact could be explained by the assumption that two excerptors have taken two-thirds each of an existing homily, combining them differently, can hardly be decided, unless further evidence appears.

I cannot here go into a discussion of internal criteria for attributing the homily to Severian, but it should be mentioned that there are two external witnesses to his authorship to be added to the attribution in the Jerusalem MSS, one in Greek and one in Armenian. We shall return below to the Armenian evidence, which consists of two quotations within the series of fragments attributed to Severian in MS Galata No. 54.[8] One of these is from section (a), the other from section (c) of the above survey. The Greek evidence is a quotation in Theodoret of Cyrus, who also gives the full name and title of the author: Severian, bishop of Gabala.[9] In spite of Theodoret's evidence, which brings us very close to Severian's own time, some modern scholars have denied Severian's authorship. This is true of B. Marx, J. Zellinger, and H.-D. Altendorf, whereas W. Durks, A. Wenger, and R. Laurentin support the attribution to Severian.[10] Those who deny it mostly do so with reference to very general arguments, saying that there is nothing particularly characteristic of Severian to be found in the Greek homily.

Great caution is required before conclusions about authorship are drawn from general observations on style and language, especially where short homilies are concerned which may very likely have been given their form by excerptors. Therefore, the Armenian evidence here referred to, seems to give considerable support to the case for Severian's authorship.[11]

As mentioned already, for the next homily again, MSS Jerusalem Nos. 1 and 154 are the principal witnesses. And again there are complications concerning the relationship to the Greek tradition. Here, however, the text of the homily as presented by the two Armenian MSS has a very close identity with one form of a Greek homily to be found in a single MS, but--to the best of my knowledge--never published. The Greek MS in question is a tenth-century MS in Trinity College, Cambridge.[12] Part of the Greek text has been edited, however, as approximately the first half of the homily CPG 4669: In illud: Ignem veni mittere in terram (PG 62, 739-742) is identical with the first half of the homily found in the Greek Cambridge MS and the Armenian MSS of Jerusalem, whereas the second half of Migne's text is an excerpt from the homily De Pharisaeo, PG 59, 589-592.[13]

The exact correspondences are as follows:

PG 62, 739 init.--741, 41: ai tōn nēpiōn . . .
Khloēphorein autēn poiēsō
= MS Trinity Coll. B.8.8. fol. 274v-276r
= MS Jerusalem arm. 1, 46b, 7-48a, 10.

The Greek tradition—including a quotation in the catena on Luke[14] —is unanimous in attributing the homily to John Chrysostom, whereas the Armenian witnesses quote Severian as the author. In the Jerusalem MSS the author is referred to as "Severian the Priest," i. e. the same designation as in the homily just treated of; one of the Venice MSS says "Seberianos, bishop of Gabala," and the other "Severianos," only.

The Venetian MSS present one complication, in that they add an exordium, two-thirds of which is identical with the opening paragraph of PG 60, 759-764 (CPG 4629): De remissione peccatorum. The section covered by the MSS of San Lazzaro (where a few lines have been added, to which I have not been able to trace any equivalent) is the following: PG 60, 759, 1-20: Mian ekhousan ē pēgē . . . oi eskotismenoi photizontai. (Oti de tauta outōs ekhei).

Of course, it would be precipitate to infer Severianic paternity of PG 60, 759-764 from the occurrence of these 20 lines in the two Venetian MSS. I cannot here go into any detailed discussion of internal or other criteria that might be added. As possible starting points for an analysis with a view to determining the question of authorship for this homily I might be allowed to quote the following three items: 1) the dogmatic opponents referred to are Arians, Eunomians, and Pneumatomachoi,[15] which would fit in very well with Severian's theological position; 2) the way in which, in commenting upon Matt 18:18 and 18:19, the homilist collects examples from all parts of the Bible, where luō/deō and sumphōneō are used, is very reminiscent of the exegetic (or homiletic) method of collecting "testimonia" characteristic of Severian;[16] 3) finally, it should be noted that this homily appears in a collection containing much Severianic material.[17]

Thus, if there are, admittedly, further questions to be solved concerning the introduction in the Venetian MSS and concerning CPG 4629 on the whole, before a final verdict on the question of authorship could be given, then it should be emphasized, that, for the bulk of the homily—CPG 4669—in the version witnessed by the four Armenian and the one Greek MS, the unanimous attribution to Severian in the Armenian material highly strengthens the case for his paternity.

Leaving aside now the Armenian transmission of entire homilies—or at any rate excerpts of such a length that they present themselves—and have been used—as homilies, I turn to two series of fragments to be found in MS Galata no. 54 (fourteenth century). Quantitatively these series do not furnish us with a great amount of new material—comprising only a little more than thirty pages in the MS; but a number of the fragments support identifications made already, and others invite to new identifications or contain unknown material.

The first series—given under the name of "Seberianos of Emesa"—contains 20 fragments from eight homilies of the Aucher Collection. I have treated of these fragments elsewhere,[18] so I shall confine myself here to repeating that there are highly interesting coincidences between the excerptor of MS Galata no. 54 and the author of the famous florilegium, the "Seal of Faith," as concerns their quotations form Severian's homilies.

The second series in the Galata MS is given under the name of "Seberianos, bishop of Gabala."[19] It contains eleven fragments from six different homilies. I shall give a brief survey of the contents of this series of fragments. I should like to note at once a fact that certainly adds to the value of this collection: for each homily quoted, both title and incipit is given.[20]

Below is given a list of titles, incipits, and the amount of correspondence established; and a few remarks on the main characteristics will be added.

(1)   i čařen or i mayr ordwoc'n Zebedia. yormē t'ē, vkayic'n . . wn[21]

(Cf. CPG 4249)

(a)   375,15 - 376,18:   Ew na asē . . . i kamac' nora = Jordan 32,9 - 33,19

(2)   i čařen or i cnundn K'ristosi: yormē t'ē, yoržam i jmeřnayin

(Cf. CPG 4657)

(b)   376, 19-25:   Cnuc'ič'k'n šawšap'ēin . . . ařanc' jeřin mardoy[22]

= MS Jerusalem arm. 1, 42a, 26-34

(c)   376,25 - 377,7:   K'ristos cneal i kusē . . . ew oč' apakanel

= MS Jerusalem arm. 1, 42b, 20-40

(3)   i čařen or vasn nnǰeloyn Yisusi i nawin: yormē t'ē, xoragnac' nawordk'

(Cf. CPG 4699, PG 64, 19-22:   oi pelagioi plōtēres

(d)   377, 9-19:   i bun ēr tērn . . . dar-
juc'anēr

= PG 64, 21, 26-37:   ektheuden o
kyrios . . . epistrephonta

(4)   i čaŕēn yor t'ē ziard sa girs gitē oč' useal:
yormē t'ē, ber darjeal
(Cf. CPG 4201, PG 59, 643-652:   Phere
palin tōn euaggelikōn

(e)   377, 21-24:   zi   oč'   zamenaynn
. . . ĕnd anhawats = PG 59, 645, 58-
61:   Ou panta gar . . . apistois

(f)   377, 24-33:   aŕ hrēays . . . mar-
tuc'eals = PG 59, 645, 64-74:   Pros
ioudaious . . . makhomenous

(g)   377,33 - 379,8:   bayc' zi mi kar-
cic'i . . . ayl miabanen mitk'd
= PG 59, 646,42 - 647,20:   All' ina
mē nomisethēi . . . alla symphōnei ta
noēmata

(h)   379, 9-16:   yandimanē zhrēic'n . . .
ĕnd hawr martnč'i
= PG 59, 647,72 - 648,3:   Elegkhei
Ioudaiōn . . . theōi makhetai

(5)   I čaŕēn or i tērunakan xač'n ew i hogin surb
ew yerrordut'iwnn: yormē t'ē, erēk mez
bann
(Cf. CPG 4196, PG 56, 499-516:   Khthes
ēmin o logos)

(i)   379, 18-23:   bayc' sakayn . . . yałags
ink'ean
= PG 56, 504,61 - 505,6:   Plēn
otan . . . di eauton

(6)   I xawsic'n, yor t'ē xostowanim zk'ez hayr,
tēr erkni ew erkri: ew i tesut'iwnn Daniēli,
yormē t'ē, erēk mez eranelin Ambakum
(Cf. CPG 4295, 17a, CSCO 102, 237)

(j)   379,25 - 381,21:   Ayl ē xostowanut'-

> iwn mełuc'eloc'n . . . amenec'un
> anowaneal
>
> (k)   381,21 - 384,6:   Du es or hanēr
> zis . . . zi nmanē ē
> 379,33 - 380,14:   Ew et'ē ok' ha-
> wasteaw . . . zi zmez yarusc'ē
> = CSCO 102, 237, 21-23:   Et si quis
> accurate . . . ut nos suscitet

The first fragment stems from the Pseudo-Irenaeus. Here the incipit is at variance with that in Jordan's edition, and I would take that to mean that the homily is not complete, as it appears in Jordan's edition.[23]

Then follow two fragments of the homily treated of above on the Birth of Christ, giving the same incipit of the homily as in the Jerusalem MSS. As was mentioned already, this fragmentary evidence to my mind strongly supports the attribution to Severian.

Thirdly we meet with a fragment from a homily on Matt 8:24. The Greek original of the fragment quoted is found in PG 64, 21; i. e. it belongs to the homily CPG 4699. On the basis of the Greek text it has been suggested that this homily should be attributed to Proclus.[24] To my mind, however, the reasons for this attribution are not so cogent as to weigh more heavily than the Armenian evidence for Severianic paternity, but it should be noticed concerning the Greek homily that once again we are confronted with a very short text, presumably an excerpt, which makes the argument from internal criteria problematic.

In the fourth place, in the Galata MS we meet with four fragments from a homily, which has with very good reason been attributed to Severian by modern scholars.[25]

The fifth homily quoted was attributed to Severian already in the seventeenth century by J. Sirmond, who was followed by Montfaucon. In the twentieth century this attribution has been substantiated very fully, especially by J. Zellinger.[26]

Finally, two excerpts from a sixth homily take up almost exactly as much space as do the fragments of the five homilies mentioned until now. This quantitative fact is the more valuable since we are here confronted with a homily of which only a small fragment was known beforehand. The fragment in question has been transmitted in Syriac only, by Severus of Antioch.[27] Severus and the excerptor of MS Galata No. 54 agree, both in the attribution to Severian and as concerns the title of the homily in question.[28] As, furthermore, the contents of the Armenian excerpts seem to me very Severianic, I find that this homily is in reality one of those, for which Severianic authorship is least disputable.

For an overall estimation of the value of the MS Galata-quotations it should, of course, be kept in mind that in the first series of excerpts, Aucher's homily 1, which is not by Severian, has been included; an inclusion of a spurious homily in a collection such as those treated of here is thus, of course, a possibility that should always be taken into account. On the whole, however, it seems to me that there are so many indications of Severianic authorship for the group of six homilies quoted by the Galata excerptor, that the appearance of a text in this series is in itself rather a weighty positive argument for Severianic authorship in cases where there is little or no supplementary evidence for this.

By way of rounding off it might be reasonable to point to the fact that the registration of Severianic texts in this paper does not--as no such register should--claim to be exhaustive. It should be noted explicitly, however, that I have omitted references to a number of fragments that exist in florilegia, catenae, and collections of ecclesiastical canons. The reason for that is that I have not been able to go through this material in a systematic and comprehensive way. As is known, parts of this material have been published already,[29] whereas other elements have only been hinted at or registered in a more or less provisional manner.[30] Presumably, also, a still secret portion awaits its finder. My humble purpose has been to point out for some texts, that exploration of a number of Armenian MSS, seems to provide a more solid basis for identifying their instrument of origin with the stylus of Severian.

NOTES

[1]Severiani sive Seberiani Gabalorum episcopi Emesensis homiliae (ed. J. B. Aucher; San Lazzaro, Venice, 1827).

[2]N. Akinian, "Die Reden des Bischofs Eusebius von Emesa," Handēs Amsoreay 70-73 (1956-1959). For the attribution of homilies 8-13 of this collection to Severian of Gabala, cf. H. J. Lehmann, "The Attribution of

certain Pseudo-Chrysostomica to Severian of Gabala confirmed by the Armenian Tradition," Studia Patristica 10 (ed. F. L. Cross; Texte und Untersuchungen zur Geschichte der altchristlichen Literatur, Berlin: Akademie-Verlag), 107 (1970), 121-130; and H. J. Lehmann: Per Piscatores: Studies in the Armenian version of a collection of homilies by Eusebius of Emesa and Severian of Gabala (Aarhus, 1975).

[3]H. Jordan, Armenische Irenaeusfragmente (Texte und Untersuchungen zur Geschichte der altchristlichen Literatur; Leipzig: J. C. Hinrichs), 36, 3 (1913), Text No. 29.

[4]John Chrysostom, Interpretation of the Pauline Epistles (in Armenian; 2 vols.; San Lazzaro, Venice, 1862). The four Severianic homilies are the following: 2.694-715 (= Akinian XI, CPG 4202), 2.783-791 (CPG 4206), 2.883-891 (CPG 4195), 2.892-897 (CPG 4216). The CPG numbers quoted here and elsewhere are those used in M. Geerard, Clavis Patrum Graecorum, vol. 2 (Corpus Christianorum; Brepols-Turnhout, 1974).

[5]Recently, M. van Esbroeck has published a translation of the Georgian version of this homily, which is interesting in being much shorter than Akinian XIII without shortening as radically as is the case in Aucher XI. See M. van Esbroeck, "Deux homélies de Sévérien de Gabala (IVe-Ve siècle) conservées en géorgien," Bedi Kartlisa, Revue de kartvélologie (Paris), 36 (1978), 71-91, esp. pp. 90f.

[6]Without any intention of drawing up an exhaustive list of references to the scholarly discussion of the authenticity of these--and other--texts, the following titles should be mentioned: G. Dürks, De Severiano Gabalitano (dissertation; Kiel, 1917); J. Zellinger, Die Genesishomilien des Bischofs Severian von Gabala (Alttestamentliche Abhandlungen 7.1; Münster i.W. 1916); J. Zellinger, Studien zu Severian von Gabala (Münsterische Beiträge zur Theologie 8; Münster i.W. 1926); B. Marx, Severiana unter den Spuria Chrysostomi bei Montfaucon-Migne (Orientalia Christiana Periodica 5; Rome, 1939), 281-367; H.-D. Altendorf, Untersuchungen zu Severian von Gabala (unpublished dissertation; Tübingen, 1957). When I include homilies XII and XIII of the Aucher Collection among texts for which Severianic authorship must still be considered, this is due to the conviction that the utmost caution is required, before negative conclusions regarding questions of authorship are drawn on the basis of internal criteria, esp. for short texts, as mentioned below. A supplementary reason for mentioning them is that de Aldama's

otherwise very useful and accurate manual of Pseudo-Chrysostomica (J. A. de Aldama, Repertorium pseudochrysostomicum, Paris, 1965) in the information given concerning CPG 4581 (de Aldama No. 457), seems to confuse this homily with CPG 4247 = Aucher XII (and with CPG 4588 = Aucher XIII, as far as his page references are concerned).

[7]For reasons of clarity I have only given references to one of the Jerusalem MSS. It should be noted, however, that the number of variants between the texts of MS Jerusalem No. 1 and No. 154 is very small.

[8]Cf. below.

[9]Theodoret of Cyrus, Eranistes (ed. Gerard H. Ettlinger; Oxford: Clarendon Press, 1975), 181.

[10]For the four first mentioned authors, cf. the references in note 6, above, and B. Marx, Procliana: Untersuchungen über den homiletischen Nachlass des Patriarchen Proklos von Konstantinopel (Münsterische Beiträge zur Theologie, Münster i.W.), 23 (1940). For the two last mentioned authorities, cf. R. Laurentin, Court traite de theologie mariale (Paris, 1953).

[11]It should be noted that the attribution to John Chrysostom is not only to be found in the Greek MS material, but also in a number of quotations in Syriac, viz. in Severus of Antioch (cf. Sévère d'Antioche, La polémique antijulianiste (ed. & trans. Robert Hespel, Corpus Scriptorum Christianorum Orientalium (Scriptores Syri 104-105; Paris and Louvain), 244-245 (1964), cf. esp. 245.110; 186; 197. The Coptic tradition in one place contains an attribution to John Chrysostom (cf. E. Porcher, "Analyse des manuscrits coptes 131, 1-8 de la Bibliothèque Nationale," Revue d'Egyptologie (1933) 123-160, esp. pp. 124f., where also an "exégèse de Sévérien de Gabala," containing "allégresse au sujet de la naissance du Christ" is referred to--cf. CPG 4282), in another to a Cappadocian bishop (cf. W. E. Crum, Theological texts from Coptic papyri (Anecdota Oxoniensa; Semitic Series 12; Oxford, 1913), 18-20), whereas the Georgian tradition seems to put Epiphanius's name at the head of this homily (cf. G. Peradze, "Die alt-christliche Literatur in der georgischen Überlieferung," (Oriens Christianus 3 (1930), 5.86 n. 9 [here quoted from CPG--ad 4657]).

[12]MS Trinity Coll. Cambridge B.8.8., fol. 274v-277v.

[13]Cf. CPG ad 4669.

[14]J. A. Cramer, Catenae Graecorum Patrum in Novum Testamentum (Oxford, 1844), 2.105.

[15]The latter group is here referred to as Marathonians (cf. W. Ensslin in Paulys Realencyklopädie der klassischen Altertumswissenschaft (new edition by G. Wissowa & W. Kroll; Stuttgart, 1893ff), 14.2. col. 1430f). The three groups of heretics mentioned here are also referred to in PG 59, 569 (where the Scythians are added) and in PG 61, 774 (in an interesting exegesis of the Parable of the Sower taking the three groups of heretics to be those sown by the wayside, among thorns, and on stony ground, respectively). In both cases the designation of the Pneumatomachoi is "Marathonians," leaving us with an interesting connecting link between the three homilies, CPG 4584, 4629, and 4660, that might deserve further attention, also when the questions of authorship for the three homilies are considered.

[16]Cf. Lehmann, Per Piscatores, 292; (see note 2).

[17]I am thinking of the collection of texts in MS Berlin, Phill. 1438, cf. R. E. Carter, Codices Chrysostomici Graeci (Codices Germaniae, Documents, Études et Répertoires publiés par l'Institut de Recherche et d'Histoire des Textes, Paris), 14 (1968), 2.15.

[18]Henning J. Lehmann, "Severian of Gabala--Fragments of the Aucher Collection in MS Galata 54," Haig Berberian Memorial Volume (in press).

[19]Only the first four letters of the name of the town are readable, but as they are Gaba(, it is easy to conjecture the two missing letters.

[20]The same, incidentally, is the case for the quotations from the Aucher Collection.

[21]It is difficult to read the word vkayic'n in my microfilm of the MS. I have no doubt, however, that Babgēn's reading of the incipit of the text is correct (Babgēn, Catalogue des manuscrits de la bibliothèque nationale arménienne de Galata (in Armenian; Antilias: Catholicossat armenien de Cilicie, 1961), 329); the second word, the reading of which also caused difficulties for Babgēn, seems to have included two or three letters before the -wn. Enough is readable, however, to make it clear that the incipit cannot be identical with that in Jordan's edition; this fact combined with the ascertainment of the incipits of the other homilies in this series being rendered very correctly in MS Galata no. 54, suggests the conclusion

concerning the incompleteness of the homily in Jordan's edition as stated below.

[22]There is no marking in the MS to keep the two fragments (b) and (c) apart, as is otherwise the case, where more than one fragment from the same homily is quoted (usually through the excerptor's yet sakawuc' or the like). Thus it is only on the basis of the Jerusalem MSS that it has been possible to ascertain that this excerpt is compounded of two fragments.

[23]Cf. note 21.

[24]Cf. B. Marx, Procliana, 73 (see note 10).

[25]Cf. Marx, OCP V (see note 6), 309-314, and Altendorf, Untersuchungen, 146f.

[26]Cf. Zellinger, Studien (see note 6), 27-34, and Altendorf, Untersuchungen. Cf. also A. Wenger, "Hésychius de Jerusalem," Revue des Etudes Augustiniennes 2(1956), 461, and J. Kirchmeyer, "L'homélie acéphale de Sévérien sur la croix dans le Sinaiticus Gr. 493," Analecta Bollandiana (1960), 78. 18-23.

[27]Severi Antiocheni Liber contra impium Grammaticum III, 1 (ed. & trans. J. Lebon, Corpus Scriptorum Christianorum Orientalium (Scriptores Syri, 50-51); Paris and Louvain), 101-102 (1933).

[28]In Lebon's translation the title runs as follows in Severus: Ex homilia in illud: Confiteor tibi, pater domine caeli et terrae (Matt 11:25), et de visione, quam vidit Daniel in Susa civitate, Severi Antiocheni (CSCO 102), 237.

[29]Cf. e. g. V. Hakopyan, Kanonagirk' hayoc' (Erevan, 1971), 2.288f; Aucher, Severiani, xviii. Cf. further the notes in CPG--conc. Nos. 4295, 5; 4295, 6.

[30]Cf. e. g. A. Zanolli, Di una vetusta catena sul Levitico perduta in greco e conservata in armeno (Venice: San Lazzaro, 1938); and R. W. Thomson, "The shorter recension of the Root of Faith," REArm, 5 (1968), 250-260. Cf. further the note in CPG conc. No. 4194.

TRADITION AND INNOVATION IN THE ARMENIAN

LANGUAGE

Giancarlo Bolognesi (Italy)

In a letter from Hauteville House dated December 17, 1868, Victor Hugo wrote as follows:

> J'ignore votre vieil idiome, mais je l'aime. J'y
> sens l'Orient. J'y entrevois les siècles. J'y vois
> rayonner la mystérieuse lueur du passé.[1]

in reply to Krikor Tchilinguirian, who intended to dedicate to him the Armenian translation of Les Misérables. In this impression of the Armenian language, which he gained without knowing it or being expert at linguistics, the great French writer indicates, often with particular insistence, that the main, distinctive feature of the Armenian language is antiquity: "vieil idiome . . . J'y entrevois les siècles . . . la mysterieuse lueur du passé."

At first sight, a connoisseur of Armenian, even without great expertise in Indo-European comparative linguistics, could have quite a different impression, grasping the innovation, so characteristic of the Armenian language, which has so deeply differentiated it from all the others of the Indo-European family. For example, although it is quite easy to point out, even at first sight, the relationship among several cognates of "two" (Sanskrit duvá, dvā, Avestan dva, Old Church Slavonic dŭva, Greek duō, Latin duo, etc.), it is certainly much more difficult to see the relationship between these forms and the Armenian numeral erku. This characteristic innovation, so evident in the Armenian language, has been pointed out by the most skillful Armenists beginning with H. Hübschmann. In his famous work "Ueber die stellung des armenischen im kreise der indogermanischen sprachen," which opened a new era in Armenian linguistic studies, he pointed out:

> Betrachet man aber das armenische nach seinem
> ganzen baue, so macht es den eindruck einer
> sprache, die grosse veränderungen erlitten, von
> dem alten materiale der stamm und wortbildenden

125

> elemente viel verloren, das verlorene aber durch
>
> neue flexionselemente ersetzt hat,

and afterwards he listed a whole series of "neubildungen" in Armenian.[2]

As a matter of fact, both of these different and contrasting impressions about the Armenian language can be explained and justified by a careful, although quick, analysis of the main phenomena marking Armenian. In the dynamics of the Armenian language, more than in other languages, the combination of two opposite tendencies, tradition and innovation, have resulted in the existence of numerous archaisms side by side with many radical changes.

Recently, Robert Godel, a disciple of F. de Saussure, a subtle interpreter of his theories, and a competent Armenian scholar, wrote:

> Aujourd'hui, on demande à l'arménien des élé-
>
> ments utiles à cette reconstruction (scil. à la
>
> reconstruction de l'indo-europeen): on y cherche
>
> des traits archaïques--et il y en a sans doute, à
>
> côté d'innovations radicales.[3]

To begin, it will be useful to mention some of the most interesting archaisms of Armenian, which will be much more meaningful when compared with the result of other Indo-European languages documented much earlier. First, the three primary vowels a/ e/ o/, which have merged to one or two vowels in most of the other Indo-European langauges, are kept quite distinct in Armenian. This is an archaic feature of Armenian; the neighboring Iranian and Indian languages, although documented over a millenium before, look much more innovative because they have merged these vowels to the sole timbre a. This distinctive characteristic of the Armenian vowel system, in comparison with Indo-Iranian, was just one of the elements on which Hübschmann based his thesis that Armenian was not an Iranian dialect but and independent branch of the Indo-European family: "Das armenische dagegen spaltet das a ganz in der europäischen weise in a, e, o und unterscheidet sich schon dadurch scharf von den arischen verwandten."[4] From these words one may infer that Hübschmann was still a prisoner of the then prevailing idea that a, e, o represented the Spaltung of a sole primary vowel a and that therefore the Indo-Iranian languages reflected the original situation better than the Armenian and European languages (especially Greek and Latin) which had changed. Not long after talking about the arische grundsprache, however, Hübschmann wrote more exactly: "Sie hatte a für indog. $\underline{a}^1$, $\underline{a}^2$, $\underline{a}^3$ = gr. a, e, o"; therefore, "Wer diese ansicht theilt, muss sagen, dass die verschiedenen indogermanischen $\underline{a}$ ($\underline{a}^1$, $\underline{a}^2$, $\underline{a}^3$ = $\underline{a}$, $\underline{e}$, $\underline{o}$) im Arischen in $\underline{a}$ zusammengefallen sind."[5]

Almost at the same time, but independently, Hermann Collitz, Johannes Schmidt, and other linguists upset the traditional opinion, proving by means of the so-called "Palatalgesetz," that the three vowels $\underline{a}$, $\underline{e}$, $\underline{o}$ antedated the sole Indo-Iranian vowel $\underline{a}$. In this case, therefore, Armenian (with Greek and Latin) was more conservative than Indo-Iranian.

Although the Armenian consonant system is marked by deep changes, it also contains some noteworthy archaisms. With special regard to the Lautverschiebung, the consonant system has posed problems for Armenian historical phonology which have increasingly drawn the attention of scholars in recent decades. An article of Gharibyan about the Armenian consonant system[6] set off a lively and useful discussion which, from 1959 to 1962, developed mainly, but not solely, in the pages of the Soviet journal Voprosy Jazykoznanija. Although it gave rise to many contrasts and disagreements, this discussion had the merit of bringing up the whole problem of the Armenian consonant system again, especially in the light of the aspirated voiced stop series attested in some modern Armenian dialects. Before Gharibyan's article, the results of modern dialectology served as a starting point for a critical revision of the traditional pattern by which the Armenian consonant system had been codified. Émile Benveniste concluded a lucid essay on the Armenian consonant shift and modern dialects by postulating an aspirated voiced stop series in Classical Armenian: "Nous posons donc l'existence de sonores aspirées en armenien classique, où les phonèmes qu'on a toujours transcrits $\underline{b}$ $\underline{d}$ $\underline{g}$ $\underline{j}$ $\underline{\check{j}}$ doivent recevoir la valeur de [bh], [dh], [gh], [jh], [ǰh]."[7]

At the same time, but independently of Benveniste, Hans Vogt came substantially to the same conclusions, proposing an aspirated voiced pronunciation for the Classical Armenian stops, normally spelled as voiced, on the grounds of the modern dialects.[8]

We can go back still earlier, to the beginning of the century, when Holger Pedersen, pointing out that in the modern Western Armenian dialects the old voiced stops have become voiceless and the old voiceless ones voiced, wondered how that change was possible without the eventual confusion of the two series of stops. He concluded that the only solution was to suppose the Classical Armenian stops spelled as voiced, to be the unchanged Indo-

European voiced aspirated ones.[9]

Meillet liked this idea, which was later discussed by Pedersen in opening number of the journal Philologica.[10] In the new Avant-propos of the reprinting of his Dialectes indo-européennes, Meillet declared, without any hesitation, that the Classical Armenian stops traditionally spelled as voiced were really voiced aspirated.[11]

Unfortunately Meillet's position on this is not contained in the second edition of his Esquisse d'une grammaire comparée de l'Arménien classique (Vienna, 1936), yet Benveniste, as a disciple and successor of Meillet, had good grounds for pointing out: "C'est donc dans le texte cité de 1922 qu'il faudra voir l'opinion réfléchie de Meillet sur ce problème, et non dans la réimpression (1936) de l'Equisse d'une grammaire comparée de l'arménien classique, où malheureusement la rédaction de 1903 a subsisté sans changement de fond."[12]

The reservations of some scholars about the presence of voiced aspirated series in Armenian are not beyond criticism, and the difficulties raised do not look insurmountable. I deem the clues right and the reasons for assuming the existence of aspirated voiced stops in Classical Armenian well-grounded. These stops represent the retention of the primary Indo-European voiced aspirated stops similar to those in modern Armenian dialects. Hence we can draw two important consequences:

> (1)   This series of voiced aspirated stops, which is kept in Armenian, is a truly exceptional archaism paralleled only in Sanskrit. In the other Indo-European languages, even in those documented long before Armenian, these primary voiced aspirated stops have developed differently.
>
> (2)   In Armenian, therefore, the consonant shift does not affect three series of stops but is limited to just two groups: Indo-European voiced and voiceless stops.

Besides the series of voiced aspirated stops, a series of voiceless aspirated stops is reconstructed for Indo-European; these, however, occur in only a few Indo-European languages, such as Indo-Iranian, Armenian, partially Greek, Latin, and Slavic. For this reason, these stops have been thought to be limited to a part of Indo-European territory and to have a more expressive than distinctive value. According to some, they should not be postulated for

Indo-European; rather, they may have arisen secondarily, in particular conditions, and only in some languages. Whether the voiceless aspirated stops have been inherited from the primary Indo-European consonant system, or whether they are secondary, expressive variants of the voiceless stops established in a limited part of the Indo-European linguistic field, it is interesting to point out that these voiceless aspirated stops are unchanged only in Sanskrit and in Armenian[13] (excepting the velar one, which becomes a voiceless spirant in Armenian). In contrast to the voiceless aspirated stops of Sanskrit and Armenian and the Armenian voiceless velar spirant, Greek has either the voiceless aspirated or the voiceless unaspirated stop (especially the dental); Iranian generally has the voiceless spirant; Latin has the initial voiceless spirant and the medial voiceless stop; Osco-Umbrian always has the voiceless spirant; Slavic has the voiceless spirant only for the velar (for the other consonants it has the voiceless stop); while in all the other languages they are grouped together with the primary voiceless stops and follow the same change.

Hence we can point out some interesting facts:

(1)   In retaining of the series of voiceless aspirated stops, Armenian agrees perfectly with Sanskrit, which generally presents a very archaic consonant system.

(2)   The voiceless aspirated stops, like the primary voiced aspirated ones, were not involved in the Armenian consonant shift, which affected only the primary voiceless and voiced stops.

(3)   The voiceless aspirated stops are kept nearly the same in all modern Armenian dialects, unlike the voiced aspirated ones, which have changed differently in the modern Western Armenian dialects, owing to the second consonant shift.

Another archaic feature of the Armenian consonant system is of great interest for the open question of the primary Indo-European gutturals. V. Pisani, in his lectures during the 1945-46[14] academic year and later in a lecture at the "Sodalizio Glottologico Milanese"[15] on February 28, 1948, had already expounded a new theory of the guttural palatalization in Armenian. His new theory was later resumed and improved in a longer, documented work of 1950.[16] By correcting the traditional doctrine, mainly put forth in the second edition of Meillet's Esquisse,[17] Pisani pointed out that only the primary labiovelars (with the exception of the voiced one) were palatalized in Armenian before *e, *i, besides *i̯ (but in the final syllable, e dropped before palatalization), while the primary velars ignore such a palatalization except after s. This state of affairs is perfectly paralleled in Albanian, where H. Pedersen had already succeeded in proving that the primary labiovelars were palatalized, turning into sibilants, while the primary velars remained even before front vowels, turning into q (= kj) or gj only recently.[18] In addition, Greek presents a similar pattern : the primary labiovelars were palatalized, turning into dentals, while the primary velars were exempt from such a palatalization. The similarity between Armenian and Greek as regards the palatalization of labiovelars becomes much clearer when we notice that in Greek, just as it does in Armenian,[19] the primary voiced labiovelar does not undergo the palatalization process. We can, therefore, establish an interesting new Armenian-Greek-Albanian isogloss on the grounds of which we can draw some noteworthy conclusions as to the prehistory of Indo-European languages:

>(1)   Armenian, Greek, and Albanian show the clear, primary distinction of these two series of consonants by means of the palatalization of velars. This is, of course, much more important for Armenian and Albanian, where the two above-mentioned series of consonants joined in one prehistoric series of velar sounds, like in the other so-called satəm languages.

>(2)   The palatalization of labiovelars is a very ancient phenomenon which surely precedes their delabialization in the so-called satəm languages and their labialization in a so-called centum language such as Greek.

We can point out other interesting archaic features in Armenian, always referring to the prehistoric development of the primary labiovelars. Meillet considered Armenian awcanel 'to grease, oil, anoint,' awj (gen. awji) 'snake,' to be clearly related to Latin unguo, anguis, two cases in which Armenian w replaces Indo-European *n in a very enigmatic way.[20] Much more decisively, G. Bonfante has pointed out the anticipation of the labial feature of the following primary labiovelar in the w of Armenian awcanel, awj; this is also well known and clear in such Greek words as kyklos, onyx, aukhēn (Aeolian amphēn), and so on.[21] The case of Greek aukhēn, Aeolian amphēn stands out, first of all for the double form of the same word: The former presents the anticipation of the labial feature of the primary labiovelar instead of the nasal and the consequent delabialization after w, the latter with the nasal and ph from the primary labiovelar. Second, it is important because we can find the exact cognate of Greek aukhēn, with the same characteristics, in an Armenian word awjik'. Bonfante, however, was unaware of this correspondence. Today, at any rate, it is a matter of fact that the presence of w in the above-mentioned Armenian words has to be related to the labial feature of the following labiovelar. Either we agree with Bonfante as that the labial feature has arisen through anticipation following G. R. Solta,[22] or with W. Winter that "the -w- in awj and awcanem [are] the result of the assimilation of -n- to the labial element of the following labiovelar."[23]

The Armenian words awj (-i- stem) and awjik' exhibit a remarkable phenomenon: the primary voiced aspirated labiovelar is not palatalized before i (to give the expected ǰ or ž between vowels). It follows that, owing to the anticipated labial feature w, the original, conditioning labiovelar must have dissimilated losing its labialization itself before the labiovelar palatalization took place. This can be found--and confirmed, in a certain way--in Greek, where aukhēn, kyklos onyx prove, the labial anticipation has no doubt delabialized the labiovelars before their palatalization. The Mycenaean forms in Linear B which exhibit labiovelars already delabialized after u but not yet palatalized before e, i prove it clearly. These velars which developed from labiovelar delabialization after u obviously remain in Greek, while in Armenian they turn into sibilants or affricates after u, as did the primary velars. From what has been said so far, we can infer the following points on the prehistory of Armenian and Indo-European languages in general:

(1)   It is important that a trace of the labial feature of labiovelars can be found in a satəm language like Armenian; this is a clue to profound archaism. Therefore, it has been said: "parmi les langues satəm l'arménien est celle qui se rapproche la plus du groupe centum qui conserve l'élément labial des labiovélaires, c'est-à-dire du grec, qui du point de vue de l' arménien est la

langue centum la plus proche."[24]

(2)   The anticipation of the labial feature of the primary labiovelars is another of the many phonetic isoglosses joining Armenian and Greek.

(3)   The labiovelar delabialization after u (either original or arising from anticipation of the labial element of the labiovelar) is a very archaic phenomenon, both in Greek and Armenian. It surely precedes the palatalization of labiovelars, which itself has been proved to be ancient and to precede not only the unconditioned delabialization of labiovelars in every satǝm language but also the labialization of labiovelars in Greek.[25]

(4)   The merging of the labiovelar with velar series is a relatively recent event in the prehistory of the so-called satǝm languages.

Another important trace of the primary labiovelar in Armenian can be found in the following fact: the Indo-European syllabic liquids r, l after a primary labiovelar seem to issue in Armenian ur, ul instead of in ar, al, which is the regular in Armenian reflex after a primary velar and in every other case.[26]   Interestingly, in Sanskrit rǝ issues in ūr after a primary labiovelar and labial; in īr in every other case.[27]   Hence, we can draw another interesting phonetic isogloss, Armenian-Sanskrit. Clearly, in the prehistory of Armenian and Sanskrit, the labiovelar series remained distinct from the velar one for a rather long time. Even in the consonant system, Armenian presents an archaism in comparison with Sanskrit: the retention of the two distinct primary liquids r, l which generally merge to r in Sanskrit.

So far I have just pointed out some phenomena which, among others, are outstanding in the Armenian phonological system for their archaism. Even among the numerous innovations which have changed the primary morphological system deeply, some important archaic elements can be seen in Armenian.

Meillet has already noticed that, as a matter of fact, Armenian lost only one of the eight Indo-European cases; that is, the vocative. This occurred in spite of the disappearance of the last-syllable vowel, with a possible consequent adjustment and leveling of forms, and even though each kind of declension contains no more than three or four distinct endings (though, in the personal pronouns there can be as many as six). This conservatism is one of the outstanding peculiarities of the history of Armenian. Among all the Indo-European languages, only Baltic and Slavic have kept such a complete declension from the date when Armenian is known. Greek, although archaic in other ways, had already lost three of the eight Indo-European cases before the historical age.[28] In the nominal inflection, which also has undergone perceptible transformations, some archaic elements survive; such as, isolated traces of the primary ablaut-series in nasal stems: Nom. Acc. matn " finger," Gen. Dat. Loc. matin, Inst. matamb, Nom. Pl. matunk'. In this declension, Armenian has maintained a more ancient state of affairs than Greek. While Greek has generalized the vowel o in every case of the declension of aphrōn (Gen. aphronos, Dat. aphroni), Armenian has kept the ancient vowel e in Gen. Dat. Loc. Sg. mianjin; cf. the contrast of Lithuanian Nom. akmũo "stone" and Gen. akmeñs, of Gothic Nom. haírto 'heart,' Gen. haírtins.[29] Other traces of the primary ablaut can also be found in the liquid-stem declension: Nom. Acc. hayr 'father,' Gen. Dat. Loc. hawr, and so on; in the declension of the numeral erek' 'three': Nom. erek', Acc. eris (cf. Sanskrit tráyah, trīn; Gothic þreis, þrins).

The opposition of hur 'fire' and its derivative hnoc' 'oven' refers to the ancient alternation r/n which occurs in Sanskrit yakrt, yaknáh and on which Greek hēpar, hēpatos is based.

The traces of the ancient dual are very interesting. They are kept not only in the numeral erku 'two' but also in some nouns such as ač'-k' 'eyes,' which is exactly an ancient dual (cf. Greek osse; Old Church Slavonic oči, Lithuanian aki   I. E. oqᵘi), to which the plural ending -k' has been added, and similarly akanj̆-k' 'ears' (with j̆ after n), and cung-k' (or cunk-k') 'knees' (probably   I. E. ĝonu̯i).

The classical genitive of the noun arew 'sun' is arewu, but its archaic genitive areg survives in the compound aregakn, which is to be etymologically interpreted as 'source of the sun.'[30]

Although the Armenian verbal inflections exhibit remarkable innovations, there are also some noteworthy archaisms; for instance, the preservation of the ancient root-aorists ed 'he has put,' et 'he has given,' ekn 'he has come,' perfectly parallel to Sanskrit ádhāt, ádāt, Vedic ágan.

In spite of these and other archaisms, the Armenian phonological and morphological system looks well developed and deeply diversified from the primary Indo-European one from the time of its oldest written documentation, owing to a whole series of innovations among which we have just described a few of particular interest.

One of the main reasons for the deep transformation of the Armenian phonological system was the shift of the primary free, tonal Indo-European stress into dynamic stress fixed on the primary penultimate syllable. The strong, centralizing action which this stress had on the word caused the fall of the last syllable vowel and the weakening, more or less emphasized, of some pretonic vowels. As for the chronology of this stress, it is evident that, at least, its effects on the vowel system of the pretonic syllables are still clearly discernable in the most ancient Middle-Iranian and Syriac loanwords in Armenian.[31]   Elsewhere I have also noted that these effects of the Armenian stress on the pretonic vowel are also valuable for a better knowledge of the different phases of the phonetic development in Iranian.[32]

Another very innovative feature of the Armenian vowel system is the neutralization of the primary phonemic quantitative alternations which have issued into qualitative alternations only as regards some vowel timbres.

As for the consonant system, the Lautverschiebung is not the only phenomenon which produced notable changes in Armenian. It will suffice to record this fact alone; in the Indo-European reconstruction we set up many consonant clusters, which Armenian did away with leaving, in the historical age, nothing but the sequence of a semi-vowel or a liquid or a nasal or a sibilant plus a consonant, as the former of these two consonants was uttered with the preceding vowel.

Among the most outstanding morphological innovations, besides the many and various transformations of the nominal and verbal inflectional system, is the disappearance of grammatical gender in Armenian, which coincides singularly and remarkably with Southern Caucasian languages, which also do not mark the grammatical gender.

Aside from the few examples mentioned above, it is pertinent to note that, by the time when Armenian is first attested, the dual had already disappeared or was disappearing, not only in Armenian, but also in every other Indo-European language, with the exception of Baltic, Slavic, and Celtic.

The double tendency toward retention and innovation which can be noticed in phonology and morphology, that is, in the deepest structure of the language, can also be seen in the lexicon. Together with the retention of an important part of the most archaic Indo-European terminology, Armenian exhibits an extraordinary propensity toward assimilating and harmonizing lexical elements of the most different linguistic and cultural traditions, both Indo-European and non-Indo-European. Put differently, in different ages and in different ways, the Armenian lexicon has always added to its wealth of words derived from substratum, adstratum, and superstratum languages, such as Hurrian, Iranian, Syriac, Greek, and Arabic and many more. We can, moreover, say that the complex history of this people and their cultural relationships with other peoples are well reflected in the stratification of the Armenian lexicon. As we all know, the Iranian contribution was particularly prominent and most decisive in the establishment of the Armenian lexicon. If the great phonological and morphological innovations notably changed the primary state of affairs, making the similarity between Armenian words and the ones of other Indo-European languages often quite difficult to grasp, the vast penetration of Iranian lexical elements caused the Armenian language to be considered an Iranian dialect for a long time. The Iranian loanwords in Armenian have usually kept the phonetic and semantic characteristics of the period when they came into Armenian, while their cognates in Iranian underwent considerable changes.[33]   Just a few examples will be enough to illustrate the important phenomenon of the Iranian loanwords in Armenian: Armenian bazuk 'arm'[34] maintained the ancient Middle-Iranian form bāzūk better than Persian bāzū by keeping the final guttural, which disappeared in Persian, and the original pronunciation of a, which turned into a very open o in Persian. Armenian vat 'bad' kept the ancient Middle-Iranian form vat better than Persian bad with the primary unchanged v-, which turned into b- in Persian; the primary a turned into a very open e; and the primary -t turned into -d in Persian. Therefore, the perfect phonetic and semantic similarity between Persian bad and English bad is the final result of phonetic developments operating on two originally distinct words; the former with an ancient v-, the latter with an ancient b-, Middle-English badde). With the unchanged v-, and -č-, and with the primary pronunciation of a, Armenian vačaṙ 'market,' has kept the ancient Middle-Iranian form vāčār better than Persian bazar. Armenian vard 'rose' has perfectly maintained the ancient Middle-Iranian form vard which has become gol in Persian through deep, radical changes, that is, a word with neither a vowel nor a consonant similar to those of Middle-Iranian.

If we pass from the phonetic side to the lexical one, we can point out the interesting case of some Iranian words which have disappeared in Persian, but have been retained as loanwords in Armenian.   Some Armenian words such as azd 'news, advice,' apastan 'shelter, refuge;' zēn-k' 'weapon' are some examples of this Persian Verlorenes Sprachgut[35] which have survived in Armenian.   A far more interesting fact is that Armenian has kept Iranian words which are not attested in the whole Iranian linguistic tradition. According to phonetic reasoning, we can consider Armenian nirh a sure loanword of which the Iranian original is recorded in no Iranian linguistic phase, but it can be traced back to an ancient form *nidrā well attested in the parallel Indian tradition (cf. Vedic nidrā).   It is also possible to recover an otherwise unknown Iranian word through Armenian with patuhan 'window,' which finds its matrix in a Middle-Iranian form *pătfrān, from an older Iranian form *pătifrāna-, of which the latter element is a cognate of Sanskrit prāṇa- 'breath.'   This allows us to establish the primary meaning of 'opening for the air' for the compound noun.   Another Iranian word, without any documentation until the present day, is well attested by the Armenian loanword hraparak 'square,' supposing an ancient Iranian form *frapādaka- which also survived in the Syriac loanword hrpdq.   In the same way, Armenian hrapoyr 'attraction, charm, allurement' presupposes an Iranian form *fra-pauda-, of which, however, no documentation has yet been found.   Thus the Armenian linguistic area has maintained a part of the Iranian lexical inheritance of which we could not learn from any other source.

At the beginning, we said that two opposite tendencies, retention and innovation, coexist in Armenian and that they have somehow integrated and harmonized themselves.   Now we see that the tendency to preserve lexical elements, subject in Iranian to many changes and even to disappearance in several cases, is itself born of the innovative tendency to receive lexical elements from other languages.

This phenomenon, closely fits one of the rules of areal linguistics (or linguistic geography) set by M. Bartoli: that of the "seriore" area, usually preserving the preceding phase.[36]   In other words, when a language or the words of a language are taken somewhere else, this language or its words usually tend to remain more archaic than in the native land.   That is why, for instance, American English and American Spanish have kept some archaisms which have been replaced by other forms in British English and Continental Spanish.   Thus, American gotten (I've gotten bad/good reports) has been replaced by got as the past participle of to get in English.

While the tremendous contribution of foreign words to the establishment of the Armenian lexical inheritance have been thoroughly discussed, the studies of the presence of Armenian words in other languages (not only in Georgian and other neighboring languages, but in Western languages), as well, are rare and more isolated. A fact that is not of common knowledge but of great interest in this regard is the presence of an Armenian word in a text dating back to the origins of Italian literature. In the canzone "Amor non vole ch'io chlami" by Jacopo da Lentini, who is, perhaps, the oldest and greatest of the poets of the Sicilian school (thirteenth century), we read the word scolosmini. This word is of obscure origin and is not recorded in other Italian texts. A. Pagliaro, the careful and sensitive interpreter of Italian texts and a skillful Iranist, has proved, with profound insight and sharp subtlety, that the origin of this word must be found in Armenian xolozmik.[37] It is interesting to note that the few dictionaries which record this obsolete Armenian word give the vague meaning of 'smooth and dressed stone which could be employed as a whetstone or a base on which to pound other material.' Now, on the grounds of the elements drawn from the context where scolosmini occurs, as well as from other clues, Pagliaro has succeeded in pointing out "turquoise," the so-called stone from Khorasmia, as the primary referent of Armenian xolozmik. Thus, if on one hand the Armenian word xolosmini has shed light on an obscure, isolated, archaic Italian word handed-down as scolosmini,[38] on the other the Italian context of this word throws light on the primary meaning of an obsolete Armenian word. The oldest meaning of the word, archaic and changed in Armenian, turns out to be quite well preserved in the Italian "seriore" area, just as is predicted by the "seriore" area rule.

I hope that this quick outline is enough to give an idea of the main archaisms and innovations characterizing the Armenian language. At this point, the romatic idea that language reflects the speaking people's spirit strikes us in an alluring and evocative way. The Armenian people, whose roots are deeply embedded in the past, are profoundly anchored to their age-old customs, but at the same time they accept innovations, are open to renewal, and are particularly gifted with creativity. They are a people whose heart is bound to Masis and to Lakes Van and Sevan, but whose eyes are turned to the future.

NOTES

[1]A. Tchobanian, Victor Hugo, Chateaubriand et Lamartine dans la littérature arménienne (Paris: Librairie Ernest Leroux, 1935), 27.

[2]H. Hübschmann, "Ueber die stellung des armenischen im kreise der indogermanischen sprachen," KZ 23 (1875), 11.

[3]R. Godel, rev. of the KZ 89 (1975) to celebrate the centenary of H. Hübschmann's well-known article "Ueber die stellung des armenischen . . .," Kratylos 21 (1976), 104.

[4]H. Hübschmann, "Ueber die stellung des armenischen . . .," KZ 23 (1875), 31.

[5]Hübschmann, "Iranische Studien," KZ 24 (1879), 409.

[6]A. S. Garibjan (Łaribyan), "Ob armjanskom konsonantizme," VJa (1959), 5.81-90.

[7]E. Benveniste, "Sur la phonétique et la syntaxe de l'arménien classique. I La mutation consonantique et les dialectes modernes," BSL 54 (1959), 53. In a final note (p. 56), he wants to fix the research chronology, observing that the problem of the Armenian consonant system had been the object of several lessons during an Indo-European dialectology course at the Collège de France since early 1958 and that in the Annuaire du Collège de France 58 (1958), 324, a summary of these lessons was already present: ". . . il a été montré à l'aide de travaux publiés sur la dialectologie moderne de l'arménien et sur les articulations du dialecte arménien oriental, que les sons de l'arménien classique transcrits par des sonores devaient être en réalité des sonores aspirées." Moreover, the same note let us know that at the end of Dec. 1958 Benveniste received the eighteenth volume of the Norsk Tidsskrift for Sprogvidenskap containing Hans Vogt's article "Les occlusives de l'arménien" (143-159), which came to the same conclusions pointed out by Benveniste.

[8]H. Vogt, "Les occlusives de l'arménien," Norsk Tidsskrift for Sprogvidenskap 18 (1958), 143-159.

[9]H. Pedersen, "Armenisch und die nachbarsprachen. 1 Vorbemerkungen über das armenische lautsystem," KZ 39 (1904-1906), 337.

[10]Pedersen, Philologica 1 (1921-22), 45-46.

[11]A. Meillet, Les dialectes indo-européens (Paris: Champion, 1922), 13 of the Avant-propos.

[12]E. Benveniste, "Sur la phonétique et la syntaxe," BSL 54 (1959), 54-55.

[13]The arguments advanced by W. Winter in favor of a presumed fricative feature of the traditional aspirated voiceless stops "in the older period of Armenian" are weak and contested: cf. W. Winter, "Problems of Armenian Phonology, I: The Phonetic Value of Old Armenian p' t' k'," Lg 30 (1954), 197-201; "Problems of Armenian Phonology, II: The Representation of IE p t k kʷ," Lg 31 (1955), pp. 4-8.

[14]V. Pisani, Lezioni di Armeno (Milano: Cisalpino, 1946), 31-32.

[15]V. Pisani, "La palatalizzazione armena," ASGIM 1 (1948), 1.15.

[16]V. Pisani, "Studi sulla fonetica dell'armeno. I Palatalizzazioni ed esiti di s + gutturale; esiti delle semivocali," RL 1 (1950), 165-193; now also idem, Mantissa (Brescia: Paideia, 1978), 255-286. See also the recent work by G. B. Jahukyan, "Die Bedeutung der ersten (indogermanischen) und der zweiten (inner-armenischen) Palatalisierung fur die Konstituierung des armenischen Konsonanten-Systems," KZ 89 (1975), 31-42. F. H. H. Kortlandt, "A Note on the Armenian Palatalization," KZ 89 (1975), 43-45 is not very convincing.

[17]Antoine Meillet, Esquisse d'une grammaire comparée de l'arménien classique (2d ed.; Vienna: Mekhitarist, 1936), 30, passim.

[18]H. Pedersen, "Die gutturale im Albanesischen," KZ 36 (1900), 305-326.

[19]For this and other correspondences between Greek and Armenian see: G. Bonfante, "Les isoglosses greco-armeniennes," Mélanges linguistiques offerts à M. Holger Pedersen à l'occasion de son soixante-dixième anniversaire (Copenhagen: Levin & Munksgaard, 1937), 15-33.

[20]A. Meillet, Esquisse, 37, cf. also p. 44 and p. 153, Armenian awcanem ("w traitement arménien de *n indo-eur. 2ᵉ élém. de dipht. [?]," idem s. v. awj p. 154).

[21]Bonfante, "Les isoglosses gréco-arméniennes," 25.

[22]G. R. Solta, "Palatalisierung und Labialisierung," IF 70 (1965), 277 n. 5.

[23]W. Winter, "Problems of Armenian Phonology, III: Consonant Clusters," Lg 38 (1962), 258.

[24]G. Bonfante, "Les isoglosses greco-armeniennes," 25-26.

[25]It is astonishing that Pisani later asserted the contrary without any plausible reason (cf. V. Pisani, "Ueber eine paelignische Inschrift," Rheinisches Museum 95 (1952), 18; now also idem, Saggi di linguistica storica (Torino: Rosenberg and Sellier, 1959), 155) after upholding exactly that the delabialization of labiovelars after u preceded the palatalization of labiovelars before e, i (cf. V. Pisani, "Studi sulla fonetica dell'armeno," RL 1 (1950), 192).

[26]V. Pisani, "Armenische Miszellen I. Spuren von Labiovelaren im Armenischen," Die Sprache (1966), 12.227-228 (now also idem, Mantissa [Brescia: Paideia, 1978], 336).

[27]T. Burrow, "Skt gr̄-/gur- 'to welcome," BSOAS 20 (1957), 133 ff. (the article summarizes what O. Szemerenyi had already stated during several lectures in Budapest and London); V. Pisani, "La ricostruzione dell'indeuropeo e del suo sistema fonetico," AGI 46 (1961), 22-23, adding other cases in which it is "possibile scorgere le tracce di una labiovelare in sanscrito: e precisamente in tre radici che in sanscrito cominciano con kṣv- corrispondente a un ps greco, ovè e lecito scorgere le continuazioni di un antico qᵘs-."

[28]Meillet, Esquisse, 68-69; cf. also 97 "Jusqu'aujourd'hui les cas ont consérve en arménien leur principale valeur indo-européenne sans changement essentiel, et cette conservation est d'autant plus remarquable qu'on n'en retrouve l'équivalent nulle part en dehors du slave et du baltique."

[29]A. Meillet, Esquisse, 79.

[30]E. Benveniste, "Arménien Aregakn "soleil" et la formation nominale en -akn," REArm 2 (1965), 9-10.

[31]G. Bolognesi, "Ricerche sulla fonetica armena. I Cronologia degli effetti dell'accento armeno sul vocalismo delle sillabe finali e su quello delle sillabe pretoniche," RL 3 (1954), 123-138.

[32]G. Bolognesi, "Sul vocalismo degli imprestiti iranici in armeno," RL 2 (1951), 141-162.

[33]G. Bolognesi, "Problemi di geografia lingüística relativi all' area iranica e armena," Actas del V Congreso Internacional de Estudios Lingüísticos del Mediterráneo (Madrid: Departamento de Geografia Lingüística C. S. I. C., 1977), 527-540.

[34]Obviously I am referring to the eastern pronunciation of Armenian which is free from the transformations of the so-called Second Consonant shift that affected the western Modern Armenian dialects.

[35]P. Horn, Grundriss der neupersischen Etymologie (Strasbourg: Karl J. Trubner, 1893), 261-302.

[36]M. Bartoli, Introduzione alla neolinguistica (Geneva: Leo S. Olschki, 1925), 13-14, 69; Lineamenti di linguistica spaziale (Milano: Le lingue estere, 1943), 39-40, 50; Saggi di linguistica spaziale (Torino: Rosenberg and Sellier, 1945), 45-55.

[37]A. Pagliaro, "Inviluti sono li scolosmini . . . (Giacomo da Lentini)," Nuovi saggi di critica semantica (Messina-Florence: D'Anna, 1956), 199-212.

[38]". . . il gruppo iniziale sc della forma tramandata e un puro scambio grafico dovuto alla scissione del segno x che rendeva la velare spirante" (Ibid., 205).

TWO HURRIAN WORDS IN ARMENIAN

John A. C. Greppin

Cleveland State University (USA)

Since Msériantz[1] reported on the Urartian substratum in Armenian, in a paper read before the XII. Internationaler Orientaliste-Kongress in Hamburg in 1902, there has been fairly steady research made on the detritus of the ancient Anatolian languages left in Armenian as loan words. Additional Urartological comments were made by Safrastian, Bănăţeanu and Ghapantsian.[2] Ghapantsian[3] brought in Hurrian, a language considerably similar to Urartian. Hittite, which was deciphered later than Urartian, soon was analyzed, and the first correspondences with Armenian were suggested by Martirossian who was followed by Ghapantsian, Schultheiss and others.[4] It would appear that all the principal surviving languages of eastern Anatolia, with the exception of Hattic, might have left their imprint in the Armenian lexicon.

It is not difficult to assume that the Armenians were present in eastern Anatolia at the time the Urartians were at their peak, for it is acknowledged that the Armenians replaced the Urartians, after 650 B. C., as the principal power in that area. The single significant recorded historical instance that supports this view is the statement by Darius the Great (DB 2.42-47) that it took him three campaigns to subdue the energetic Armenians. For the most part, Darius was able to subdue the various other tribes in single campaigns; that it took him three campaigns to put his yoke on the Armenians implies that they were not only present in significant number, but also that they were well organized and well trained by the year ca. 530 B. C. The passage in Kent's version of the Old Persian inscriptions[5] reads: "Said Darius the King: Again a third time the rebels assembled [and] came out against Dadarshi to join battle. A fortress by the name Uyama, in Armenia--there they joined battle."[6]

It is from this base that we can project backwards in time and suggest that it is likely that the Armenians had contact with the Urartians before 650 B. C. To establish more distant connections with the Hittites we would have to suggest an Armenian presence in eastern Anatolia before 1200 B. C., the approximate date of the collapse of the Hittite Empire.[7] And, presumably, there should have been earlier contact. The contact with the Luwians could have been later, for these more southern people remained vigorous, in various forms, well into the middle of the first millennium.

It is impossible to say which of these four languages (Hittite, Hieroglyphic Luwian, Hurrian, ahd Urartian) were the direct contributors of the eastern Anatolian vocabulary absorbed by the Armenians. In a most simplistic sense we could state that the Armenian lexicon was fleshed out by independent additions from all four cultural groups, though this is probably not the best conclusion. Equally we could suggest that the Hurrian and Urartian words came in through only one source, but because the two languages are so similar, it is impossible to determine which language the words actually originated in. And, because of a high degree of similarity between Hieroglyphic Luwian and Hittite, we would face the same problem of exact identification there as well. Simply because an Armenian word is identified in Hittite does not mean that Hittite was the actual source; it appears so only because we have no record of the Hieroglyphic Luwian word remaining. The same is possible for Hurrian or Urartian. And, there is a still different possibility. Remembering that Hurrian was no doubt a well known language within the Hittite Empire, we could suggest that all four of these linguistic tailings would have come into Armenian from just one source: Hittite. The Urartian words are just Hurrian words in disguise, and these Hurrian words were part of the collected vocabulary of the frequently bilingual educated Hittite class. Thus, the original source of the vocabulary--whether multi-sourced, or of a single source--cannot yet be stated.

We call these two loans into Armenian which I deal with below "Hurrian" simply because they occur in Hurrian texts; they could as well be Urartian, for they conform perfectly well to Urartian patterns. And since at least one of them was spoken on Hittite territory, and found on an inscription in the archives from Boğazköy, we could easily suggest that the words were in the Hittite vocabulary as well.

(1)   Hurrian awari 'field.'

This word can easily be related to Armenian agarak 'idem.' The pre-Armenian intervocalic -w- in Hurrian awari would regularly have become Armenian -g-;[8] the final -i of Hurrian awari would have been dropped in accordance with the Armenian law of final syllables. The suffix -ak was a later addition, a suffix that can be added to a word of any origin.[9]   Thus Hurrian <u>awari</u> > Proto Armenian   *<u>awar</u> > <u>agar-ak</u>, according to standard phonetic rules.[10]

The Hurrian word is quite solidly established, appearing over twenty times in Hurrian literature.[11]   Its meaning is made further secure from a bilingual text of Ras Shamra,[12] where we find the correspondence Hurrian <u>awari</u> = Akkadian eq[lu] = Ugaritic šadu.   Similarly, in Nourgayrol's study[13] we find the parallel MAL//GÁN: e]q[(?)-lu]: <u>a-wa-ar-ri</u>, where the meaning of the Hurrian <u>awari</u> is again made clear by the Akkadian and Sumerian equivalents.   There are, thus, no phonetic or semantic problems with the etymology, it seems secure.

(2)   Hurrian, <u>Kade</u> 'a grain, frequently of wheat.'

This word can be related to Armenian <u>kut</u> 'idem,' and though this word is abundantly common in the modern dialects, its early history is a bit vague, becoming secure only in the Middle Armenian period where it appears in such writers as Davit' Anyałt' and Samuēl Anec'i.   In the earliest period it is cited only in two sources, one of which was a translation from the Greek: the <u>Hexaëmeron</u> of St. Basil; and the other was from the Syriac: Ephraem's <u>Commentary on the Harmony of the Gospels</u>.   Neither is an unimpeachable source for the legitimacy of the word.   St. Basil's Armenian text is hopelessly corrupt, a fact that has been well noted.[14]   The text of St. Ephraem is more reliable,[15] and it is assumed that the manuscript has suffered little scribal malfeasance.   Yet, those few instances cannot establish the early legitimacy of the word.   A use in a compound appears in Eznik, <u>ktik</u> 'a small grain,'[16] which is helpful.   It seems, then, that we have some evidence for the use of the root <u>kut</u> from the fifth century; Middle Armenian literature is more precise, but the attestation is made entirely clear in New Armenian where we find such additional compounds as <u>ktap</u> 'a bun made of wheat'[17] and <u>ktaman</u> 'the crop of a fowl.'

And though Hurrian <u>kade</u> is uncommon, being recorded only twice in extant Hurrian texts, its meaning is quote clear.   F. Thureau-Dagin,[18] in a lexicographic tablet, records (column 2, line 10) the Sumerian ŠE 'a grain' in apposition to Hurrian <u>ka-te-ni-we</u>.[19]   The other source is published in KUB XLV 47 III 8, a badly fragmented tablet where we can only read ^Dga-te-e-na which Laroche[20] notes as an 'attribut de Nikkal.'[21]   This second citation is not particularly helpful.

The semantic accord between Hurrian <u>kade</u> and Armenian <u>kut</u> is exact, and, as near as we can tell, the correspondence between obstruents is satisfactory; our problem lies in the interior vowel of the Armenian word kut. However, there is a parallel found in the Armenian proper name Tork'/Turk' which is, presumably, a Hittite or Luwian loan.[22]   In Hittite we find the proper name Tarḫu-, a god of violent storms which is probably related to the adjuective Hittite tarḫuili- 'heroic.'   The same god appears in Hieroglyphic Luwian as Tarḫuzarma, in Hattic as Taru, a storm god, in Asiatic Greek as Tarkozarmas, Lycian trqq.   Armenian Tork'/Turk' is a powerful hero whom Nerses Snorhali describes as 'more powerful than Samson,'[23] and there seems to be little question that Hittite Tarḫu- engendered Armenian Tork'/Turk', of which the spelling Turk' is of special interest, for it supports a view that Armenian u can replace an Anatolian a.

There has been further recent comment on Hurrian kade by Ivanov[24] where a parallel is drawn from Lycian khththa as well as Lycian khade-wati 'god of grain.'[25]   We have the following matrix:

Armenian	Hurrian	Hittite	Lycian	Asiatic Greek	Hattic
kut	kade	(ḫalki)	Khththa	Kadrema	---
Turk'	---	tarḫu-	trqq	Tarkozarmas	taru-

It thus appears that we can suggest, in addition to the appropriate semantic rapport, a fairly precise phonetic rapport as well.[26]

This will give us, altogether, eleven possible correspondences between Hurrian and Armenian:[27]

Hurrian ašte 'female'; Armenian ast-em 'to get married'; cf. Russian žen- 'female'; ženit'sja 'to get married.'[28]

Hurrian ḫinzuri 'apple'; Armenian xnjor 'idem.'[29]

Hurrian ner 'sister-in-law,' Armenian ner 'idem.'[30]

Hurrian pal- 'beg,' Armenian pał-at-em 'idem.'[31]

Hurrian pali 'canal,' Armenian pał-em 'excavate,'[32] also note Urartian pili 'canal.'

Hurrian puḫ- 'to change,' Armenian p'ox-em 'idem.'[33]

Hurrian tarmane 'spring of water,' Armenian tarma-ǰur 'well-water;'[34] also note Urartian tarmana 'spring of water.'

Hurrian tuldi 'type of plant,' Armenian tułt 'marsh-mallow, genus malva.'[35]

Hurrian zarr/šarr 'slave,' Armenian caṙay 'servant.'[36]

ADDENDUM

Among the Armenian people are many amateur linguists, intelligent and creative individuals who express a strong and imaginative interest in the history of their language. One such was a certain Bedros Effendi Kerestedjian who was the head of the Translations and Foreign Correspondence Department at the Treasury of the Ottoman Government (1864-1909). He prepared a collection of etymological notes that were recently published in Amsterdam.[37] His work cannot be taken seriously since he had no grasp of the restraints that technical training in linguistics places on a scholar. And, among all the material that he churned out, little is of interest. Another such "linguist" was Morayr Vrouyr who published a lengthy series of etymologies in Antwerp.[38] Again, the bulk of the material is nonsense. However, there do remain a few shining nuggets that are worth considering quite seriously which pertain to Urartian loans in Armenian. Vrouyr, from his listing of twenty-one Armenian-Urartian correspondences, has about a half dozen that stand up under close inspection. Among these half dozen are two that have not been suggested before. They are:

Urartian ulgu 'life,' Armenian oł̃ 'alive, living.'

Urartian ḫarḫaršu- 'to destroy,' Armenian xarxar-em 'idem.'[39]

Both Urartian words are well established, and their exact meaning is not open to question. The correspondence ulgu/oł̃ is of particular interest since it shows a Hurrian plosive expressed in the more sensitive Armenian alphabet as an affricate, a reflex for which there has been only minimal support in spite of the logical potential for such a phoneme in the ancient languages of eastern Anatolia.[40]

NOTES

[1]L. Msériantz, "Les éléments ourartiques dans la langue arménienne," Verhandlungen des XIII Internationalen Orientalisten Kongresses (Leiden: Brill, 1904), 128-129.

[2]For references to the Hittite and Luwian substratum in Armenian see J. A. C. Greppin, "'Hittite' Loan Words in Armenian (synopsis)," Lautgeshichte und Etymologie, Akten der VI Fachtagung für Indogermanische und Allgemeine Sprachwissenschaft Wein, 24-29 September 1978. (Weisbaden:

Dr. Ludwig Reichert Verlag, 1980), 203-207.

[3]G. A. Ghapantsian, "Xurritskie slova armjanskogo jazyka," Izvestija AN ArmSSR (1951) 5.25-50. reprinted in Istoriko-lingvističeskie raboty. (AN ArmSSR, 1975), 2.270-305.   "K ustanovleniju Xurritskogo termina ŠAPP-/ZAPP v značenii 'sluga, rab' po dannym Armjanskogo i Gruzonskogo i Lazomingrel'skogo jazykov," Izvestija AN ArmSSR (1951), 3.21-28. reprinted in Istoriko-lingvističeskie raboty, 2.306-316.

[4]For further references to the Hittite and Luwian substratum in Armenian see note 2 above and Greppin, "A Further Comment on the God Šanta-/Santōn," La Parola del Passato (1978), 138.411-413. "ArmenoLuwica," REArm 13 (1978), 000.   "Hieroglyphic Luwian ma-tu-sa 'Arbutus' (?)," KZ 94.119-122.

[5]R. G. Kent, Old Persian Grammar, Texts, Lexicon (New Haven: American Oriental Society, 1953).

[6]This is the first unimpeachable reference to the historical Armenians that we have, though there appears to be some confusion even among specialists. S. Der Nersessian, The Armenians (London: Thames and Hudson, 1969), 20. followed by B. Brentjes, Drei Jahrtausende Armenien (Vienna: Verlag Anton Schroll, 1974), 47, 206. suggested that the Greek historian Hecataeus made the first referenence to the Armenians, a supposition that cannot be true (for which see Greppin, "Fragmenta historicorum graecorum pertinentia ad res armeniacas," Drevnij Vostok 4 (1981), forthcoming.

[7]And though the Empire fell, there is no reason to assume that the people and their langauge disappeared immediately; we must assume that Hittite speech communities remained beyond the date of 1200 B. C.

[8]Compare Greek áwesa núkta 'spent the night,' Armenian aganim 'spend the night' IE *awes-.

[9]The suffix -ak is of Iranian origin, and highly productive; note Armenian aregaknak 'balcony' from the components areg 'sun,' akn 'eye' (also taken together with the meaning of 'sun') plus -ak. See Greppin, Classical Armenian Nominal Suffixes (Vienna: Mechitharisten Buchdruckerei, 1975), 31.

[10]This word, so attractively close to IE *ağr- 'field' (Latin ager, etc.), has drawn the attention of many etymologizers. P. de Lagarde, Armenische Studien (Gottingen: Dieterisch'sche Verlagsbuchhandlung, 1877), 4. was the

first to note *aǧr-, a phonetically impossible Indo-European parallel; B. Xalat'ian, "Gitut'iwn dimaki tak," Handēs Amsoreay (1902), 309 suggested a rapport with Syr. akārā/ikkaru 'farmer,' which is weak semantically and fails phonetically; J. Karst, "Zur ethnischen Stellung der Armenier," Yuŝarjan (Vienna: Mechitharisten, 1911), 399-431. brought in Sumerian A. GÀR 'field' which has phonetic validity, but is improbable since we cannot in any way argue for contact between the Sumerians and the Armenians.   It is chronologically improbable.

[11]Principally investigated by C.-G. von Brandenstein, "Zum Churrischen Lexicon," ZA 46 (1940), 12.83-115.

[12]See E. Laroche, "Documents en langue hourrite provenant de Ras Shamra," Ugaritica V (1968). 450.

[13]J. Nourayrol, "Textes suméro-accadien des archives et bibliothèques privées d'ugarit," Ugaritica V (1968). 234.

[14]K. Muradyan, "Srbagrut'yunner Barseł Kesarac'u 'Vec'ōreay'-um," Banber Matenadarani 10 (1971), 43-51. and H. Y. T'oragian, "S. Barseł Kesarac'i, ir 'Vec'ōreay' čaŕerě ew Hay Targmanut'iwně," Bazmavep (1934), 11.327-336; 12.412-422.

[15]L. Leloir, Le témoignage d'Ephrem sur le diastessaron (Louvaine: Secretariat du Corpus SCO, 1962), passim.

[16]In the Venice text of 1826.175 we read: Orpēs . . . mrǰean . . . i ǰer ẑamanaks haneloy ztikn yorǰe anti. "And so in summer time, an ant pulls a tiny grain out of its hole."

[17]The suffix -ap can be found on xučap 'fright' (xuč 'scarecrow'). It is possible that xučap was in this shape before it came into Armenian since, had -ap been an Armenian suffixation, we would have expected *xcap.

[18]F. Thureau-Dagin, "Vocabulaire de Ras-Shamra," Syria 12 (1931), 238, 245, plate 50.

[19]Hurrian ni is an anaphoric suffix-connective; we is a genitive relational particle.

[20]E. Laroche, Glossaire de la langue hourrite, première partie (A-L), RHA 34 (1976), 133.

[21]E. Laroche, Les noms des hittites (Paris: Kliniksieck, 1966), 349.

notes that Nikkal is a "déesse lunaire très repande en Syrie du nord."

[22]J. A. C. Greppin, "Armeno-Luwica," REArm 13 (1978), 000.

[23]In the Venice text of 1830.538 we read: "(Tork') Manuk mi kayr i Hayk' govan, / k'an ĕzSamp'son ayl yaɫt'akan." The form Turk' is found in Samuēl Anec'i and Davit' Anyaɫt', the two Middle Armenian authors where we find kut.

[24]Vjač. Vs. Ivanov, "Razyskanija v oblasti anatolijskogo jazykoznanija. 3-8," Ètimologija 13 (1976), 155-162.

[25]G. Neumann, "Beiträge zum Lykischen V," Die Sprache 20 (1974), 113. notes in the following passage: me ttlidi : ĕni qlahi : ebijehi : nuñtȃta : Am̃m[ȃ]ma : uwa se nijepi : zalatu : se ttiti ĕni qlahi : ebijehi rm̃mazata : khththase : ada, for which he gives the translation "und es erhält (?) die Mutter des hiesigen Heiligtums montaliche Lieferung, aus Getreide bestehende, und zwar fünf (?) Ada." He adds that "Das se habe ich hier als ein 'exepegetischen und' übersetzt."

[26]There actually remains some question, in my mind, whether the word in Thureau-Dagin's text should be read as ka-te. In his edition of the text, the sign ⟨cuneiform⟩ is read as ka, yet this is at best an unusual shape for it only approximately approaches the common form for ka: ⟨cuneiform⟩. As an alternate reading, suggested quote tentatively, I might propose that the first element (⟨cuneiform⟩) is an otherwise unknown logogram, followed by ku (⟨cuneiform⟩).   Thus we would read ⟨cuneiform⟩ as $^?$ku, thus giving us a welcome $^?$ku-te but a reading which would leave ^{D}ga-te-e-na even more perplexing.

[27]Many others have been suggested, but most cannot at all be regarded as likely since semantic and phonological congruences have been treated too loosely.

[28]Kapancjan, "Xurritskie slova," 31.

[29]Ibid., 30-34.

[30]Ibid., 28-29.

[31]Ibid., 39.

[32]Ibid., 39-40.

[33]Ibid., 39.

[34]I. Diakanoff, Hurrisch and Urartäisch (Munich: Kitzinger, 1971), 85.

[35]Kapancjan, "Xurritskie slova," 33.

[36]Kapancjan, "K Ustanovleniju Xurritskogo Termina ŠAPP."

[37]B. Kerestedjian, Études philologique et lexicographique (Amsterdam: Philo Press, 1969).

[38]N. Vrouyr, Répertoire étymologie de l'arménien (Antwerp: T. Vrouyr, 1948).

[39]Note also the surprisingly similar correspondence Hitt. halhaliya- 'fight, struggle,' Arm. xołxołem 'slaughter.'

[40]N. Mkrtchyan, "Neue hethitiseh-armenische lexikalische Parallelen," Acta Antiqua Ac. Sc. Hungaricae 22 (1974), 313-319. has noted, among others; Hitt. kuskus- 'pound, bruise,' Arm. koškoč 'ruined, destroyed,' which is interesting.

ASPECTS OF CLASSICAL GREEK HERITAGE IN OLD ARMENIAN

ARCHITECTURE

Edith Neubauer

Karl-Marx-Universität (DDR)

The fourth century A. D. is a landmark in Armenian history. Opening with the adoption of Christianity as the state religion in 314, the legal preconditions were created for developing early Christian architecture. Almost at the same time, Christian art developed in Armenia, Georgia, Asia Minor, Syria, Mesopotamia, and Egypt. A gradual transition from late classical Greek art to early Christian art took place. Right from the beginning, nationally conditioned particularities may be seen in the Christian countries; common elements, however, also exist. The complicated interdependence of Eastern Christian countries in the field of art as well as their contacts with Byzantium have still to be investigated in a more differentiated way.[1] At the same time, each of these national developments of art established important sources of subsequent developments of art in Central Europe. From Armenia, it is especially elements of architecture and relief-sculpture that found their analogous succession in German Romanesque architecture. Although the processes of development are roughly the same, they do not coincide with regard to time. These manifold parallel phenomena in the repertoire of artistic forms of Romanesque architecture have always kept alive intense interest in Armenian medieval art.[2]

Indeed, European visitors seeing Armenian churches and entering the interior feel a surprising congeniality: Nothing is strange to them. This first emotional impression of familiarity disappears, however, if they look more closely. There is no building of Romanesque style that is based on direct Armenian influence. There are a number of parallel features, however, that could not be explained without knowing Caucasian examples. When we compare portals and sculptural relief decoration we may find predominantly similar artistic solutions. In Caucasian territories, the architecture of the portal has been developed since the fifth century; the same applies to its

151

sculptural repertoire. In Central and West European Romanesque art, the portal becomes the predominant basis of sculptural decoration in the twelfth century.   The architecture of the German Romanesque portal, with its different forms of doorposts shows, in addition to impulses from France, essential elements suggesting a genesis from other spheres of art.[3]

With regard to a number of essential features of representation, tympanon reliefs of German Romanesque portals are analogous to Caucasian examples. With the exception of Armenia and Georgia, it is not possible to establish proof of the existence of sculptured tympana in connection with architecture within the whole of early Christian art; therefore, there is no reason not to look for the genesis of the Romanesque tympanum in the Caucasian area.

Nevertheless, it is an inappropriate exaggeration to designate Armenian architecture, from a European point of view, as "proto-Romanesque architecture," "the Romanesque style of Asia," "Anticipation of the Romanesque style," or "Eastern Romanesque style."[4]   The Romanesque style was created independently, like the medieval style of Armenian art.   Both of them have their independendent, national, distinct features.   Both of them are perfect and effective forms of the artisticial sense of two peoples with the Christian religion and early medieval modes of production in a territory where, after the collapse of the West Roman empire, the traditional linkage between East and West was not interrupted until the fifteenth century A. D., when Constantinople was conquered by the Turks.   Thus, Transcaucasian elements could influence the Romanesque style in a fruitful way.   The dynamic and expansive character of Armenian art, above all, is based, last but not least, on the fact that, beginning in the fourth century, a continuous flood of Armenian immigrants came to Western countries, undoubtedly with many artists among them.

Close contacts between the whole Christian world and their neighbors in the East were of great importance with regard to the development of national cultures.   Important meeting centers were established by the Metropolitan associations, missionary centers, places of pilgrimage, and monks' colonies with an almost supranational autonomous structure.   Merchants from many countries met in commercial centers like Edessa, Alexandria, Dvin, Mzcheta, Constantinople and other towns.

The Armenian and Georgian churches had monasteries in Jerusalem, Antioch, Edessa, Constantinople, Sinai, on Mt. Athos, and in Bačkovo,

Bulgaria. Since the twelfth century, a new center of Armenian art was developed in Cilicia, intensely influencing Europe in the fields of fortification and manuscript illumination, above all. Nevertheless, it is not very probable that there existed direct links between Caucasian art and that of the German Romanesque. It may be assumed that whatever influence there was is the result of a broad stream of works of art gradually coming from Caucasian countries to the West up to Italy.[5] Recently, art historians have discovered and investigated a great number of parallel artistic features in Greece, Bulgaria, Romania, Hungary, Serbia, and Lombardy. This indicates intense contacts between South European countries and countries of the Middle East, due to Oriental commerce and pilgrimage.

Two of the South European countries mentioned above were of special importance for Germany at the time of the development of Romanesque style in the German empire: the Byzantine Empire and Italy. It is most probable that these two countries played the intermediary role, that through Constantinople and the Lombardy Caucasian forms came into German art.

Surviving monuments of classical Greek art provide an important source for explaining the phenomenon of parallel artistic features in the Caucusus and Europe, because classical Greek art was taken as an example in both neighboring areas on the periphery of the old Roman Empire. The relationship between classical Greek and early Christian architecture, however, is not yet the subject of detailed research. Adoption and assimilation of classical Greek elements are essential sources of early Christian Armenian architecture initiated in the early fourth century. The Armenians could use traditions of technical skills of Urartian architects and experience gained in classical Hellenistic construction. Christian architecture is further enriched by the productive appropriation of artistic elements of neighboring early Christian countries. Proceeding from these complex preconditions, it developed into an independent link in the chain of East Christian cultures--an autonomous early center of Christian architecture of remarkable quality. When the German Empire in Central Europe emerged as a powerful Christian state, Armenia already had a very advanced civilization for centuries and rich traditions in architecture. When the Romanesque style came into being in Germany, Armenian art, like the art of Byzantium, had a very diverse attractive repertoire of forms to be adopted by artists. Armenia had close contacts with Syria and Egypt and with large cities such as Constantinople, Antioch, and Alexandria, where Hellenistic culture, having achieved a very high level of development, exerted widespread influence. In Armenia itself, classical Greek art had also been deeply rooted.   Therefore, it was quite natural that Christian monumental architecture be stimulated by traditions of classical Greek architecture, although there existed a fundamental difference between this architecture and classical Greek architecture.   The Christian church was not the only house of God, like the classical temple, but also a room for the meetings and prayers of the parish.   This new function of the place of worship brought an end to classical Greek architecture but not to the effect of the detailed concepts and forms of classical architecture.

Two architectural types dominate in Christian Armenian architecture: the basilica and the centrally planned building.   Caucasian basilicas are reminiscent of classical markets, lawcourts, and palaces as well as prehistoric royal audience-rooms.   The system of piers and vaults had already been known for centuries in ancient Rome, but it was not transferred to the early Roman basilicas.   Similar Armenian elements—piers and vaults—probably were not based on Roman examples.   As Deichmann claims, it rather seems to be a parallel development.[6]   The Armenian architects preferred a T-shaped pier, and this form is an innovation.   The manifold ground plans of Caucasian basilicas give the idea that they were not simply "model-reproductions" and that no special elements were obligatory for them.   Thus, the Caucasian basilicas show a national character: they belong to an independent group, distinguished by a simple structure without transept or narthex, but with a simple rectangular ground plan.   The distinctly tectonic structure brings about a quietness of forms, architectural substantiality and plastic-statical feature that reminds us in general of Greek Hellenistic architecture.   The creation of the Caucasian type of central building went on during the fourth century, developing parallel to the basilica.   The large variety of plans suggests that there existed no uniform, fixed liturgy and that therefore the vital point was not the function of a building but its aesthetic appearance.   Furthermore, the concepts of central building types were also based on the classical circular building; cruciform and octogonal building types notwithstanding, their existence cannot be proved on Armenian territory.   In the late Roman Empire, the central building type with dome was used predominantly in the advanced type of the circular house in the imperial thermal baths or in funeral buildings.   The commemorative worship in classical mausoleums, martyria, or memorial buildings—mostly connected with a centrally planned building--continued in early Christian architecture, since the ancient funeral churches and baptisteries were central buildings like the Church of the Holy Sepulcher in Jerusalem or the mausoleum of Constantine in Rome.[7]

In Armenia, ancient central buildings were also constructed over the tombs of saints and martyrs: Ējmiacin; the church of St. Hřip'simē over the tomb of the holy virgin Hřip'simē, and the church of St. Gayanē over the tomb of the holy virgin Gayanē. Memorial buildings were also constructed over the places of holy events, e. g., Ējmiacin, a cathedral of the fourth and fifth centuries. Here the luminous figure of Jesus Christ appeared to St. Gregory the Illuminator, the first Catholicos of Armenia.

Early Armenian basilicas and centrally planned buildings are usually constructed over a multistepped stylobate, isolating them from its surroundings in the form of a monument in the same way as classical high tombs and temples: Zuart'noc', the seventh-century church of St. Gregory, and the first century A.D. Temple of Garni, with nine steps.

The interior of early Christian Armenian churches shows anthropomorphic proportions which are visible at a glance--clear forms and a brightness that does not allow mystical absorption or unworldliness. The walls are mostly without mosaic art or painting; the only ornament results from slightly polycolored, carefully carved stone. There is no doubt that these clear forms are a heritage of classical architecture. In Byzantium, architects gave preference to the predominant shaping of the interior by means of rich decorations and illusionistic effects; this does not occur in Armenian architecture.

Relief sculptures are broadly applied in shaping the exterior structures of Armenian churches. It is quite evident that in the Byzantine empire, the application of sculptures was clearly diminishing, and sculptures were only used with regard to applied arts and at places of minor importance; in Armenia, however, the classical tradition of relief sculptures in connection with monumental religious architecture continued. Thus, pioneering work was carried out for Romanesque relief sculptures that come into being later. One may find in Armenia, above all, many sculptured tympana and lintels, reliefs with Biblical symbolic-mythological or ornamental reproductions. The tympanum or lintel as the center of sculpture decoration in Armenian Christian churches corresponds to the tympanum with symbolic mythological reproductions in the classical temple. Formal structure and iconography were changed when relief sculptures were transferred from the pediment to the tympanum; the relationship of function, however, is quite evident.   The pediment of the classical temple and the tympanum of the Christian church represented an essential event of the respective religious conceptions of the world.

Furthermore, the portal forms of Armenian churches were essentially influenced by the classical portal.   Early examples, like the western portal of the cathedral of Awan from the sixth and seventh centuries, show an open semicircular compartment between arch and lintel.   This form is widespread also in Syria.   In the course of their development, elements of classical structure, like the architrave over the doorposts, were transformed into medieval form.   The formerly open semicircular compartment was now closed by a plate, the tympanum.   The tympanon-portal was a specifically medieval form, whereas the portal with doorposts and lintel, also used during the Middle Ages, showed a closer relationship to the classical example.[8]

In 1975, Kalayan published a study on symmetry and the relationship of measures in Armenian architecture.[9]   He connected different points of a monument-roofs, for instance--differently inclined according to their heights, and established lines within a circle covering the entire monument.   He concluded that an exact plan determined the porportions of the church building.   He indicates 29.5 up to 29.7 cm. as the Armenian unit of measurement; this is a unit which continues relationships of measurement used in Greek and Roman architecture.   Although it is true that uniform and generally binding units of measurement did not yet exist in the ancient world, there were fixed relations which, according to Kalayan, were used up to the end of the Middle Ages and were taken as fundamental units of European architecture.

There is no doubt that ideas and elements of classical Hellenistic architecture continued to exist in early Christian architecture also, but only as a remote echo.   This fact must not be overestimated.   If the new centers of architecture were far from the main centers of classical art, the reception of classical ideas was more independent, and the development of national elements is stronger.   Based on ancient traditional forms, Armenian medieval architecture created completely new works with regard to quality.   Therefore, the regional school of architecture of Old Armenia finally developed independently of Rome and Constantinople a nationally distinguished architecture of immense artistic influence.[10]   We should, therefore, be careful when speaking about the reception of classical elements, and should proceed from the fact that Christian Armenian art is not a beginning ex nihilo, but a continuation as well. New and specific spatial creations emerge under the "power of cruciform symbolism" as the crux of Christian ideology as they are possible only under the concrete historical conditions prevailing in early medieval Armenia.

    An analysis of the relationship between Armenian medieval architecture and classical Greek architecture may, among other things, help us to understand the relationship between Caucasian and European art and clarify to a certain extent the existence of many similar or parallel solutions. Classical Greek art was also the basis of the development of medieval European art and there is no doubt about its effects of exemplary character with regard to aesthetics. The early Christian art of Rome and Constantinople was strongly dedicated to highly civilized, late classical art, culminating in a refined, final stage and just starting a transition in the sixth century A. D. In comparison, the art of peoples living on the periphery of the Roman Empire, while proceeding from the same classical heritage, shows deliberate simplification, manifested as a conscious reduction of forms and a stronger emphasis on national particularities, thus marking the comprehensive beginning of something new. This transition, occurring to the same extent in the East and West of the Roman Empire, constitutes one of the reasons why quite similar developments are exhibited in the art of both Armenia and Europe.

NOTES

[1]First steps in this respect: N. A. Aladšvili, Monumental'naja Skul'ptura Gruzii. Sjužetnye Relefy V - XI vekov (Moskva: Iskusstvo, 1977). W. Beridse, E. Neubauer, Die Bakunst des Mittelalters in Georgien (Berlin: Union-Verlag, 1980).

[2]J. Strzygowsky, Die Baukunst der Armenier und Europa (Arbeiten des Kunsthistorischen Instituts der Universitat Wien, Band 9 and 10; Wien, 1918). Ph. Schweinfurth, Grundzüge der Byzantinisch-osteuropäischen Kunstgeschichte (Berlin, 1947).   H. Sedlmayer, "Östliche Romanik. Das Problem der Antizipationen in der Baukunst Transkaukasiens," Festschrift Karl Öttinger

(Erlanger Forschungen Reihe A, Band 20; 1967), 54.

[3]E. Neubauer, "Untersuchungen zur georgischen und deutschen Portalarchitektur des Mittelalters," Second International Symposium of Georgian Art, Seperatum (Tbilisi, 1977).

[4]See note 2.

[5]E. Neubauer, Zur mittelalterlichen kaukasischen und europäischen Bauplastik und Portalarchitektur und zu den Beziehungen zwischen der armenischen, georgischen und europaischen Kunst des Mittelalters (Dissertation zur Promotion B, Karl-Marx-Universitat; Leipzig, 1976), 35-42.

[6]F. W. Deichmann, "Zur Entwicklung der Pfeilerbasilike. Die Basilika Sion von Volbisi," Second International Symposium of Georgian Art, Seperatum, 1-6 (Tbilisi, 1977).

[7]S. Guyer, Grundlagen mittelalterlicher abendlandischer Baukunst (Zurich, 1950).

[8]See note 3.

[9]H. Kalayan, "The Symmetry and Proportion of Armenian Architecture First International Symposium of Armenian Art. Seperatum; Bergamo, 1975).

[10]D. Tumanischwili, "Zur Typologie der orientalisch-christlichen Baukunst," Second International Symposium of Georgian Art, Seperatum (Tbilisi, 1977).

THE ENTHRONED VIRGIN AND CHILD IN THE ŌJUN CHURCH

Carolyn Kane

Metropolitan Museum of Art, New York (USA)

A unique sculpture from the early Christian period in Armenia survives within the church of Ōjun in the village of Uzunlar.[1] It is a less-than-life-size high relief of an enthroned Virgin and Child, now placed within a niche on the interior north wall of the church. Its original location is unknown. This image of the Virgin and Child conforms generally by pose and dress to the type current in the Christian East and West during the fifth and sixth centuries.[2] The high relief, the scale, and certain details of iconography are unmatched in existing early Christian sculpture in Armenia, and only one other example of large-scale relief sculpture is recorded outside of Armenia.

The first purpose of this paper will be to date the group precisely within an art-historical context. An attempt will also be made to point out those aspects of the iconography which are typically Early Christian and those which are unusual during this time, as well as to offer a tentative proposal for the function of this relief.

The sculpture

It is immediately evident that this relief is outside the artistic tradition of early Christian Armenian sculpture, which is usually executed in low relief and is of small dimensions. Such reliefs were usually subordinate to the architecture or other setting and are found today on steles, bases, capitals, around doors, windows, and walls of churches, similar to the reliefs on the exterior of the Ōjun church.[3] These latter reliefs from the Ōjun church may or may not be contemporary with the relief group. The Ōjun Madonna and Child group differs in style and proportion and, in addition, was probably a large, independent sculpture. With the exception of fragments from an ambo from Saloniki, now in the Archeological Museum in Istanbul, this Armenian sculpture is unprecedented.[4] Only sculpture from small ivory reliefs, carved stone sacophagi, and architectural relief sculpture are extant from the early Christian period.[5]

The work appears to be reduced in size because of the uneven, asymmetrical outline of the head and right side of the Virgin (Figure 1). The published proportions are given as 92 x 60 cm.[6] The composition is simple, rather crudely carved, and somewhat disproportionate, especially the child's head and the arms and hands of the Virgin, as well as her stocky body.

The Virgin is seated on a cathedra with a high, semi-circular back, with the carved legs terminating in "capital"-shaped arms (Figure 2). Although the face of the Virgin is badly damaged, there are indications of a straight nose and mouth on a longish, oval face, and eyes which must have gazed straight out towards the viewer. Her dress is typical for fifth to seventh century representations of Mary. A snug cap hides the hair, a maphorion covers the head, and a long tunic and cloak cover the body. The corners of the cloak dangle between her limbs and the legs of the chair. The tight-fitting sleeves of the dress are indicated by a series of soft, round, parallel folds at the wrists. The folds of the gown and cloak are perfunctory, varying only slightly in size and direction. Those around the head are uneven in width and mostly vertical; then they gradually become wider and diagonal until they are nearly horizontal under the chin and fall into larger, broken parallel pleats at the shoulder. The cloak hangs in even, slightly diagonal bands over the lower arms and body all the way to the feet which rest far apart on the ground line. Only her face, enormous hands and long fingers are uncovered. The tips of the fingers of the right hand point towards the child and graze the edge of his halo, and her left arm cradles the body of the child. There appears to be no nimbus around the head. The position of the arms and the outspread legs soften the hieratic pose. Although the figure exudes an air of monumentality, and an impression of calm, motherly dignity, no modelling of the body is evident beneath the drapery.

The body of a young but not newborn child nestles within the left arm of the Virgin (Figure 3). The Savior's face seems melancholy and more mature than childlike. Tight, regular, kinky, round curls, and a round halo frame his long, somewhat triangular face. The mouth is small, thin-lipped, wavy, and slightly pursed. The nose is long and straight. Beneath a low forehead and heavy, wide eyebrows, two enormous eyes are enclosed within deep orbital cavities. The tops of the large, elevated pupils appear to touch the top of the upper rim of the socket, and stare fixedly, almost hypnotically ahead. These exaggerated, oversized, and slightly brooding eyes with the peculiar feature of the pupils brushing the top of the socket dominate the face and are its most distinguishing feature.

The upper torso and head of the Child are frontal. The lower torso and thighs stretch diagonally across the Virgin's body, and the lower legs, covered by a long gown, and the bare feet are visible below the Virgin's knees. His right hand rests limply on his lap beneath her gesturing hand, and his left arm is hidden. Unusually, he does not hold an attribute nor does he gesture with the one exposed arm. The child is dressed in a square-necked, probably tailored garment which is indicated by the bands or ribbons around the neck and shoulders. From these fillets, narrow, straight, parallel pleats fan out slightly. His rigid, wooden upper body contrasts markedly with the limp, lower portion.

As mentioned above, there is no comparable image to the Ōjun group in early Armenian Christian art. It is possible that a small relief of an enthroned Virgin and Child on top of the west side of the north Ōjun stele may have a similar iconography, but as only an unsatisfactory drawing and photographs have been published, no conclusions can be made at this time.[7]

There are several characteristics found in this group which set it apart from other representations of the enthroned Madonna and Child in early Christian art. First, there is the placement of the Virgin's left hand, then the distinctive passive, rather than active, attitude of the Child, and his one exposed arm. The Child's extraordinary eyes and the invisible arm may help to place this group, by stylistic comparisons with material from the East Christian world, in a specific time.

Dating

The four paintings at the end of the Ējmiacin Gospels (Erevan, Matenadaran No. 2374) offer telling similarities to the Ōjun group. The illustrations are the Annunciation to Zacharias, Annunciation to the Virgin, Adoration of the Magi, and the Baptism of Christ.[8] This manuscript was copied and illustrated in the Noravank' monastery in 989, but the last two leaves are of earlier date. Professor Der Nersessian, after studying the original manuscript and comparing them to Armenian frescoes of seventh-century date, and ornamental decor on the facades of Armenian churches of the sixth and seventh centuries, has stated that these end paintings are definitely Armenian of the late sixth or early seventh centuries.[9]

The enthroned Virgin in the Adoration of the Magi echoes the compact, stocky figure with large surface areas of the Ōjun Virgin, as well as its monumental character and longish, oval face. Allowing, of course, for the differences in material and execution, the Christ figure in the Adoration of the Magi, the Baptism, and the Ōjun relief have the same facial traits. Each image has a long, triangular outline; the small, thin, curvy mouth; the straight, narrow nose; the huge, almond-shaped eyes with a straightforward gaze, and the prominent pupils, raised to touch the top of the cornea; the low forehead and strong brows; and the full head of springy, curly ringlets, surrounded by a nimbus. Similar stylized, parallel folds of the gown of the Ōjun Christ are found in the dress of the Angels of the Annunciation to Zacharias, Annunciation to the Virgin, and the Adoration of the Magi. The Christ child in the Adoration of the Magi and the Ōjun relief both have a visible right arm, and a concealed left arm.

There is a definite stylistic kinship with Syrian manuscript illustrations and the terminal paintings of the Ējmiacin Gospels and the Ōjun relief, though the Armenian works do not retain the decided late antique aspects of the Syrian paintings. The standing Virgin and Child from the Rabbula Gospels (folio lv, copied 586 in the monastery of St. John of Beṭ Zagba, now in Florence, Biblioteca Laurenziana, MS Plut. I.56) have certain affinities to the seated Madonna and Child of the Adoration of the Magi and the same figures in the Ōjun group.[10] The Rabbula Virgin is definitely more sculptural and refined than the Armenian images, but the faces and features of the Ējmiacin Virgin and the Rabbula Mary are of the same type. The characteristic eye described in the Armenian works is also seen in the Rabbula Gospels in the Virgin and Child, folio lv, the Enthroned Christ, folio 14r, and in the marginal illustrations of folios 4v, 5v, and 6r.[11] The same startling, staring eye is also found in other undated Syrian manuscripts of the same time, including a leaf from a Syrian Gospel containing the head of Christ, now in the Archducal Library in Wolfenbüttel,[12] a standing Christ from a Syrian manuscript copied in Mar Yakub of Sarug,[13] and paintings from a Syrian Bible now in the Bibliothèque Nationale, Paris, Syr. 341.[14]

The Christ child in the Rabbula Gospels, folio lv, and the Ējmiacin Adoration of the Magi and the Baptism of Christ, as well as the Ōjun sculptural version have the same type of head, hair, and features, particularly the eyes. Though the Rabbula Christ child seems to be somewhat damaged, his left arm seems to be enclosed within a cloak in the same fashion as the Adoration of the Magi Jesus. This attribute remains from late Antique art, and other figures with arms encased in a cloak can be noted in the Rabbula Gospels paintings of the Election of Matthew, folio 1r, and the Pentecost, folio 14v.[15] The Ējmiacin painter may have adopted this feature directly from a Syrian source, but the Ōjun sculptor redefined it by simply hiding the arm within the Virgin's grasp rather than inside a garment.

On the basis of the above comparisons, it would seem reasonable to place the Ōjun sculpture and the Ējmiacin Gospels to the same date, and to assume that Armenian artists were working within a Syrian-Armenian tradition, related to Syrian manuscript painting, particularly the dated Rabbula Gospels of 586. Thus the Armenian works should date to the same time, the last two decades of the sixth century, or at the very latest, the beginning of the seventh century. If this dating for the Ōjun is accepted, then it is possible to re-date a capital bearing an image of the Virgin and Child within a round medallion from Dvin.[16] This capital, excavated in that city, has usually been called sixth century, but as the facial type of the Savior is stylistically so close to the Ōjun child, it should now be dated to the same period as the Ōjun sculpture.

Function and Iconography

There is a high relief stone ambo from Saloniki which is not particularly helpful in dating the Ōjun sculpture but may be useful in suggesting a function for the group.[17] Carved on the pulpit is an enthroned hieratic Virgin and Child accompanied on each side by the Magi. This narration of the Adoration of the Magi is now in fragments, but in size, now 179 cm. in height, the Madonna and Child, 104 cm., the iconography and material, it is close in spirit to the Ōjun group.[18] Grabar has placed this relief to an Eastern origin at the beginning of the sixth century, though others have dated it as early as the fifth century.[19]

The Virgin holds Jesus in mid-lap position and both are frontal (Figure 4). She is located on the front of the right support, and is distinct from the other figures by her size and formal pose. The Magi are around the corner of the right support. Across from the Virgin, though they would have been separated by the main pulpit area, is a single Magus, with two Magi and a Shepherd around the corner on the side of the left support. These figures are smaller than the main group, 90 cm. in height, and are shown in three-quarter profile and given lively, somewhat agitated movements.[20] The relief is somewhat coarsely executed. All figures are placed within niches crowned by a semi-dome containing a conch resting on engaged colonettes.

The figures of the Virgin and Child are seated on a cathedra with a round back. Her cloak and tunic with their broad planes and types of folds and pleats generally resemble the dress of the Ōjun Madonna. The features of both effigies are too damaged to describe, but the round halo of Jesus is intact. Her right arm rests on the shoulder of the Child, and the tips of her fingers touch the edge of the nimbus, in a pose remarkably close to the gesture of the Ōjun Virgin. No other comparison for this particular attitude exists either in Armenian or Syrian art, though there may be a distant correlation to representations of Coptic nursing Virgins, though the function does differ.[21] The Child is held by the left knee, and he appears to gesture to the Magi with his right hand and may have held something in his left. Unfortunately, existing photographs are not too clear, though Wellen assumes that the Child was probably gesturing and holding a roll in his hands.[22] It would seem a natural movement on the part of the Christ Child as this image was part of the Adoration of the Magi.

Though the image of Mother and Child on the Saloniki Ambo is not given an epithet, the Ōjun Virgin was called by Lasareff and others a Hodegitria. This type, originally attributed to a painting by St. Luke, shows a standing Virgin, probably only shown in half figure holding a blessing Christ on her left arm.[23] Obviously, the Ōjun relief does not fulfill this definition. If a designation should be given to these images, it should probably be the Theotokos, the Mother of God or God-bearing.[24]

The seated female holding an infant on the lap or arm can be traced to late antique art, and early Christian representations are found in catacomb paintings where the Virgin, who sits in a three-quarter pose, is dressed in a long gown, but never a cloak and rarely a veil. She is sometimes seated on a cathedra, and holds a newborn or young child who may be naked, wearing swaddling clothes or a robe, but only a more mature Christ in catacomb paintings has a halo. Mother and Child are illustrated within the context of the Adoration of the Magi, and the Child may gesture in welcome or benediction toward them, similar to the Capella Greca fresco.[25]

Fourth and fifth century representations of this narration also show the Virgin seated in profile and the child in mid-lap position in metalwork and reliefs from sarcophagi.[26] The Virgin now has a long robe, cloak, and veil and may also have a halo. The young Christ is always shown with a nimbus. Volbach has attributed the hieratic Virgin and Child to a fifth-century development in the Christian East, and Lasareff specifically to Egypt, but both of these origins are problematical.[27]   By the fifth century, an autonomous representation of an enthroned Madonna and Child also is known. Textual references refer to this image in the apse of the fifth-century church of Capua Verde and in Santa Maria Maggiore in Rome.[28]   The early sixth-century mosaic in the apse of the church at Gaza is described by Choricius as showing an ethroned Virgin and Child.[29]

By the sixth century, a hieratic, enthroned Madonna and Child were current in the West and East and both the Ōjun and Saloniki sculptures conform to this type which is found on ivories, textiles, icons, frescoes, mosaics, stone reliefs, manuscript paintings, metalwork, medallions, and ampullae.   Attitudes vary considerably, though the two figures usually are frontal, and the Child holds a book or roll and gestures.   Except for representations on ivories, both figures are nimbed and are usually associated with saints or angels, or placed within a scene from the Gospels.   A rarer portrayal shows an independent group, but whether alone or accompanied, there is the overwhelming impression that Mother and Child are the focal point.[30]

The closest representations to the Saloniki ambo reliefs are those found on pilgrim flasks and medallions dated to about 600 and attributed to a Palestinian origin.   On some of these, a monumental representation of Virgin and Child is shown with Magi or Shepherds who mirror the steps and figures of the Saloniki Magi figures.[31]   Volbach believed that the architectural setting of the ambo copied a Syrian prototype, but was made in Saloniki, while Wellen found a local source on the frieze of the Arch of Galerius (297-305).[32]   It is possible to see also a relationship to the architectural setting of the Adoration of the Magi from the Ējmiacin Gospels end paintings in which the shell within the arch resting on columns crowns the head of the Virgin, and there may even be a comparison, though it is less convincing, with the architectural settings depicted in the Rabbula Gospels.[33] All the architectural settings stem from late antique types which were known both in Greece and the Eastern Mediterranean world.   As pointed out above, the Ējmiacin end paintings seem to originate in a Syrian-Armenian background, while the Saloniki ambo would probably best fit into a provincial Byzantine environment with ties to the Palestine area.

Because the Ōjun group has been cut down, it is necessary to inquire whether it too might have been part of an architectural setting as well as part of a narration of the Adoration of the Magi or indeed was a separate individual image or associated with a smaller group of saintly or donor figures.   There is no ambo in early Christian Armenian churches of the Saloniki type, nor is there a sculptural relief showing a scene of the Adoration of the Magi.[34]   Stone relief images from Armenia and even Syria of the sixth and seventh centuries portray a seated or standing Mary holding Jesus in her arms, sometimes the group is accompanied by angels or a donor figure.[35]   The only Adoration of the Magi scene surviving is the one in the Ējmiacin Gospels showing Mary and Child, not in the drawn-out image of the Saloniki version, but a compact one with an angel and one Magus on her left hand and two Magi on the right.   This format is found on two ivories, one in the British Museum, attributed to the first half of the sixth century, from the Eastern Mediterranean, and the other in Berlin, of the sixth to the eighth century, from Syria.[36]   The angels on the ivories are found on the left of the Virgin.   Again, such evidence points to a Syrian source for the Ējmiacin illustration.

It is doubtful that the Ōjun relief was part of a large, architectural setting, and the few Armenian texts from this period make no mention of a scene of the Adoration of the Magi, and the remaining frescoes and architectural reliefs do not contain this episode.   Though the ultimate source for an independent enthroned Madonna and Child may have been the Adoration of the Magi, as Lasareff and others have suggested,[37]   the possibility that an autonomous sculpture could have developed as the cult of the Virgin gained in popularity in Armenian cannot be excluded.   The worship of the Virgin in Armenia was renewed by the Second Council of Dvin in 554, and must have contributed to the growth of devotion to Mary.[38]   It does not seem unreasonable to suggest that the Ōjun group served more than a decorative purpose.   Perhaps the relief could have served as a cult image with devotion or homage being given to Mary in her role as the Theotokos, the Mother of God.   Lasareff even suggested that the relief was based on a Syrian iconic type; Lange and Leroy mentioned that the Saloniki ambo relief as well as the Rabbula Virgin and Child folio 1v have the presence, setting, and demeanor of an isolated icon; and Wellen selected a stone relief showing the Virgin and Child from Khanasir as an icon of the sixth century.[39]

Literary evidence from Armenian sources suggests that this devotional aspect was not lacking for images during the sixth to eighth centuries. Vrt'anēs K'ert'oł wrote of the paintings and images in Armenian churches in an early seventh-century treatise.[40] While he does not specify that sculpture was among these images, he did refer to the "Virgin holding the Christ-child on her knees; the martyrdoms of Saint Gregory the Illuminator, of Saint Hṙip'simē, Gayanē, and their companions; the stoning of Saint Stephen; portraits of the prophets, apostles and other saints; the divine cross; the principal Gospel scenes: Nativity, Baptism, Passion, Crucifixion, Entombment, Resurrection, Ascension."[41]   Thus, within the decorative program in the early seventh century figured an autonomous image of the Virgin and Child, and perhaps the scene of the Adoration of the Magi was included by the reference to the Nativity.

At the end of the seventh century, an incident is related in which painted images in Armenian churches provoked an iconoclastic reaction. This report is preserved in the tenth-century History of the Albanians by Movsēs Kałankatuac'i.[42]   The story is recounted by the vardapet Yovhannēs Mayragomec'i in a letter written about 682 or 683 to David, Bishop of Albania, about three Armenian monks who, during the reign of the Catholicos Movsēs (574-604), were so outraged by the images in churches that they wished them to be destroyed.

In his treatise Against the Paulicians, the Catholicos Yovhannēs Ōjnec'i (717-728) referred to the veneration of cult images and their miraculous nature, though he specifically mentioned only the image of Christ and the Cross. "When the churches, altars, crosses, and images are anointed with oil, we believe that divine power enters into them. . . . If anyone else makes a cross of wood, or of any other materials, and [does] not give it to the priest for him to bless and anoint it with the holy oil, he must not honor that cross or prostrate himself before it, for it is void and empty of the divine power. . . . As for those which have been blessed and anointed, so that they may become instruments of the divine mystery, one must honor and worship them, prostrate oneself before them and kiss them. For the Holy Ghost dwells in them, and through them dispenses His protection to men, and the graces of healing of the ailments of souls and bodies. . . ."[43]

These references confirm that devotional images were known in Armenia, although no specific references to sculpture was made in these texts.   The Ōjun Virgin and Child, however, could have served such a function.

Summary

The Ōjun Virgin and Child are part of the iconography of the sixth-century enthroned Madonna and Child. It is a variation of the hieratic representation with Mary carrying the Child on her left arm. The closest comparison to the figure of Mary is the enthroned Virgin on the Saloniki Ambo, by size, material and gesture. The figure of Christ appears to be related stylistically to manuscript paintings dating to the end of the sixth and beginning of the seventh centuries in Syria and Armenia, though no exact parallel can be cited. The sculpture was not part of an architectural composition nor did it appear to serve in the narration of the Adoration of the Magi. Rather, it might have been an autonomous, independent sculpture, serving as a devotional image of Mary as the Theotokos. This proposal is supported by existing Armenian texts referring to devotional images in Armenia during the late sixth to the early eighth centuries. This high relief is a unique survival of early Christian art of the Syrian-Armenian tradition.

NOTES

*My profound thanks to Professor Thomas Mathews for his encouragement, time, and welcomed comments on the content of this paper, and to Marcel George Berard for his skillful drawing of the Ōjun and Saloniki reliefs.

[1]Published for the first time by V. Lasareff, "Studies in the Iconography of the Virgin," The Art Bulletin 20.1 (March 1938), fig. 29; for different views, G. Hovsepian, Materials for the Study of Armenian Art and Culture (in Armenian with English summaries), fasc. 3 (New York, 1944), fig. 16; S. Der Nersessian, Armenian Art (Paris, 1977 and 1978), fig. 31.

[2]S. Spain, "The Promised Blessing: The Iconography of the Mosaics of S. Maria Maggiore," The Art Bulletin, 61/4 (December 1979), 530-535.

[3]J. Strzygowski, Die Baukunst der Armenier und Europa I (Vienna, 1918), Abb. 205-6, 370, 373, 475; Der Nersessian, Armenian Art, 51; the church is usually dated to the sixth or seventh century although Strzygowski placed it in the reign of the Catholicos Yovhannēs Ōjnec'i, 717-728; the exact dating of the church is unresolved.

[4]W. F. Volbach, Early Christian Art (London, 1961), pl. 28 right; the

drawing published in C. R. Morey, Early Christian Art (Princeton, 1942), fig. 111 does not appear to me to be completely accurate.

[5]Age of Spirituality, Late Antique and Early Christian Art, Third to Seventh Century (ed. K. Weitzmann; New York, 1979), passim.

[6]Hovsepian, Materials, 22.

[7]L. Azarian, Vał Mijnadaryan Haykakan K'andagē (Erevan, 1975), no. 56; V. Harouthiounian and M. H. Hasrathian, Monuments of Armenia (Beirut, 1973), 52-53.

[8]L. A. Dournovo, Armenian Miniatures (London: Thames and Hudson, 1961), 35 Annunciation to Zacharias; 33 Annunciation to the Virgin; 37 Adoration of the Magi, and 39 Baptism of Christ.

[9]S. Der Nersessian, "La peinture arménienne au VIIe siecle et les miniatures de l'Evangile d'Etchmiadzin," Études byzantines et arméniennes (Louvain, 1973), 525-532.

[10]J. Leroy, Les manuscrits syriaques à peintures conservés dans les bibliothèques d'Europe et d'Orient (Institut français d'archéologie de Beyrouth, Bibliothèque Archéologique et Historique, 77, Paris, 1964), pl. 20.

[11]Ibid., pls. 31/2, 23/1, 24/1, 24/2.

[12]Ibid., pls. 2/1,2.

[13]Ibid., pl. 42.

[14]Ibid., pl. 46.

[15]Ibid., pls. 21/1, 34.

[16]Der Nersessian, Armenian Art, 52, fig. 33.

[17]See note 4.

[18]A. Grabar, Sculptures byzantines de Constantinople (IVe-Xe siècle (Bibliothèque archéologique et historique de l'institut français d'Istanbul 17; Paris, 1963), pl. 24/3, 5; p. 133.

[19]Ibid., 80-84; O. Wulff, Die altchristliche Kunst von ihren Anfängen bis zur Mitte des ersten Jahrtausends (Altchristliche und Byzaninische Kunst 1; Berlin, 1914), 135.

[20]Grabar, Sculptures, 133.

[21]R. Lange, Das Marienbild der frühen Jahrhunderte (Recklinghausen, 1969), 2, 27, 28, 58.

[22]G. A. Wellen, Theotokos, eine iconographische Abhandlung über das Gottesmutterbild in frühchristlicher Zeit (Utrecht/Antwerpen, 1961), 58.

[23]K. Weitzmann, The Monastery of Mt. Sinai, The Icons (Princeton, 1976), 67; C. Mango, The Art of the Byzantine Empire, 312-1453: Sources and Documents (Prentice-Hall, 1972), 40; Wellen, Theotokos, 157-8.

[24]Lange, Marienbild, 7-8; the epithet was first recorded as used by Origen in the third century.

[25]Wellen, Theotokos, Abb. 1b, from the Catacomb of Priscilla; Lasareff, "Studies," fig. 23.

[26]G. Schiller, Ikonographie der christlichen Kunst (Gütersloh, 1966), 2. figs. 246-7; 249; 253; Volbach, Christian Art, nos. 112, 120.

[27]Ibid., 326; Lasareff, "Studies," 28.

[28]Spain, "Blessing," 518, Lange, Marienbild, 25.

[29]G. Downey, Gaza in the Early Sixth Century (Norman, 1963), 128.

[30]Lasareff, "Studies," fig. 25.

[31]A. Grabar, Ampoules de Terre Sainte: Monza-Bobbio (Paris, 1958), pl. II, VIII; Weitzmann, Age of Spirituality, no. 287.

[32]Volbach, Christian Art, 326; Wellen, Theotokos, 58; see also a ciborium column for figures under an arch with a shell niche, said to be East Christian though provenance and dating are unresolved, Volbach, no. 82, 327.

[33]Leroy, Manuscrits syriaque, pl. 26/1,2.

[34]Strzygowski, Baukunst, abb. 107, 108, 257 for the so-called ambo at Zuart'noc', dated to the reign of the Catholicos Nersēs III, 641-661.

[35]Hovsepian, Materials, figs. 16, 57, 79, 93, 94.

[36]Weitzmann, Age of Spirituality, cats. no. 457, 476.

[37]Lasareff, "Studies," 57.

[38]A. Atiya, History of Eastern Christianity (University of Notre Dame, 1968), 426-428; B. Brentjes, Drei Jahrtausende Armenien (Leipzig, n.d.), 103-104.

[39]Lasareff, "Studies," 53; Lange, Marienbild, 30; idem, Die byzantinische Reliefsikone, Recklingshausen, 1964, 18; Leroy, Manuscrits Syriaque, 172-3; Wellen, Theotokos, 215.

[40]Der Nersessian, "Une apologie des images du septième siècle," Études, 379-403; Hovsepian, Materials, 53.

[41]Der Nersessian, "Apologie," 383-4; idem, "Image Worship in Armenia and its Opponents," Études, 408.

[42]Ibid., 406-7; N. H. Baynes, "The Icons before Iconoclasm," Harvard Theological Review (1951), 44, 105-6.

[43]Der Nersessian, "Image Worship," 409.

FIGURES

1.   Ōjun Virgin and Child. (Drawing by Marcel George Berard.)

2.   Full view of Ōjun Virgin and Child. (Photograph courtesy of Professor Thomas Mathews.)

3.   Detail of Ōjun Virgin and Child.   (Photograph courtesy of Professor Thomas Mathews.)

4.   Virgin and Child, Saloniki Ambo. (Drawing by Marcel George Berard.)

Figure 1.   Ōjun Virgin and Child.   (Drawing by Marcel George Berard.)

Figure 2.   Full view of Ōjun Virgin and Child.   (Photograph courtesy of Professor Thomas Mathews.)

Figure 3.   Detail of Ōjun Virgin and Child. (Photograph courtesy of Professor
Thomas Mathews.)

Figure 4.   Virgin and Child, Saloniki Ambo.   (Drawing by Marcel George Berard.)

ARMENIAN SCULPTURAL IMAGES, FIFTH TO EIGHTH CENTURIES

Lucy Der Manuelian

Armenian Architectural Archives (USA)

The corpus of sculptural images in Christian Armenia of the fifth to the eighth centuries provides a key document for the understanding of Armenian culture in that period.[1] The information it offers is even more precious considering that most of what survives of Armenian Christian art from that time is in the form of sculpture--except for the churches themselves, some fragments of mosaic and wall paintings, and four miniatures.[2]

The purpose of this paper is to compare this corpus to the Christian images in Byzantium and the Christian East, with the exception of Georgia,[3] in order to help define the nature of Armenian art and culture during that period. Such a comparison would reveal whether, and in what way, Armenian art was influenced by the art of the other cultures, whether particular images were copied exactly or whether changes were introduced, and whether the iconography was the same or different. It should also tell us whether Armenian art displayed a creativity of its own. The conclusions should in turn make it possible to put forth some ideas about the reasons for any differences, and what those differences can reveal about the Armenian brand of Christianity.

The Armenian corpus consists of relief sculpture in stone on the facades and interiors of churches. In addition, it includes free-standing funerary stelae of two kinds. Some are tall and obelisk-shaped, about 3 meters high. They are carved with compartmentalized images on several faces, as at Ōjun (Pl. 1 and 2) and Brdajor.[4] The others are smaller, often on cubic bases. They also have figured images, sometimes on all four sides. There are examples at T'alin, Haṙič, and Adiyaman.[5] More than seventy of the smaller ones still exist; most are found near the early basilical churches.[6]

The images in the corpus of sculpture as a whole consist mainly of individual figures of Christ, the Virgin, saints, angels, and ecclesiastics, as well as representations of the Virgin and Child, Christ with Apostles, and Biblical scenes taken almost entirely from the Old Testament.   There are also secular personages such as King Trdat, architects, stonemasons, praying figures, and princely donors of churches.[7] In addition, there are scenes which are as yet unidentified as to their meaning.[8]

A look at the corpus of sculpture in Byzantine, Coptic, and Syrian art reveals the first and perhaps most significant difference in comparison with Armenian art. The Armenian corpus includes many examples of figured relief sculpture in stone carved upon its churches. Byzantine art did not have a tradition of architectural relief sculpture in stone during this period, as far as we know. Syrian art has relief carvings, but they are not representational, for the most part. Coptic art made use of some figured reliefs in the beginning, but the practice soon died out,[9] and, as far as the West is concerned, relief sculpture does not appear essentially, until the Romanesque period.

The other stone sculpture in these arts, besides architectural sculpture, is often in the form of fragments, usually isolated from their original context. In the case of Byzantine art, the examples include sarcophagi, miscellaneous slabs of indeterminate use, and chancel pillars.[10]   In Coptic art, there are small figured stelae, but, in contrast to the Armenian examples, the images are limited to one side of the slab, and there are no figured bases.[11]

The first question is: what kinds of Christian images are seen in the Byzantine and in the Coptic examples as compared to the Armenian ones? The Byzantine images which also appear in Armenian sculpture are: Christ with Apostles, the Baptism, and the Old Testament scenes of the Sacrifice of Isaac, Daniel in the lions' den, and the three Hebrews in the fiery furnace. In addition, there are hunting scenes at the top of chancel pillars which show a horseman or a man on foot fighting a lion.[12]   The scenes which do not appear in Armenian sculpture of this period are Christ as the Good Shepherd, the Flight into Egypt, Entry into Jerusalem, and Jonah and the whale.

In Coptic art, the images shared in common with Armenian art are the Virgin with saints, Virgin and Child, the Old Testament scene of Daniel, and images of praying figures, of standing figures holding sceptred crosses, and, just as in Byzantine art, hunting scenes.[13]   The scenes which do not appear in the Armenian examples are the nursing Virgin, the Annunciation, the miracles of Christ, the Ascension, the Old Testament scenes of Moses and the Law, David and Goliath, Jonah and the whale, and the last, Saint Menas flanked by camels.

The range of sacred images in the sculpture of these non-Armenian cultures is more diverse. There are more scenes from the New Testament in addition to some Old Testament scenes which do not appear in Armenian sculpture of this period, such as Jonah and the whale, and the Moses and David scenes. Conversely, some of the Armenian images mentioned--the series of secular figures, and the unidentified scenes--do not appear in Byzantine or Coptic art. The unidentified images appear to be unique examples for Christian art as a whole, demonstrating the creativity of the Armenians.

For the purposes of this paper, the discussion centers on five Armenian monuments which contain sculptural images shared with Byzantine and Coptic art. They are examined to see if there are significant differences between them and the non-Armenian examples, and what the nature of those differences are. Because of the limited number of sculptured images in non-Armenian Christian art, examples from other media are included in the comparison.

The results of the comparison show that although the five Armenian examples are very different from one another, three common threads hold them together: 1) they all show historical figures--secular, Armenian personages; 2) they all put a direct emphasis on the concept of eternal salvation; 3) there are additions, or changes in details and in spirit which make an image the expression of an Armenian point of view although the scene may, as in some cases, have been taken over from non-Armenian art.

The Armenian examples are 1) the tall stelae beside the church at Ōjun (Pl. 1-2); 2) the stelae at Brdajor;[14] 3) the reliefs on the south facade of the church of Ptlni (Pl. 4); 4) the portal sculpture on the north and west sides of Mren (Pl. 5-7); and 5) the exterior and interior reliefs of the church of Sisawan (Pl. 9-14).

The twin stelae at Ōjun (seventh century) (Pl. 1-2) includes images found also in Byzantine and Coptic art. They include the Virgin and Child, the three Hebrews cast into the fiery furnace (Pl. 1-2), the Baptism, and Apostles standing two by two (which are like figures on Coptic stelae).[15] All these are part of the common vocabulary of Christian art. Some of these scenes at Ōjun are discussed in detail by Hovsepian[16] who points out differences in the details of composition, style, and iconography between them and non-Armenian examples. For this discussion, the most significant difference is that here they are tied together with other scenes which almost certainly refer to Agat'angełos' account of Armenia's conversion to Christianity.[17] Historical personages and events are shown or described.

King Trdat is represented in the form of a boar on the south stele, in the fourth framed image on the east face (Pl. 2). He was transformed into a boar after the martyrdom of the Virgin Hřip'simē and her companions;[18] he is shown here holding a processional cross. Similar representations of him are found among the smaller stelae at T'alin.[19] Beneath him on the Ōjun stele, there is an image of a two-story, domed structure represented (Pl. 2) which probably refers to the church of St. Hřip'simē built by St. Gregory the Illuminator in commemoration. The other historical personages on the stele are probably members of Trdat's court. They wear the garb of Sasanian royalty as Hovsepian points out, and are shown also holding sceptred crosses. The composition is the same as in Coptic art but here the figures refer to specific personages associated with an identifiable historical event.

The cycle of images at Ōjun as a whole, according to Azaryan,[20] begins with the birth and baptism of Christ (on the west face), indicates the spread of Christianity in Armenia through the work of the apostles (the west face), and ends with the conversion of the Armenians through the efforts of St. Gregory. The scene of the Hebrew youths in the fiery furnace is used as a salvation image, as in non-Armenian Christian art, but at Ōjun it is in an important location at the top of the south stele and may refer specifically to St. Gregory. Gregory had been thrown into a pit by King Trdat before the martyrdom of Hřip'simē and had emerged unscathed. On the stele, salvation is emphasized again and again through scenes such as the Baptism, and with the repeated use of the cross. As a result, the Ōjun stelae offer a striking example of how the Armenians used the common Christian images of the time in a highly unified and creative way.

The church of Ōjun (sixth or seventh century), located on the south side of the stelae, has some relief sculpture on the east elevation of interest to this discussion. Christ is shown above the central window (Pl. 3) holding an open Gospel inscribed with the first words of John: "In the beginning was the Word, and the Word was with God, and the Word was God." Two angels, one on each side, appear on the horizontal bands on either side of the

window. Each one holds the neck of a snake with one hand and its body with
the other. The two bodies follow the window curve, intertwine at the center
to form a knot, and rise, one on each side, to terminate in palmettes which
frame the figure of Christ. The composition may possibly refer to St.
Gregory the Illuminator and the snakes in his pit:

> and in that pit where they had thrown him he was kept
> alive by the grace of his Lord. But other men, once
> they had been let down there, all perished because of
> the atrociously bad air of the place, because of the
> muddy mire, the snakes who lived there and the
> depth.[21]

In any case, the combination of an image of Christ with angels, snakes, and
palmettes in association with the east window of a church--a symbolic source
of light--is a highly unusual composition in Christian art.

The next monument consists of the tall stelae of Brdajor, now in the
Georgian State Museum at Tbilisi, which is of the same period as Ōjun.[22]
Again, there are scenes shared in common with Byzantine and other East
Christian art: Christ enthroned, enclosed in a large medallion held by four
angels; the Sacrifice of Abraham; the Virgin and Child; and several baptism
scenes.[23] As at Ōjun, there are representations of secular figures: pairs are
shown in baptism scenes; a female figure is in a nimbus held by angels; two
male figures stand on either side of a hanging censer; and a male and female
figure hold a sceptred cross[24] just as at Ōjun and on Coptic stelae. Some
of the secular figures are identified by name through inscriptions. Azaryan
interprets the cycle as commemorating the conversion and baptism of a
particular princely family. Thus, Brdajor presents another example in the
Armenian corpus with historical personages and an emphasis on salvation in
both theme and content.

The third monument is the church of Ptłni, or Ptłnavank', which
probably dates to the early seventh century.[25] The arch over one of the
windows on the south side (Pl. 4) is carved with a series of images. Christ
appears at the top, flanked by a pair of angels in flight and three Apostles
on each side enclosed in medallions. At the foot of the arch on the right
and left sides, there is a rectangular slab carved with a hunting scene. The
hunter on the left is identified by the inscription as "Manuēl, lord of the
Amatunis." He is shown in profile mounted on a horse, aiming with his bow
and arrow at the lion in front of him. The tail of the horse is knotted

according to Sasanian tradition.[26]   The hunter on the right is unidentified. He is on foot and attacks a lion with his lance.   Similar scenes appear on Coptic stelae and at the top of Byzantine chancel pillars.[27]

In the case of Ptłni, the composition, except for the hunting scenes, is found often both in paleo-Christian and Byzantine churches usually in the form of mosaics or wall painting on the arch preceding the eastern apse.   A notable Byzantine example is found in the church of S. Vitale in Ravenna.[28] It is also painted before the east apse of the Armenian church of T'alin.[29] As Grabar points out,[30] the image of Christ presiding over an assembly of Apostles is a reflection of the official art of Byzantium.   Very little of that spirit remains here, however.   The location itself indicates the difference. The image is on a window on the south side, not in a more important location such as the tympanum of the main portal which would be analogous to the triumphal arch of an east apse.   Another difference is the addition of an Armenian historical personage, the secular prince Manuēl, which gives the composition a shift in emphasis.   Manuēl is associated with the construction of the church.   He is either the actual donor of the church, and the hunter on the right is his son Sahak, thus dating the church to the late sixth century, according to Hovsepian,[31] or he is the heroic ancestor of the actual Amatuni donor, according to Mnac'akanyan,[32] the figure on the right is his father Parkew, and the church is early seventh century.   The latter interpretation seems more likely.   Also, as Mnac'akanyan points out, since both father and son died martyrs' deaths,[33] they are shown in the company of Christ and the Apostles.   Literary sources state that the Armenians elevated their martyrs into the company of saints and celebrated them accordingly in church ceremonies.[34]   Here at Ptłni, that practice is represented visually. Consequently, the emphasis of the composition is on eternal salvation, with the Amatuni princes as exemplars—a definite shift from its being primarily an official image.

But why is the martyred prince shown hunting instead of in some other way, in a medallion, for example?   The hunting scene motif, representing a royal personage killing a lion, has a long history going back to the art of the ancient Near East and, closer in time, to Sasanian art.   In Christian art, the scene took on the general meaning of the victory over evil which is salvation. The lion was considered a symbol of evil in the process of being overcome by the faithful, who would then be rewarded by eternal salvation.

At Ptłni, the Armenian sculptor's use of the hunting scene is very creative. The two concepts expressed by the image--royalty and salvation-- are combined in this figure of a martyred Christian prince of Armenia who died in battle against the Persians. His father also died a martyr's death.[35] The scene signifies the prince's ultimate victory over adversity and shows to the congregation that salvation comes to those who stand firm in their faith. Thus, here at Ptłni, image and meaning are combined in a striking way in this composition of Christ, Apostles, and hunting scenes. It is also important to note that here the ancient and contemporary pagan hunting scene seems to be clearly identified as being transformed into a symbolic Christian image.

This interpretation of the motif as a donor and/or martyr image may be of use in explaining the hunting scenes in Coptic and Byzantine art[36] which, unlike the Armenian examples, are not found in context but in fragmentary form.   They have not been considered as Christian symbolic images.[37] Since Byzantine chancel pillars sometimes do have donor portraits carved at the top, these hunting images may also represent donors; and the Coptic examples might also be considered in this light.[38]

Another example at Ptłni of the creative imagination of the Armenian sculptor in representing a favorite Christian image is a fragment of what appears to be a Daniel scene on the left of the arch. The relief is probably part of a larger composition from an earlier church on that site.[39] The Daniel scene, used commonly in early Christian art to refer specifically to salvation, serves as a kind of footnote to the message of the composition beside it.

In addition, it contains certain details which differentiate it from the usual Daniel scene, indicating that the Armenians were not slavish imitators. Instead of limiting the scene to the standing figure of Daniel flanked by two lions, here there is a lion standing in front of a large tree with two animals at his feet, probably rams.[40] Daniel's hand is just visible on the right corner of the fragment. The scene seems to incorporate more details from the Book of Daniel in which both a large tree and rams appear (Dan. 4, 6, and 8).

Another delightfully different representation of the Daniel scene in Armenian sculpture appears on a seventh century stele found at Haric in which the two lions lick the garments of Daniel.[41] It is important to note that the Daniel scene, very specifically a salvation image, appears to be the most common of the few Old Testament scenes selected for representation in the Armenian sculpture of this period. The choice is significant in view of the examples already described as well as those to be discussed.

The fourth monument, the seventh-century church of Mren (completed in 639-40)[42] has some very interesting sculpture on the north and west portals. The scene on the west facade (Pl. 5) is similar in some respects to many in non-Armenian art but the sculpture over the north portal (Pl. 6) is unique both for Armenian art and Christian art in general. In both cases, just as in the previous monuments, historical Armenian figures, this time contemporary, take an active part.

On the lintel of the west portal (Pl. 5 and 6), there are two standing angels above and six figures below, including Christ at the center, St. Paul on His right, and St. Peter on His left. Standing next to Peter are the figures of Bishop Theophilus and David Saharuni (Pl. 6), who was appointed by the Byzantine emperor as ruler of Armenia. Nerseh Kamsarakan, the patron of the church, is to the right of Paul.[43]

As M. and N. Thierry point out, this composition recalls the sixth and seventh century mosaic apses of Byzantine and Western churches.[44] It is particularly instructive to compare it to a similar scene in the sixth century church of S. Vitale in Ravenna (Pl. 7) to see differences in subject matter, composition and iconography.

At S. Vitale, the composition shows Christ enthroned on the orb of heaven flanked by angels, with St. Vitalis on His right and Bishop Ecclesius, presenting a model of the church, on His left. This is an imperial image, with Christ represented as a universal sovereign, with His attendants shown frontally, wearing ceremonial robes.

Even with the very poor condition of the Mren composition, the differences are striking. There are no imperial regalia here, at least in what is visible. Christ, though an imposing figure, has no scroll and is not enthroned. He stands holding the folds of his robe with His left hand. The Armenian princes move toward him, faces frontal, bodies in profile, extending their hands as though simply presenting Christ to the viewer. The gestures appear more spontaneous and there seems to be a more direct line of communication between humans and God, Armenian men in this case, than at S. Vitale. In addition, David Saharuni is portrayed in local Armenian (and Caucasian) attire.[45] Yet he could well have been shown in ceremonial Byzantine dress, as is seen at S. Vitale, which would have been appropriate to the high rank and titles awarded him by the Emperor, all of which are carefully mentioned in the dedicatory inscription on the church. Neither he nor Nerseh Kamsarakan, also in local dress, are hieratic figures.

At S. Vitale, the emphasis is on Christ, who will reign at the end of time, while here at Mren, there are portrait-like images of historical personages.   In a contemporary time-frame, the Armenian princes gesture toward an ever-present Christ who shows the way to eternal salvation. Therefore, though S. Vitale and similar images may have been the ultimate source of this composition, the Armenian sculptor transformed an imperial image into a more intimate scene with secular Armenian personages.

The sculpture over the north portal (Pl. 8) is an original creation, probably the dedication ceremony of Mren itself.[46]   Again, there are historical figures, this time shown in a ceremonial act with the symbol of salvation—the cross—as its most prominent feature.

Prince David Saharuni is shown on the left side of the lintel. Dismounted from his horse, he moves toward the cross held by Nerseh Kamsarakan, the founder of the church. The tall cross is set into the ground. It recalls Agat'angełos' account of how St. Gregory the Illuminator set crosses into the ground to mark the sites where Hṙip'simē and her companions were martyred and, later, erected churches there.[47]   Behind Nerseh is Bishop Theophilus, hands outstretched, a censer hanging from his right hand.   Beside him is a Tree of Life mounted on a stylized representation of Golgotha.[48]   David Saharuni wears here the garb of a marzpan of Persia, a rank he held before the title given him by the Byzantine emperor.[49]

Just as on the west facade, the image is straightforward, simple, and direct.   There is nothing interposed between the viewer and the message—no saintly intercessor, not even the image of Christ.

Mren has other carvings which, just as at Ptłni, are analogous to footnotes or margin illustrations for the central message of salvation.   The two windows on the east side have relief sculpture above them.   The north window has three figures which appear to represent Daniel in the lions' den.[50]   Over the window of the south apse, there are two serpents whose tails intertwine above the center,[51] just as at Ōjun.   Their heads, now missing, and upper parts curve into large buckle-like forms.   Here again, the serpents may refer to St. Gregory and the pit, particularly if they can be considered companion pieces to the Daniel scene.   Daniel must have been a reassuring exemplar for the Armenians during their troubled history, and a particularly apt one.   This scene appears to be the single most popular image during this period aside from the representation of Christ and the Virgin and

Child.[52]

The last monument is the church of Sisavan (Pl. 9), probably completed in 691.[53] Its relief sculpture demonstrates the inventiveness of the Armenian sculptors of the classical period with regard to disposition as well as subject matter on the interior and exterior of the church. Carved busts of the four evangelists (Pl. 10) are placed in a very unusual location high up on the cornice, just below the roof. They are positioned symbolically as well, corresponding to the four corners of the earth, one at the center of each wall.[54]

On the west and south sides of the church, there are busts of unidentified figures carved at the head of the two niches (Pl. 11), now, unfortunately, in very poor condition. They are of particular interest in view of the later development in the West of figure sculpture on the facades of Romanesque and Gothic churches. Mnac'akanyan considers them to be donor figures.[55]

The location of the interior relief sculpture is also unusual. Three busts, considered to be donor portraits of a prince and two ecclesiastics (Pl. 12-14) are carved just under the cupola on the north side: two on the small squinches on the northeast, and the other nearby. Each is identified by name in the inscription framing his head. The prince is Kohazat, Siwneac' Tēr, 'Kohazat, Prince of Siwnik;' the bishop is Tēr Yovsēp', Siwneac' Episkopos 'Lord Joseph, bishop of Siwnik,' and the monk is T'odoros, Sioni Vanakan 'Theodore, monk of Zion.'[56]

The prince (Pl. 12) is bareheaded, with expressive eyes, a mustache, and beard—a rather dashing figure. His right hand is across his breast and his left hand raised as though he is taking an oath of dedication. As at Mren, special attention is given to the details of his and the other's clothing.[57] The Bishop (Pl. 13), an imposing image, wears the vełar, the conical headdress of the Armenian cleargy, and he holds a book against his breast. The monk or abbot T'odoros (Pl. 14) is dressed less richly and seems more introspective. He holds a book to his breast with his left hand and a censer in his right. Mnac'akanyan identifies him as the theologian-scholar T'odoros K'ṙtenawor who was trained in Siwnik' and may be commemorated here for his aid in endowing the church. The prince and the Bishop would be commemorated as the local patrons.

These are individualized portraits; the prince looks very self-assured, the bishop authoritative, and T'odoros reflective. Both the individualization and the care given to details of clothing distinguish Armenian images of this period from those representations of historical figures in non-Armenian Christian art, except for Georgian art. In addition, the Armenian personages are more often secular, not ecclesiastical.

These donor figures are in a significant position, at the point where the cupola, the symbolic dome of heaven, rises upward. In a sense, they are "halfway to heaven," as befits them for their endowment of this church. At the same time, they are positioned below the level of the evangelists on the exterior. Another interesting point is that the saints are on the outside whereas the contemporary figures are on the inside where perhaps they were meant to serve as exemplars to the faithful.

There are no accompanying images of Christ or the Virgin at Sisavan, just as there are none in certain scenes at Ōjun, Ptłni, Brdajor and Mren. The portraits seem to state to the faithful that each of these personages here and at the earlier monuments has achieved or will achieve salvation through his or her own individual actions. At Sisavank', it is through the construction and endowment of the church.

The emphasis on the individual in the Armenian corpus of sculpture during this period is manifested through the use of different types of donor images. The first is the hunting scene at Ptłni; the second, the standing figures shown with Christ at Mren; the third, the dedication scene on the north lintel at Mren; and fourth, these portrait busts at Sisavan. A fifth type, the donor or pair of donors shown alone, holding a model of the church also appears in this period at Agarak.[58] This variant and the hunting scene are very popular throughout the history of Armenian sculpture. Yet another type, the Virgin and Child at the center flanked by donor figures, begins as early as the seventh century.[59] Whatever the form, the donor images have no resemblance to the icon-like figures of Byzantine art, such as the donors of the seventh century Byzantine church of St. Demetrius at Salonika (c. 650).[60]

In summary, this brief survey of the corpus[61] of Armenian sculpture of the Classical period has revealed that Armenia adopted some images which were common currency in the Christian world at that time, as well as images from the Near East. But the Armenian sculptors were highly selective, limiting the choice to certain images which best expressed the focus of Armenian religious thought. Whatever was taken over, however, was transformed into something different and oftentimes new through changes of various kinds, especially through the addition of secular historical figures and through an emphasis on eternal salvation.   The secular figures are individualized exemplars who symbolized the concept of salvation in terms of individual effort--whether fighting and dying for the faith, enduring the torments of a Daniel or Gregory, or by constructing a church.   As a result, Armenian Classical figure sculpture appears to be a coherent corpus in which there is continuity and unity of focus.

The sculpture of the classical period, therefore, reflects a culture which is highly religious and yet very independent, placing a premium on individual responsibility.   That culture proclaimed its qualities consistently by engraving them in stone on the outside of its churches for all to see.

NOTES

[1]In general, few studies have been published on Armenian sculpture. Some of it is discussed and illustrated in Strzygowski's monumental work on Armenian architecture: J. Strzygowski, Die Baukunst der Armenier und Europa (2 vol.:   Vienna: A. Schroll, 1918); and in the studies of T'. T'oramanian which were assembled in two volumes in the 1940's.   T. T'oramanyan, Nyut'er Haykakan Čartarapetut'yan Patmut'yan, 2 vol.: (Erevan: HSSH GA, 1942-1948).   Discussions on the early period are of varying scope.   The two surveys are mainly concerned with sculptured stelae. Archbishop Garegin Hovsepian (Yovsep'ian) was the first to study the reliefs on these stelae, relating them to images in early Christian, Byzantine, and other Eastern Christian art as well as to those of pagan art.   G. Hovsepian, "Sepulchral Steles and their Archeological Value for the History of Armenian Art," Materials for the Study of Armenian Art and Culture (Fascicle 3, New York: No publisher cited, 1944).   Two soviet Armenian scholars, B. Aṙak'elyan (1949) and L. Azaryan (1975) also published descriptive surveys of the stelae, including some examples of architectural sculpture, with interpretations of some of the motifs.   L. Azaryan, Vaḷ Miǰnadaryan Kaykakan K'andagě (Erevan: HSSH GA, 1975), and B. Aṙak'elyan, Haykakan Patkerak'andakneṙ IV-VII Darerum (Erevan: HSSH GA, 1949).   Aside from these works, there are some articles on the sculpture of specific churches mainly by Soviet Armenian scholars.

[2]S. der Nersessian, The Armenians (Praeger Series Ancient Peoples and Places 68; New York: Praeger, 1969), 136-7, 139.

[3]Georgian sculpture is not included in the discussion for lack of space. Some of the images discussed here have Georgian counterparts, e. g., historical personages, donor portraits, and hunt scenes.   For a survey of Georgian art, see R. Mepisashvili and V. Tsintsadze, The Arts of Ancient Georgia (New York: Thames and Hudson, 1979).

[4]For other views of the stelae at Ōjun, see V. Harouthiounian and M. Hasrathian, Monuments of Armenia (Beirut: Societe Techno-Presse Moderne, S. A. L., 1975), 52.   For Brdajor and other illustrations of Ōjun, see L. Azaryan, "Ōjuni ew Brdajori Kot'oℓnerě," Patmabanasirakan Handes (1965), 4.31:1-7.

[5]S. Der Nersessian, Armenian Art (Paris: Thames and Hudson, 1977), f. 39, 42 and 43; also Hovsepian, "Sepulchral Steles" and Azaryan, "Sculpture," passim.

[6]Der Nersessian, Armenian Art, 59.

[7]Many of these are to be found on the stelae at T'alin.   Illustrations are found in Hovsepian, "Sepulchral Steles."   Figures of an architect and several stonemasons are represented on spandrel fragments at Zuart'noc'. See Der Nersessian, Armenian Art, f. 28 and Aṙak'elyan, Figure Sculpture, f. 55-59 for illustrations.

[8]At Adiyaman and Haṙič, for example.   See Hovsepian, "Sepulchral Steles," f. 99 and 92, respectively.

[9]Der Nersessian, The Armenians, 123-124.   See also A. Badawy, Coptic Art and Archaeology (Cambridge and London: MIT, 1978), 165-225.

[10]For examples, see André Grabar, Sculptures Byzantines de Constantinople (IV-X Siècle) (Paris: A. and J. Picard, 1963).

[11]See Badawy, Coptic Art, for illustrations, 210-225, and K. Wessel, Koptisches Kunst (Recklinghausen: Bongers, 1963), f. 12-13, 33-36.

[12]Grabar, Sculptures, Pl. XXVII, 4; Pl. XXX, 4.

[13]Wessel, Koptisches Kunst, f. 11.

[14]For illustrations, see Azaryan, "Ōjun," f. 1-7 and Azaryan, Sculpture, f. 14-21.   The stelae are now in the Georgian State Museum of Art at Tbilisi.

[15]Badawy, f. 3.76.

[16]Hovsepian, "Sepulchral Steles," 33-35.

[17]Azaryan, "Ōjun," 215.

[18]See Agathangelos' History of the Armenians (trans. and comment, R. W. Thomson; Albany: State University of New York, 1976) for a full account of Hŕip'simē and her companions, and the conversion of Armenia to Christianity.

[19]For illustrations, see Hovsepian, "Sepulchral Steles," f. 38.

[20]Azaryan, "Ōjun," 215.

[21]Thomson, Agathangelos, #124. The image may also refer to Gregory because of the passage in his Teaching in which he gives the simile of the serpent who sloughs off his skin as "the just strip off from their souls the ephemeral impurities of the body that they may enter the narrow gate and obtain the immortal kingdom." Robert M. Thomson (trans.), The Teaching of Saint Gregory, An Early Armenian Catechism (Harvard Armenian Texts and Studies 3, Cambridge, MA.: Harvard University, 1970), #602, 14.)

[22]Azaryan, "Ōjun," 215.

[23]For illustrations, see Azaryan, Sculpture f. 14-21.

[24]In Azaryan, "Ōjun," see f. 5 and 6, and in Azaryan, Sculpture, see f. 18, 19, and 21, respectively.

[25]G. Hovsepian, "The Monastery Chruch of Budghoons (Budghavank) and the Doming of Ancient Armenian Churches," Materials for the Study of Armenian Art and Culture (Fascicle 3, New York: No publisher cited, 1944), 7-29, dates it to the second quarter of the sixcth century on the basis of its architecture and the identification of Manuel Amatuni, shown on the relief sculpture, as the donor of the church. See description in text below. Hovsepian identifies the other hunter as Manuel's son Sahak. S. Mnac'akanyan, "Ptŕnii Tačarĕ," Patmabanasirakan Handes (1961), 3-4.219-237, disagrees. On the basis of architectural evidence, the sculptural motifs and the donor composition, he dates the church as being built no earlier than the first decade of the seventh century. He identifies Manuel and the other hunter, whom he considers Manuēl's father Pargew, not as the donors but the martyred forebears of the actual donor of the church. He also suggests that

there was probably an earlier church on the site, dating to the sixth century, from which a Daniel fragment is utilized on the present church. See below.

[26]Hovsepian, "Budghoons," 10.

[27]See f. 10 in Wessel, Koptisches Kunst, and Pl. XXX, 4 in Grabar, Sculptures Byzantines.

[28]See f. 175 in Andre Grabar, Christian Iconography, A Study of its Origins (Bollingen Series 35/10; Princeton: Princeton University Press, 1968).

[29]Der Nersessian, Armenian Art, 71-72. There are also remnants of a similar composition at Mren.

[30]Grabar, Christian Iconography, 73; Irmgard Hutter, Early Christian and Byzantine Art (London: Weidenfeld and Nicolson, 1971), 12.

[31]Hovsepian, "Budghoons," 14-16. See supra, n. 25.

[32]Mnac'akanyan, "Ptlni," 234-237. Also see supra, n. 25.

[33]See passage in Moses Khorenats'i History of the Armenians (trans. and comment, Robert W. Thomson; Cambridge, MA. & London: Harvard University Press, 1978), #50, 314-315.

[34]Mnac'akanyan, "Ptlni," 235.

[35]Thomson (ed.), Moses Khorenats'i, 315.

[36]For Byzantine examples, see Grabar, Sculptures, Pl. 28, 4, and Pl. 30, 4. For Coptic art, see Wessel, Koptisches Kunst, f. 11; also Badawy, f. 3.151.

[37]Grabar, Sculptures,70, 72. Grabar refers to their origins in Near Eastern art.

[38]In Armenian art, the motif survives well into the thirteenth century and is found at Ałt'amar (tenth century), and in the thirteenth century, at T'anahat, Amału Noravank', and Spitakawor, and on several Xačk'ars. In all cases, the figures are identifiable as Armenian princes and appear to be commemorated in the same way as Manuēl Amatuni at Ptlni.

[39]Mnac'akanyan, "Ptlni," 237; see also 226-228.

[40]Ibid., 226.

[41]See Hovsepian, "Sepulchral Steles," f. 91, and Der Nersessian, Armenian Art, f. 42.

[42]M. A. Sargsyan, "Mreni Tačari Himnadirneri Patkerak'andagnerš," Patmabanasirakan Handes (1966), 4.249, and M. and N. Thierry, "La Cathedrale de Mren et sa Decoration," Cahiers Archeologiques 21 (1971), 75.

[43]Ibid.

[44]Sargsyan, "Mren," 240; Thierry, "Mren," 64.

[45]See Thierry, "Mren," 67, and Sargsyan, "Mren," 246. Sargsyan points out that Kind Trdat is represented with the same dress on a stele at Agarak. See also Thierry, "Mren," 63.

[46]Sargsyan, "Mren," 249.

[47]Ibid., 247.

[48]Thierry, "Mren," 75.

[49]Sargsyan, "Mren," 243.

[50]See Thierry, "Mren," f. 11 and 12.

[51]Ibid., f. 11 (h).

[52]The motif is found as late as the thirteenth century carved on the south wall of the church of St. Step'anos at the monastery of Ałjoc' St. Step'anos near Gełard.

[53]S. Mnac'akanyan, "Sisavani Tačarě," Patmabanasirakan Handes (1965), 4, 73.

[54]Saints John, Mark, and Matthew are on the north, east, south, and west sides, respectively.

[55]Private communication, December, 1977.

[56]Mnac'akanyan, "Sisavan," 67-68.

[57]Thierry, "Mren," 63, point out that the bishop wears the same type of Armenian/Caucasian robe as David Saharuni on the west portal at Mren.

[58]At Agarak; see Ařak'elyan, Figure Sculpture, f. 18.

[59]At Pemzašen (formerly Mahmudčuł). See Der Nersessian, Armenianm Art, 56; also Hovsepian, "Sepulchral Steles," f. 16 and Azaryan, Sculpture, 102 and f. 88.

[60]See Hutter, Early Christian, f. 100.

[61]The smaller stelae and fragments in the corpus seem to demonstrate the same characteristics as the sculpture of the monuments described. They will be included in a later study.

LIST OF PLATES

Photographs by author unless otherwise specified.

1.   Ōjun. Stelae, seventh century. East face. (After V. Harouthiounian and M. Hasrathian, Monuments of Armenia.)

2.   Ōjun. Stelae, east face. South stele on the left; north stele on the right. (After S. Der Nersessian, Armenian Art.)

3.   Ōjun. Church, sixth or seventh century. Sculpture above central window of east wall.

4.   Ptłni. Church, early seventh century. Sculpture above window on south facade.

5.   Mren. Cathedral, seventh century. Sculpture over west portal. (After B. Aṙak'elyan, Hayakan Patkerak'andaknerĕ IV-VII Darerum.)

6.   Mren. Cathedral. Lintel of west portal. Bishop Theophilus and David Saharuni. (After S. Der Nersessian, Armenian Art.)

7.   Ravenna. S. Vitale, sixth century. East apse. (After A. Grabar, The Golden Age of Justinian (New York: Odyssey Press, 1967).)

8.   Mren. Lintel of north portal. (After M. and N. Thierry, "La Cathedrale de Mrèn et sa Décoration," Cahiers Archéologiques 21 (1975).)

9.   Sisawan. Church, seventh century. View from the south.

10.   Sisawan. Evangelist on cornice.

11.   Sisawan. Niche sculpture on west wall.

12.   Sisawan. Interior relief. Prince Kohazat. (After S. Mnac'akanyan, Haykakan Ašxarhik Patkerak'andagĕ IX-XIV Darerum (Erevan: HSSH GA, 1976).)

13.   Sisawan. Interior relief. Bishop Yovsēp'. (After S. Mnac'akanyan, "Sisavani Tačarĕ," Patmabanasirakan Handes.)

14.   Sisawan. Interior relief. T'odoros, the monk. (After S. Mnac'akan-yan, "Sisavani Tačarĕ," Patmabanasirakan Handes.)

Plate 1. Ōjun. Stelae, seventh century. East face. (After V. Harouthiounian
and M. Hasrathian, Monuments of Armenia.)

Plate 2. Ōjun. Stelae, east face. South stele on the left; north stele on the right. (After S. Der Nersessian, Armenian Art.)

Plate 3. Ōjun. Church, sixth or seventh century. Sculpture above central window of east wall.

Plate 4. Ptłni. Church, early seventh century. Sculpture above window on south facade.

Plate 5. Mren. Cathedral, seventh century. Sculpture over west portal. (After B. Aṛak'elyan, Hayakan Patkerak'andaknerě IV-VII Darerum.)

Plate 6. Mren. Cathedral. Lintel of west portal. Bishop Theophilus and David Saharuni. (After S. Der Nersessian, Armenian Art.)

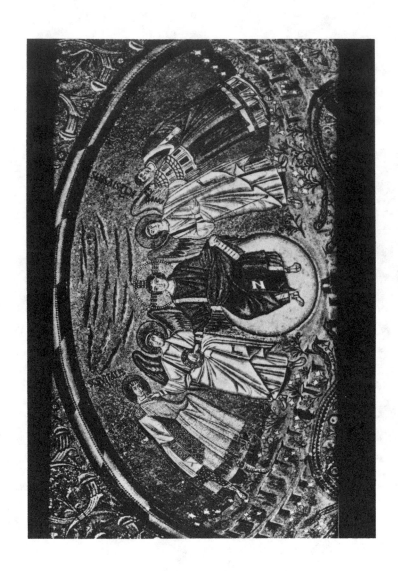

Plate 7. Ravenna. S. Vitale, sixth century. East apse. (After A. Grabar, The Golden Age of Justinian (New York: Odyssey Press, 1967).)

Plate 8.   Mren.   Lintel of north portal.   (After M. and N. Thierry, "La Cathedrale de Mrèn et sa Décoration," Cahiers Archéologiques 21 (1975).)

Plate 9. Sisawan. Church, seventh century. View from the south.

Plate 10.   Sisawan.   Evangelist on cornice.

Plate 11. Sisawan. Niche sculpture on west wall.

Plate 12. Sisawan. Interior relief. Prince Kohazat. (After S. Mnacʻakanyan, Haykakan Ašxarhik Patkerakʻandagě IX–XIV Darerum (Erevan: HSSH GA, 1976).)

Plate 13. Sisawan. Interior relief. Bishop Yovsēpʿ. (After S. Mnacʿakanyan, "Sisavani Tačarě," Patmabanasirakan Handes.)

Plate 14. Sisawan. Interior relief. T'odoros, the monk. (After S. Mnac'akanyan, "Sisavani Tačarĕ," Patmabanasirakan Handes.)

INDEX

Abeghian, M. (Abełyan), 7, 19

Abgaryan, G. V., 54-56, 66, 68, 70-72, 76-78

Abraham Ałbat'anec'i (Catholicos), 63-64

Abraham Xostovanoł and Vkayk' Arewelic', 49

Abrahamian, A. G., 6, 7, 50

Achaemenian dynasty, 1, 14, 31, 33

Achtemeier, P., 108

Acts of Persian Martyrs, 42

Acts of the Apostles, 89

Adam and Eve, 107

Adiyaman, 176

Adler, W., 108

Admon, 90

Adontz, N., 37, 38, 69, 73, 78

"Adoration of the Magi," 161

Aeolia Capitolina, 84

Afrahat, 62

Agarak, 186

Agat'angełos, 6-26, 38, 43, 52-53, 70, 72, 79, 80, 83, 94, 179, 184; Patmut'iwn Hayoc', 38, 71; Teachings of Gregory, 43, 89

Aggadat Sir, 107

Agṙawuc' K'ar, 4

Aharonian, A., 20

Ahekan, 2

Ahuramazda (Ohrmizd), 1-3, 11, 14

Akinian, N., 36, 41, 49, 55, 66, 69, 73, 77, 89, 99, 100, 113, 120

Aladsvili, N. A., 157

Al-Arminiya, 30

Alarodians, 31

Albania, Caucasian, 27, 29, 33, 62

Aldama, J. M. de, 122

Alexander: Treatise on the Cross, 88

Alexander, the Great, 1, 31, 32

Alisan, L., 7

Alp Arslan, 63

Altendorf, H. D., 115, 121, 124

Aluank', 36

Amanor, 15

Ambrose, 84, 91, 98

Amrdōl, 53, 70-71

Anania Širakac'i, 2, 64; Chronicle, 48; Mnac'ordk' Banic', 7

Anahit (Anahita), 1, 2, 4, 8, 14, 18

Ananian, P., 55, 66

Ananikian, M. Y., 6

Anastasis, 84

Anatolia, 31, 142-43

Ani, 4

Annals (Eutychius), 107

Annassian, H. S. (Anasyan), 31, 37, 109

"Annunciation to Zacharius," 161

Antioch, 91, 93, 152-53

Antonellus, N. M., 50

Aphrodite, 84

Apocalypse of Moses, The, 102, 106

Apollinaris, 4, 93

Apollo, 14, 80